LUCY CALKINS ✦ MEDEA MCEVOY

LITERARY ESSAYS: WRITING ABOUT READING

This book is dedicated to Carmen Fariña and Laura Kotch.

DEDICATED TO TEACHERS

FirstHand
An imprint of Heinemann
361 Hanover Street
Portsmouth, NH 03801-3912
www.heinemann.com

Offices and agents throughout the world

Copyright © 2006 by Lucy Calkins and Medea McEvoy

Photography: Peter Cunningham

Library of Congress Cataloging-in-Publication Data

CIP data on file with the Library of Congress.
ISBN: 0-325-00865-5
ISBN-13: 978-0-325-00865-3

Printed in the United States of America on acid-free paper
10   09   ML   5   6   7

ACKNOWLEDGEMENTS

This book is dedicated to Carmen Fariña, the Deputy Chancellor for Teaching and Learning, and Laura Kotch, the Executive Director of Curriculum and Professional Development, for the New York City Department of Education. Because of these two people and their commitment to ensuring that every child receives the richest and most rigorous education possible, thousands and thousands of New York City children are growing up as avid readers and writers. We thank them for their resolve, their untiring efforts, and their friendship.

The contributing author of this book, Medea McEvoy, is Director of Literacy for the New York City schools and works with Laura Kotch and Carmen Fariña to support literacy instruction citywide. Before assuming this role, Medea was a fifth-grade teacher at PS 6, and her classroom was a laboratory for learning par excellence. This unit of study stands on the shoulders of work in the teaching of reading that many of us at the Project developed together and that Medea pioneered in her classroom. Medea also helped me pilot this specific unit in Kathy Doyle's wonderful classroom, and the two of them joined me for a writing retreat in order to turn our teaching into a text. Medea has been a willing contributor, helping out with Tailoring Your Teachings and with other portions of the book as well, and she has provided all the artwork. Above all, she has been a thought companion in the adventure of learning to teach not only writing but also reading.

This book could not have been written were it not for the invaluable support of Kathy Doyle, a fifth-grade teacher at the Smith School in Tenafly, New Jersey. Whereas many of these books draw upon the teaching that has been done in hundreds of classrooms over a decade, this book relies very specifically on the work that Kathy, Medea and I did with Kathy's wonderful group of fifth graders. Kathy's willingness to open her classroom to Medea and me, her sense of adventure and of appreciation, and her vast knowledge of books and of her children, made all the difference.

Julia Mooney and Grace Enriquez, two Project colleagues, helped elaborate on sections of the text. Kathleen Tolan, the Deputy Director for Reading, read the entire draft and contributed dozens of ideas as well as many pages of text. Many of the ideas that fill these pages reflect the Project's thinking about teaching reading, and Donna Santman, Randy Bomer, Ginny Lockwood, Kathy Collins, Maggie Moon, Emily Smith, Katherine Bomer, Daria Rigney, Mary Ehrenworth, and Amanda Hartman (along with many others) have all contributed to those ideas. My ideas on teaching reading benefit from the work done by other researchers. I am especially grateful to Ellin Keene, Kylene Beers, and Dick Allington.

Production of this book was especially complicated, and I am indebted to both Jean Lawler at Heinemann and to Tasha Kalista, whose considerable talents for composition and organization helped editor Kate Montgomery and me bring out the infrastructure in the book.

LITERARY ESSAYS: WRITING ABOUT READING

Welcome to Unit 5

WELCOME TO THE UNIT

LITERARY ESSAYS: WRITING ABOUT READING

In personal essays, many children will have written about lessons they learned from people they know and interact with. But writing also helps us learn from the characters in the books we read. Just as writing allows us to pause in our hurried lives and really notice and experience and reflect on things that have happened to us, so, too, writing allows us to pause in our hurried reading and really pay attention to the characters in our books.

In order for children to write about reading in this way, they need to be reading! Children who are learning to write literary essays while they are still very young—in grades three, four, and five—will profit from writing these essays about short texts they've read, reread, and discussed. In this unit, I invite children to read and study small packets of short texts that merit close study. A teacher might thread one short story through many minilessons, showing children how she reads, thinks, and writes about that one story and then suggesting that children try similar techniques with a story from their packet. The stories in a child's packet need to be ones the child can read. Therefore, children may not all have the same collection. I encourage teachers to provide stories that are rich, complex, and well-crafted enough to reward close study.

On each of the first few days of the unit, I demonstrate a lens that readers can bring to a text, reminding children that all of these lenses accumulate so they have a repertoire of possibilities to choose from whenever they read. I teach children that just as essayists pay attention to our lives, expecting to grow ideas from this wide-awake attentiveness, so, too, literary essayists pay attention . . . but this time the attention is directed to texts. Each child chooses a story that especially speaks to her and then collects entries about that story. The process of choosing a seed idea in this unit has two stages. First a child chooses a story. Then the child lives with that one story and gathers entries about it. Eventually, the child rereads those entries to chose a seed idea.

I remind children of their work in the personal essay unit, when they observed their lives and then pushed their thinking in their notebooks by writing, "The thought I have about this is . . ." or "This makes me realize that . . . ." In this unit, children can pause as they read to observe what is happening in the text and then develop an idea using the same conversational prompts. I teach children that their thoughts can be extended by using phrases such as "another example of this is," "furthermore," "this connects with," "on the other hand," "but you might ask," "this is true because," and "I am realizing." If we hope children will write literary essays in which they articulate the lessons they believe a character learns in a story or name the theme or idea a text teaches, then it is important to provide children with strategies for generating these sorts of ideas.

After children have collected reading responses in their writer's notebooks for at least a week, I remind them that they already know how to reread a notebook in order to find a seed idea. In the essay unit, students found seed ideas, and they'll need to do something similar now. I encourage students to search for a portion of an entry that tells the heart of the story in one or two sentences. I ask them to look for a seed idea that is central to the story and provocative.

I also help children generate possible seed ideas. Some children find it helpful to write inside this general structure: This is a story about [identify the character] who [has this trait]/[wants/cares about such-and-so] but then [what happens to change things?] and s/he ends up [how?]. In other words, I encourage some students to try writing a sentence or two in which they lay out what the character was like at the start of the story, what happened to change things, and how this was resolved at the end: "*Because of Winn-Dixie* is the story of a lonely girl, Opal, who befriends a stray dog, Winn-Dixie. The dog helps Opal make friends with lots of people." "'Spaghetti' is the story of a lonely boy, Gabriel, who learns from a tiny stray kitten to open himself to love." We also encourage children to think of a story as containing an external as well as an internal storyline, and to write an essay which highlights the internal (and therefore, sometimes the overlooked) story.

It is important to help each child revise her seed idea so that it is a clear thesis, making sure it is a claim or an idea, not a fact or a question. I help children imagine how they can support the thesis in a few paragraphs. Usually for children in grades three through five, the first support paragraph will show how the child's claim was true at the start of the story, and the next support paragraph(s) will show that it was true later in the story as well. It may be that the first support paragraph shows how the claim was true for one reason, the next, for a second reason.

Once children have planned their "boxes and bullets" for a literary essay, they will need to collect the information and insights they need to build a case. We encourage each child to make a file for each topic sentence (and each support paragraph). For example, if the child's claim is "Cynthia Rylant's story 'Spaghetti' is the story of a lonely boy who learns from a tiny stray kitten to open himself to love," the child might title one file "Gabriel is a lonely boy," and another "Gabriel learns from a tiny stray kitten to open himself to love."

I also teach writers how to cite references from a text and how to "unpack" the ways these references address the relevant big idea. Before this unit is over, we teach children that writers of literary essays use the vocabulary of their trade, incorporating literary terms such as *narrator*, *point of view*, *scenes*, and the like. We may also teach students to write introductory paragraphs that include a tiny summary of the story and closing paragraphs that link back to the thesis and that link the story's message to the writer's own life, or to another story, or to literature as a whole.

The Plan for the Unit

The "bends in the road" for this unit *Literary Essays* are as follows:

- Children read from a packet of short stories (and other texts) and write entries responding to their reading. I teach them a repertoire of ways in which literary essayists might write about texts that they are studying, including teaching them they might observe the text closely and then push themselves to have thoughts about what they notice. I suggest that readers know it pays off to give special attention to characters, writing about their traits, motivations, struggles, changes, and lessons. It is also helpful to think, "What is this text really about?" Part way through this phase of collecting entries, children narrow in on one text from the packet that particularly speaks to them and collect entries just about that text. Classroom time is spent not only writing but also talking about these texts.

- Children reread their entries and select an idea that they'd like to bring forth in a literary essay. With help, they craft this into a thesis statement. In most of their thesis statements, the child will either state her idea of what the text is *really* about, or the child will write about how a character changes or learns across the story. In either case, the child generally sets him or herself up to support the thesis with topic sentences like this: "Early in the book . . . and late in the book . . . ."

- Children set up a system for collecting support material for each of their topic sentences. This system replicates the system of folders children used when writing personal essays. Once again, each of the child's internal topic sentences is written on a file, and as the child collects support materials these are filed in the appropriate file. All the files are in one folder labeled with the child's thesis statement.

- Children reread the text under study as literary essayists do, finding ministories which support their claims. We remind children that it is important to angle these stories to make the point and to unpack them, showing how the story makes the point.

- Children collect lists, quotations, and other materials to support their claims, as literary essayists do.

- Eventually, children take one file at a time, sort through its contents, decide on particularly compelling support material, and sequence this material. They staple it together, rewriting only some of it, to make a rough draft.

- Children create cohesion among the bits that comprise their drafts by using transition words and repeating key words from their thesis and topic sentences. They may or may not revise the draft. They edit and recopy it for publication.

YOU'LL TEACH CHILDREN THAT GOOD READERS FLESH OUT STORIES BY ENVISIONING THEM AND LIVING VICARIOUSLY THROUGH THE CHARACTERS. YOU'LL TEACH CHILDREN TO TRY THIS FIRST ON PAPER, IN PREPARATION FOR TRYING IT MENTALLY.

GETTING READY

- Anecdote you can tell to illustrate that writers live intensely
- Enlarged copy of "Spaghetti" by Cynthia Rylant (or other touchstone text), prepared on chart paper for use throughout the unit
- List of tips for writing about reading—Write Inside the Story to Help You Read Well—prepared on chart paper
- A packet of four or five short, accessible texts for each child, marked in places where child could pause to envision
- See CD-ROM for resources

WRITING INSIDE THE STORY

Because you have already taught many units of study, *you enter this unit with an expectation for how a unit of study will probably go. You can count on the fact that Session I will invite writers into the big work of the unit while also equipping them with a particular strategy for generating the new kind of writing. You can also count on the fact that the first few minilessons will give students a repertoire of strategies for generating this new kind of writing, and for lifting the level of writing.*

But this unit is a bit different from all the others. To write well about reading, children not only need to learn more about writing, they also need to learn more about reading. These sessions, then, must support reading well in addition to writing well. Specifically, this first session is intended to help children to read actively—and to write about the literature they are reading.

When children write essays about texts, they need to first experience the text, dreaming the world of the story, walking in the shoes of the characters. Only after reading the story with empathy and imagination will the reader who wants to write analytically shift to reread with a critic's eyes, looking closely at the text and constructing a logical argument about what she sees. In this session, then, children will talk and write about stories not as commentators or expository thinkers, but instead as active, participating readers. This session invites children to draw from their lives, to fill in the gaps in a story, as readers do. If I read a story in which a small girl pulls on the door to her school, I see the girl, leaning back to slowly pull the mighty wooden door open—and it is the door from my own elementary school. Readers co-construct texts as we read, using both the words in texts and images from our lives.

In this session, you will invite children to fill in the details as they read. You'll teach children that when the character walks outside early one morning just after a long rainy night, good readers are apt to see the character step over the wet grass and pass the worms that writhe on the pathway. The purpose of today's writing is to help children read with engagement, writing inside the text as preparation for the writing they will do about the text.

MINILESSON

Writing Inside the Story

CONNECTION

Use a metaphor or anecdote to remind children that writers first live intensely and only then write about their experiences.

"As we learned earlier in the year, the great writer Annie Dillard has a photograph above her writing desk of a little boy standing firm in the river rapids, only his head above water. Annie posts that picture beside her writing desk because, she says, 'That little boy is completely alive. He's letting the mystery of existence beat on him. He's having his childhood and he knows it.' Annie uses that picture to remind herself that writers need to live intensely wide-awake lives, and then we write about those lives."

Tell children that, in the same way, we first read intensely and only then write about that experience.

"In this unit of study we will be writing about our reading. Reading is one way to wake up to the intensity and meaning and truth of our own lives. The famous essayist Donald Hall has said, 'Great literature, if we read it well, opens us up to the world and makes us more sensitive to it, as if we acquired eyes that could see through things and ears that could hear smaller sounds.' Before we can write a literary essay, we first need to climb inside a story, just as that little boy climbed inside the white water. We need to let the experience of the story pound down on us. Then and only then will we decide what we want to say about the story."

Name your teaching point. Specifically, tell children that to write a literary essay, they first need to live in the world of a story. Writing inside the story can help them do that.

"Specifically, what I want to teach you today is that when we want to make something of our reading, we first need to read as deeply as possible. We first need to experience the story as intensely as possible. And writing can help us do that."

TEACHING

Demonstrate close, empathetic reading. Show especially that as you read, you infer and envision, filling in details.

"When I want to read a story well, I don't read like this," I said, turning pages quickly and disinterestedly. "I don't just skim the story, then push it aside to stare up into the heavens trying to come up with something to write about the story."

COACHING

I know that this introduction has a high beauty quotient and may be a bit low on practical nuts-and-bolts information. I'm aware that when I preach a little sermon like this, some kids won't actually take in all of what I am saying. That's okay by me. I think they still glean that I'm trying to start the unit by talking about really important issues.

With this session, I am trying to reclaim writing about reading as a beautiful, glorious thing. I'm trying to make writing about reading feel personal—even intimate—and intense. For many children, writing about reading is a dreaded enterprise. Often children are asked to do this simply as a way to prove they read the text. Often no one reads the writing children do about reading, and nothing happens to that writing. It's not read, shared, revised, discussed—and, consequently, it feels wooden and lifeless. This unit attempts to reclaim writing about reading.

Sometimes when young people are asked to write a literary essay, the assignment turns reading itself into a search for a main idea and supportive detail. This lesson aims to convey that when we read a story, we need to bring a narrative frame of mind (not an expository one) to our reading. This lesson channels children toward empathizing, envisioning, anticipating, and experiencing vicariously—all actions that writers take when writing narratives and that readers take when reading narratives.

"Instead I read closely, trying to stand inside the character's shoes. Let me show you what I mean by reading just the start of 'Spaghetti,' a short story many of you know by Cynthia Rylant." I began to read aloud as if I were doing so privately, to myself:

> It was evening and people sat outside, talking quietly among themselves. On the stoop of a tall building of crumbling bricks and rotting wood sat a boy. His name was Gabriel and he wished for some company.
>
> Gabriel was thinking about things. He remembered being the only boy in class with the right answer that day, and he remembered the butter sandwich he had had for lunch. (1998)

I paused after reading this aloud and looked up, as if musing about the story. "I'm picturing Gabriel sitting on the stoop of his building. He remembers being in the school lunchroom; in my mind, he sat at a corner of a table, by himself, at lunch. I can see him pulling out a sandwich; it's not much of a sandwich, it just has butter on it." Then I paused, thought some more, and said to myself, "What else do I see?" I glanced back at the text, then again looked up and thought aloud. "I think Gabriel ate his sandwich, taking tiny bites, a little at a time, because he wanted to make it last. Now, sitting on the stoop, he is hungry. He probably wishes he'd kept some of the sandwich, that it was in his pocket still."

Setting aside the role of reader and resuming the role of teacher, I leaned close to the children and spoke directly to them. "Do you see how I read just a tiny bit and then I pause to get a picture in my mind?"

Debrief. Emphasize that as you read, you see the story in your mind.

Continuing to process my reading aloud, I said, "Do you see that when I want a story to be important to me, I don't just rush through it? It's almost as if I live inside the story. When I read, I act the story out in my mind as if it is a play and I'm the main character. You'll remember that the novelist, John Gardner, once described reading this way: 'It creates for us a kind of dream, a rich and vivid play in the mind. We read a few words at the beginning of a book or the particular story and suddenly we find ourselves seeing not words on a page but a train moving through Russia, an old Italian crying, or a farmhouse battered by rain. We read on—dream on—worrying about the choices the characters have to make, listening in panic for some sound behind the fictional door.' (1991) In our case, we read remembering butter sandwiches and feeling the hollow hunger as if it's not just Gabriel's but also our own."

In this unit of study, minilessons often require the teacher to shift between reading aloud and thinking aloud. It's easy for these two to become indistinguishable, something that creates confusion for the observing children. So, from the first, find a way to signal when you shift from reading aloud to thinking aloud. When you are thinking about the text rather than reading it, lower the book and look up toward the sky: Don't hesitate to be a bit overly dramatic in ways that convey, "Now I'm not reading. I am, instead, musing over what I've just read."

You may squirm uncomfortably over the fact that as a reader, I am filling in details that are not there in the story, but I am totally convinced that all good readers do this. We read, "She stepped out into the whirling snow," and some of us see blinding snow, driven by winds. Some of us see a scattering of flakes, each one distinct, dancing daintily toward the ground. As we read on, the upcoming words in the text alter the images we create. But an active reader doesn't wait till all the information has been amassed before creating mental pictures. The talking I've just done (and the talking and writing I will soon ask children to do) embodies the mental activities that I hope good readers do as they read. I want children to experience a text deeply and fully. Later, I will also want children to hold the text at arm's length and to think about the messages in it, rereading in ways that lead them to use sections of the text to defend ideas. At that point, I will ask them to bring an expository frame even to narrative texts, generating ideas (and entries and essays) that are shaped like expository texts. But for now, I don't want to hurry children toward thinking and writing entries that feel like little expository essays about their reading.

The Gardner quote is one of my favorite descriptions of reading. I want children to become so absorbed in a text that they see not words on the page, but a train moving through Russia. Because I want to support envisionment, during read-aloud time as well as during these minilessons, I'll sometimes pause in the middle of a read-aloud, look up with a faraway expression, and say, "I can picture it. I'm seeing . . . ."

ACTIVE ENGAGEMENT
Set children up to practice envisioning as they read by explaining their mental pictures to a partner.

"Let me read on. As I read, try to be in the story. See Gabriel, hear him—try to sense through Gabriel's eyes, ears, skin. When I come to a good place to stop, I'll pause so we can each see the story in our minds and say what we are sensing, what we are envisioning, to our partners." I read this aloud:

> Gabriel was thinking that he would like to live outside all the time. He imagined himself carrying a pack of food and a few tools and a heavy cloth to erect a hasty tent. Gabriel saw himself sleeping among coyotes. But next he saw himself sleeping beneath the glittering lights of a movie theater, near the bus stop. (1998)

"Turn to your partner and say, 'I see . . . ,' then say what you see."

After this tiny interval for talk, I resumed reading, repeating the previous section of the text just a bit and then reading on:

> Gabriel was a boy who thought about things so seriously, so fully, that on this evening he nearly missed hearing a cry from the street. The cry was so weak and faraway in his mind that, for him, it could have been the slow lifting of a stubborn window. It could have been the creak of an old man's legs. It could have been the wind.

"Turn to your partner and say, 'I see . . .' or 'I hear . . . .'" After a moment, while children were still talking, I resumed reading. As usual, I reread a bit of the story, knowing that some of the children would miss the start of my read-aloud because they were still finishing their partner conversations and repositioning themselves to listen.

> Gabriel picked himself up from the stoop and began to walk carefully along the edge of the street, peering into the gloom and the dusk.

"Turn and envision," I said.

Sometimes instead of demonstrating how I envision as I read, I set children up to do this. Pausing while reading aloud, I say, "Let me reread that . . . ." I might invite children to turn and talk for a moment with a partner. "What city block are you picturing?" I might ask, then add, "Turn and talk." If children aren't sure how to supply the details in those mental pictures, help them understand that readers bring the city blocks from our own lives into stories we read. Sometimes as we continue to read, the text causes us to revise those pictures, and this revision is a crucial part of reading.

As you listen in, you may see a child sort of shrug to a partner and then repeat exactly what you just read aloud, saying, "I see him sleeping by the movie theater?" Don't despair, and definitely don't reveal your disappointment! For now, you want to help all children begin this new work. So nod generously, and add on. "I see that too! The movie theater I'm picturing is huge. It has eight shows all showing at once; it has great crowds of people lined up. This is a city! The people sort of circle around the lump on the sidewalk that is Gabriel, wrapped in a blanket, trying to sleep. He realizes as he lies there, sleeping alone isn't all that fun!" Be sure to ask, "What do you see? Is your theater huge, or small, or what?"

The children don't yet have much to go on in their effort to fill in the gaps in this story. If you were leaving gaps like this halfway through a novel instead of a short story, the children could use the whole first half of the story to supply missing details. Because the story I was reading aloud—"Spaghetti"—is brief and sparse, I kept the gaps that children were asked to fill very small. Alternatively, you may decide to do this work with a chapter from your read-aloud novel! If you ask children to supply too much detail without providing enough text to guide the detail selection, your request can lead children away from the story as it is written.

Show children that instead of saying what they envision and sense for the character while reading, they can write inside the story, and this can help them read more deeply.

As the children again voiced what they were picturing, I recorded the last phrase I'd just read on chart paper. Then I said, "Partner 1, keep making a movie in your mind, only this time, *write* rather than saying aloud whatever you are envisioning. Partner 2, do the same in your notebook. Do that now while I do the same thing on this chart paper." I reread the line from "Spaghetti" I'd copied onto chart paper, then paused thoughtfully to model envisioning. Then I wrote what I envisioned on chart paper:

> Gabriel picked himself up from the stoop and began to walk carefully along the edge of the street, peering into the gloom and the dusk. He peered behind a trash can, piled high with garbage. "Was the sound coming from there?" he wondered. But only a rat skittered out from the shadows. Walking down the street, Gabriel listened hard, hoping to hear the tiny cry again. He looked again into an alley, this time seeing stuff (a bike, a bucket of purple flowers).

"Writers, do you see that instead of *talking* to convey what I saw and heard in this bit of the story, I wrote—and you did this as well. We each copied a sentence from the text and then we each added into the story, almost as if we were the author of the story. In this case, I filled in what Gabriel probably thought and noticed. Most of us wrote just a small step that the author left out, to help us really feel that moment right after what was described in the story." At this point, I turned a page of my chart paper tablet to reveal this chart.

Write Inside the Story to Help You Read Well

- Read trying to experience the story.
- Choose a part that matters.
- Step into the story. As you envision, fill in details.
- Write a bit to help you go into the story. Write a few lines that could belong in it. Resume reading.
- Pause to write again when it feels right.

In the Active Engagement sections of minilessons, it is important for us to provide children with assisted practice doing what we have just demonstrated. In this instance, I know the Active Engagement stands a chance of being confusing, so I take extra steps to set children up and get them started, making it is as likely as possible that they'll be able to do this work successfully—and in short order.

I write publicly on chart paper while the children write alongside me so my demonstration provides extra support for those who don't quite grasp what I've asked them to do. Because this is a three-minute activity and I won't have a chance to get around to every kid, a few children will probably spend this interlude watching me model rather than actually getting started on their own work, and that's okay. The fact that I am writing alongside the others, then, makes the lesson more multilevel.

Be sure you give children only a very short amount of time to fill in the gaps of the story, or they'll veer far from the story as it's written!

I could decide to say, "Partners, would you show each other what you wrote, and talk about whether you did all these steps? This was your very first time doing this, so I know some of you will see that you haven't been clear about what this work entails. That's okay—just talk about it!" But, in this case, time is short, and I know some children are confused enough that I'd rather clarify by sharing an example or two.

When I show children a chart like this, I don't necessarily read it aloud. I'm just showing them that this chart exists, and children can use it if they want this scaffold. For some children, the chart is unnecessary. Let this chart be a resource rather than a lesson!

Point out that the mental movies readers create are grounded in the texts themselves. Ask children to point to the textual details that informed their mental movies.

"I heard amazing descriptions of what you are picturing and sensing through Gabriel. Of course, we didn't all picture the same things, which is as it should be."

"When Gabriel walked down that street, searching for the source of that thin cry, Max filled in that Gabriel saw a large brown dog, curled up asleep in the alley. On the other hand, I filled in that he saw a bike and a bucket of purple flowers. The movies we make in our minds won't be exactly the same. When John Gardner said that readers create—we imagine—a kind of dream, a play in the mind (when he said we listen for some sound behind the imagined door, for that thin cry to come again from the shadows along Gabriel's street), remember that we *invent* this imagined story, this dream, out of both our lives and the text."

"Both Max and I remembered, however, that the author has told us that Gabriel sat on the stoop outside a tall building of 'crumbling bricks and rotting wood' and sees himself 'sleeping beneath the glittering lights of a movie theater, near the bus stop.' We'd be misreading the story if we had Gabriel search for the source of the cry by looking in posh doorways of boutique restaurants, stopping for an éclair and a frozen frappe."

"Would you go back to your partner and point to the lines from the story that provided a rationale for the bits you created to fill in the gaps of 'Spaghetti'? For example, if you added the line, 'He peered behind a trash can, piled high with garbage,' tell your partner the grounds for this image. If your picture wasn't grounded in the text, say aloud a new way to fill out the text."

LINK
Rally children to the big work of this unit and to the goal of wide-awake, attentive reading. Explain that for the next few days, they need to read deeply the texts from the packet.

"Writers, today we embark on a new unit of study. Earlier this year, you wrote about experiences and people that have left their mark on you. Today, I hope you've learned that the first step in writing a literary essay is to be the kind of reader who lets *stories* leave a mark on us. We need to read a few sentences on a page, and all of a sudden see a train rushing through Russia; we need to read sentences and all of a sudden see a small boy peering into the alley. And today you learned that one way to help you step into the story is to write from inside it. You learned that you can write in ways that help you feel a story. Doing this writing will help you see more, hear more, think more, feel more as you read."

"I've put a small packet of stories on each of your desks; for the next few weeks we'll read and reread, think, talk, and write about these stories, and about 'Spaghetti,' too."

I added this extension to the Active Engagement because I found that some children thought my invitation to fill in the gaps in the story gave them license to imagine any old thing. I hadn't meant to suggest this. However, I did expect children to add specific details that are not actually in the text, as in the example from my demonstration of the bike and the bucket of flowers. I am convinced that all good readers embellish, add on to, infer. However, good readers make sure that the text guides this process appropriately.

The qualities of good writing are also the qualities of good teaching. I could have made this same point without referring to the frozen frappe or the éclair, but I try to make general points with revealing specifics.

Sometimes we intervene during the Active Engagement to lift the level of children's work. This extension of the Active Engagement could easily have been a separate minilesson, but I'm trying to devote only a little bit of this unit to this deep reading.

You'll want to give each child a packet of four or five short texts. Be sure there are several texts in the packet that are easy enough for your struggling readers. We've had great success, for example, with "Alone" from Frog and Toad Are Friends *by Arnold Lobel. That story works because it is beautifully written—as are the other texts we recommend. Include texts your class has reread often and come to love. On the CD-ROM, I've included a list of possible texts. If you use picture books, we usually give children typed copies of the texts (with permission from the publishers) so children can write on them (while reading the beautiful versions).*

Today, choose whatever story catches your eye, and then read and write. Writers sometimes do this kind of thinking from inside a text before we write from outside a text—before we write *about* it."

"When you read today, you won't want to read like this," I said, flipping through pages and looking away. "Instead, read slowly, as if your job is to climb inside the words of this text and *live* the text. You'll see I've marked places to pause in each text, and when you come to one of those places, copy the underlined bit from the text and then keep writing, adding what the character was probably seeing, thinking, remembering. Just write a tiny bit, then return to the text to read some more. Go intensely through one short text, and maybe another, today. You will be doing something *on the page* that good readers do *in our minds' eyes* whenever we read really well."

During the Link in most minilessons, we generally say to children, "The strategy I've taught you today should help you from this day forward, whenever you . . . ." However, I am aware that the strategy I've taught children today is not one they will actually use "from this day forward." Instead, I've asked children to do something in writing that I hope they end up doing in their minds' eyes as they read. We earn kids' trust by acknowledging that what we ask them to do from time to time may not be a strategy readers or writers use often—and by explaining why we nevertheless believe it matters.

WRITING AND CONFERRING

Supporting Deep Reading

At the start of any new unit, you'll hustle among children, helping them begin the new work you've laid out. Children will need quite a lot of help getting started with the work of today's minilesson. You have asked them to engage in something that requires a different orientation than their usual writing workshop work. You have asked them to read—and the reading you hope they do probably differs from their usual reading as well as their usual writing work. Specifically, you have asked children to read much more intensely than usual, inching through a text with frequent shifts between reading and writing.

So at the start of today's workshop, I suggest you survey the room and notice right away the children who are flying through a text. Notice also those who are writing at a distance from the texts rather than from deep inside them; the children who concern you will be evaluating or commenting on texts rather than writing as if they were the authors, filling in gaps. These two groups will each need a quick intervention to bring them on course.

If the entire class needs guidance, rely on a mid-workshop teaching point; otherwise, I suggest using table conferences. When I taught this unit recently, I spent this first workshop time going to one table after another. At each table, I did similar work. Gathering the attention of all the children, I said, "Will you watch me work with . . . ." Then I worked with one child to get that one youngster doing what I hoped all the children would do. Specifically, I asked that child, "Where are you in reading the story?" Once the child showed me the spot, I said, "Let's read it together," and I scanned the surrounding group of children, saying, "She's reading . . . " (and I named the text). The watching children often pulled out their copy of that text so they could follow along. "Watch." Then the one child and I read silently for less than a minute. Then I paused and said to the one child, "I'm picturing this, aren't you?" In a voice that was loud enough for all the listeners to hear, I described what I was picturing. Then we read on.

> **MID-WORKSHOP TEACHING POINT** *Writing Inside the Text* "Writers, can I have your eyes and your attention please? Some of you are writing about the story; to use writing to read deeply, it helps to try writing inside the story. Let me share something very smart that Judah did. First I'm going to read the bit of text she read—it's from 'Boar Out There' by Cynthia Rylant—and then I'll read how she recorded what she envisioned. You'll remember that the story starts by saying everyone knew there was a wild boar beyond the rail fence in the woods. Then the story zooms in on one moment:
>
> > Jenny would hook her chin over the top rail of the fence, twirl a long green blade of grass in her teeth and whisper, "Boar out there."
>
> "First Judah wrote *about* the character, about Jenny in 'Boar Out There.' Here's how she did it at first":
>
> > Jenny cares about animals. She seems lonely—sitting, looking at the boar.
>
> "But then Judah said to herself, 'No, that doesn't help me really feel from inside the story. I want to get more in it.' So this time Judah wrote about the moment when Jenny was in the woods, sensing the boar is close."
>
> *continued on next page*

In one such conference, I asked Carmen to show me where she was reading in "The Marble Champ" by Gary Soto. She pointed to a section where the protagonist, Lupe, poured her brother's marbles onto the bed and picked five marbles. I read the section of the familiar text aloud to myself (knowing the observing children were listening in). It said, "She smoothed her bedspread and practiced shooting, softly at first." (2000) I pointed to that passage and said to Carmen what I was picturing: "She reached for the can full of marbles. Then she poured the whole can-full onto the bed. As she did this, the marbles clattered against the tin can. She picked out five marbles, one at a time, then scooped up the rest and returned them to the can. Then she lined up the five marbles on the bedspread." Then I paused to name what I'd just done for Carmen and for the others who were listening. "Do you see how I used what I know from my life—like the clatter of the marbles against that tin can—*and* what I learned from the story—the text told me Lupe's brother's marbles were in a can—to get me deeper into the story? Let's read on," I said, and after a minute I again paused and said, "I can see it, can't you?" Then I whispered to Carmen, "Take it from there. What do you see?"

Carmen was speechless, so I looked at the children who were watching, as if to signal, "You should be able to do this. Could any of you do it?" No one leapt in, so I went back and reread the text in a way that allowed Carmen to regain momentum. This time, I started Carmen off. She stumbled through a tiny bit of envisionment and I resumed where she left off, adding on a bit more. I then turned our focus back to the text. "Let's read to the mark on the page, and again you tell me what you are imagining." This time, once Carmen began to tell me what she envisioned, I said, "Write that down!" As Carmen recorded two sentences, I debriefed with the observing children. Carmen looked up in the middle of this and I gestured as if to say, "Perfect," and then said, "Read on," returning her focus to the text. Then I asked the watching group of children to get started doing similar work with whatever text each of them chose.

In these ways, you'll provide the help that some children will need. You'll probably recognize that there is reciprocity between this work—teaching children to make movies in their minds as they read—and previous work you've helped children do as writers of short fiction and personal narratives.

continued from previous page

"Judah wrote": *[Fig. I-1]*

> Jenny is slowly walking. The leaves crumble beneath her feet. She looks around, nervously she tries to be quiet, so she doesn't startle the boar.
>
> She starts to feel all closed in. She looks up to the sky to try and feel out of the woods.
>
> She eats a leaf and relaxes a little. She leans against a tree, looks around, and freezes. She stops breathing.
>
> He ran through the trees toward her. Her heart starts beating fast.

"Do you see how Judah wrote that part from inside the story? We can really see Jenny looking around and we can hear the leaves crumbling beneath her feet! That's what you need to do in your work, too! Remember you, too, can use your eyes, your ears, your skin to experience the story you've chosen to read."

"Would you go back to the writing you've done so far? Read it over to see if you are writing in a way that helps you get deeper into the story."

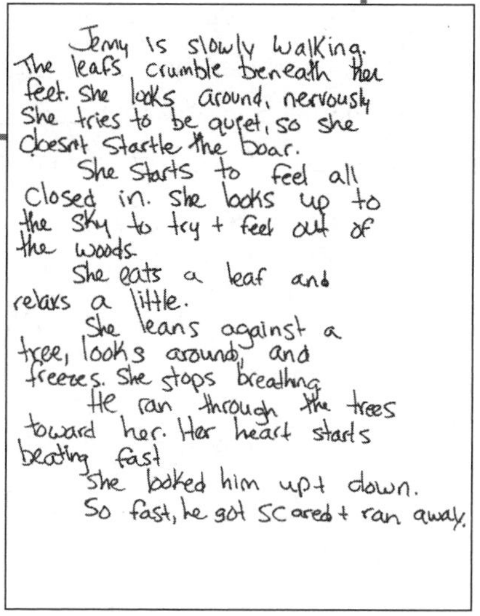
Jenny is slowly walking.
The leafs crumble beneath her
feet. She looks around, nervously
She tries to be quiet, so she
doesnt startle the boar.
She starts to feel all
closed in. She looks up to
the sky to try + feel out of
the woods.
She eats a leaf and
relaxs a little.
She leans against a
tree, looks around, and
freezes. She stops breathing.
He ran through the trees
toward her. Her heart starts
beating fast
She looked him up + down.
So fast, he got scared + ran away.

Fig. I-1 Judah continues envisioning the story

Max, for example, read "Slower than the Rest," another Rylant story, (1988) this time about a turtle. Max copied a line of the text onto his page (see italics) and then added on to it:

> "Both his little sisters squealed when the animal stuck its ugly head out to look at them, and they thought its claws horrifying."
>
> I see a dark turtle in the trunk of a big tree, scared and standing still, slowly sticking out its head. Leo would put Charlie down and he would sniff at the air for a moment, then take off as if no one had ever told him how slow he was supposed to be.

Then Max resumed reading, and soon paused again to copy a line from the text and add what he saw: *[Fig. I-2]*

> "Leo settled Charlie in a cardboard box, threw in some lettuce and radishes, and declared himself a happy boy."
>
> I see a small box with two holes for handles, just big enough for the turtle to sit in. He is in a kitchen, eating radishes.

A few youngsters may still find this difficult. With those children you'll need to decide upon your level of commitment to the work you laid out today. How invested are you in having every child grasp what it means to use writing as a medium in which they dream the dream of the story? Some of you will decide that it is crucial to be sure your children are reading with a level of alertness, empathy, and investment, but not crucial that they do this sort of writing today. Others of you will decide to linger with this session, and the extensions that follow can help you do this.

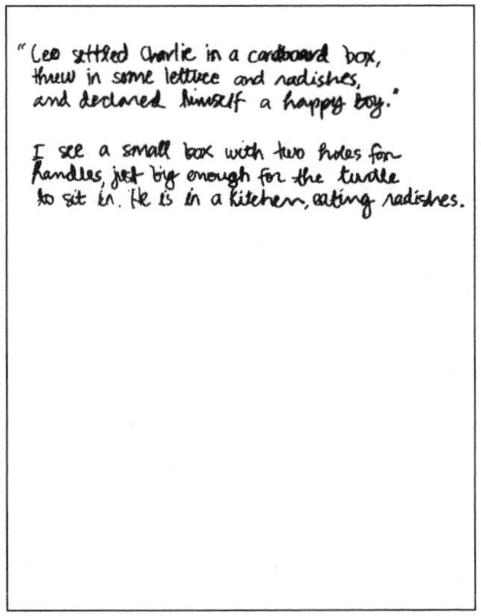
"Leo settled Charlie in a cardboard box, threw in some lettuce and radishes, and declared himself a happy boy."

I see a small box with two holes for handles, just big enough for the turtle to sit in. He is in a kitchen, eating radishes.

Fig. I-2 Max copies a line from Rylant's text and then writes about what he envisions

SHARE

Reading Empathetically

Ask children to share their writing with their partners, discussing how this writing changed their reading.

"Right now, would you share with your partner what you wrote? Would you also talk with your partner about how this work helped you experience your story more deeply? And here is an important question: How could you do this sort of reading even if you don't have a pen in hand?"

I listened as Ali read aloud entries she'd written inside "The Marble Champ." In the story, after Lupe, the protagonist, realizes her marble-shooting thumb is weaker than the neck of a newborn chick, the text says, "She looked out the window. The rain was letting up but the ground was too muddy to play." (2000) Ali had copied that line and then filled in the details of what Lupe did next: *[Fig. I-3]*

> She looked out the window. The rain was letting up. She gripped the brown silk bag of marbles in one hand and a piece of chalk in the other hand. She got up and walked to the door to the outside. She took a deep breath and walked back to the marbles on the bed.

Later, Ali extended another section of the text: "To strengthen her shooting, she decided to do 20 pushups on her fingertips, five at a time." (2000) In her notebook, Ali wrote:

> Lupe got into the push up position. 1, 2, 3, 4, and 5. She fell down. But decided to push herself 10, 15, 20. "Yes!" she screamed.

Ali told her partner that writing these extra bits made her realize how hard it was to practice all the time, and she could feel how much each little pushup hurt.

Explain that empathy for real people works in much the same way as empathy for characters.

"Wow, I can hear that you all have really been reading deeply! The writing in support of reading that you have been doing today should definitely help you read empathetically, seeing through the character's eyes. Have you ever tried this kind of envisioning in your lives?"

You will definitely want to know well the stories you've given to your children to read. This will allow you to model, and also to quickly grasp what they've done.

> She looked out the window. The rain was letting up. She gripped the brown silk bag of marbles in one hand and a piece of chalk in the other hand. She got up and walked to the door to the outside. She took a deep breath and walked back to the marbles on the bed.
>
> . . . .
>
> Lupe got into the push up position. 1, 2, 3, 4, 5. She fell down. But decided to push herself 10, 15, 20. "Yes!" she screamed.

Fig. I-3 Ali envisions and writes off from "The Marble Champ"

"Have you ever tried to really imagine the senses of another person, perhaps a girl being bullied or a boy who is new to a school? This kind of careful attention to the world through someone else's eyes can help us learn how to have friends and be a good citizen in the world. From reading we can learn empathy."

You may wonder about my use of "big words" such as empathetically. I make a point of weaving what I suspect will be unfamiliar vocabulary into my teaching. I do not usually stop to provide a definition, but I do try to surround the difficult term with an explanation of its meaning. That is, I try to enable children to use contextual knowledge to grasp the meaning of the term. This is how most human beings learn the thousands and thousands of new words we learn each year. I recognize that you will alter these minilessons so they work for your kids, and this may include altering the level of vocabulary.

HOMEWORK *Reading, Writing, and Living with Empathy* The great writer, Joyce Carol Oates, has said, "Reading is the sole means by which we slip, involuntarily, often helplessly, into another's skin, another's voice, another's soul." Anna Quindlen agrees: "It is like the rubbing of two sticks together to make a fire . . . this making symbols into words, into sentences, into sentiments and scenes and a world imagined in the mind's eye." During reading time tonight and always, be sure to let the words on the page create a movie in your mind.

All year long, you've learned that *writers* make movies in our minds and then capture those movies in print. Tonight, be the *reader*. Take in the letters, words, and sentences, and let them be like the film of a mental movie. Read the print, learn that it is winter in the story, and let yourself shiver with the cold.

You can read or reread one of the short texts we'll be studying in the writing workshop— "Eleven," "The Marble Champ," "Boar Out There," "The Birthday Box"—or you can read your novel. But after you read a bit, put down the page and write what you see in that mental movie. Then resume reading. Shift between reading and writing, reading and writing. Here's an example of the kind of writing you can do: *[Fig. I-4]*

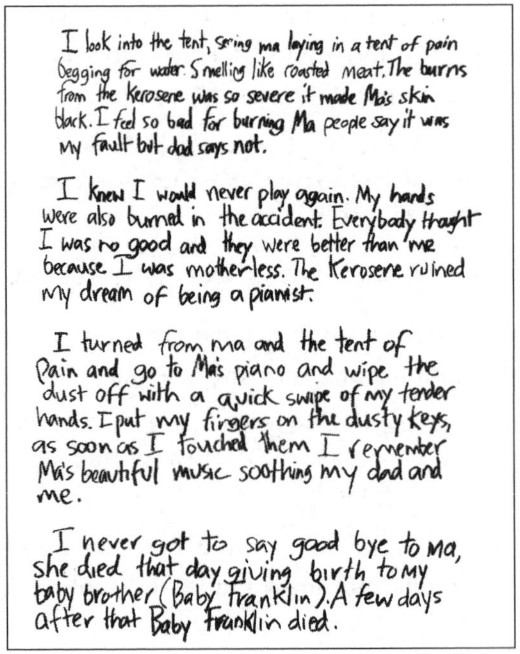

I look into the tent, seeing Ma laying in a tent of pain begging for water. Smelling like roasted meat. The burns from the kerosene were so severe it made Ma's skin black. I feel so bad for burning Ma. People say it was my fault but Dad says not.

I knew I would never play again. My hands were also burned in the accident. Everybody thought I was no good and they were better than me because I was motherless. The kerosene ruined my dream of being a pianist.

I turned from Ma and the tent of pain and go to Ma's piano and wipe the dust off with a quick swipe of my tender

Fig. I-4 David's notebook entry in response to *Out of the Dust* by Karen Hesse

hands. I put my fingers on the dusty keys, as soon as I touched them I remember Ma's beautiful music soothing my dad and me.

I never got to say good bye to Ma, she died that day giving birth to my baby brother (Baby Franklin). A few days after that Baby Franklin died.

TAILORING YOUR TEACHING

If your children need more work to help them read deeply . . . you may decide to set children up to turn and talk inside the story during your read-aloud sessions. For example, if you are reading aloud *Because of Winn-Dixie* and you have just read that Opal brought a stray dog, Winn-Dixie, home to her father, the Preacher, you might read, "The Preacher looked at Winn-Dixie. He looked at his ribs and his matted-up fur and the places where he was bald." And then you might say, "Partner 1, you are the father. You are looking at that dog. What are you thinking? Tell partner 2." After a bit, you could intervene, "Partner 2, you are Opal. Talk back to your father . . ." Once children have done this work orally in the context of the read-aloud, it will be far easier for them to do similar work in response to the short stories you are asking them to read as part of the writing workshop.

If children need more time envisioning the story and writing from the character's point of view in order to read more deeply . . . you could lead a minilesson by helping them rely on close reading when they envision. You might start off by saying, "Yesterday you put yourselves into 'Spaghetti' and wrote your mental movie of moments from those stories. You used what you knew about the characters to imagine what they might have seen, heard, and felt. Today I want to remind you that readers need to rely on the clues in a text to help us picture the world in which the story takes place. You and I have talked about how every story has a setting, and we talked about the importance of discerning that setting . . . but I want to go a step farther and tell you that readers need to not only be able to name the setting, we need to create it around us as we read. If it is a damp, gray day in the book, we read and feel a chill. When I read, the setting unfolds like a movie in my mind."

To demonstrate, you could read a bit aloud from "Spaghetti" and say something such as, "Watch how I create the setting out of the clues I'm given. I see Gabriel slowly getting up from the stairs of his building. He walks carefully along the edge of the street next to the sidewalk. It is not easy to see because it is a gray, gloomy day—since Gabriel is peering into the dusk, I know it is late in the day. Gabriel heard the cry and quickened his pace."

Then you'll want to debrief, pointing out what you did. "Writers, did you notice how I went back to where Gabriel was—sitting on the stoop—and I imagined the place where he was, then I followed him down the street, picturing exactly when and how he walked, on the edge of the sidewalk. Did you notice also that I made sure I paid attention to the word 'dusk' because it was a clue in the text, letting me know it was not morning or afternoon? I was walking in Gabriel's shoes, so when he heard the cry, I knew he would start walking faster and so would I. I was so into the story that I felt as if I (like Gabriel) wanted to discover who or what was making that sound."

During the Active Engagement, you might read a bit further in "Spaghetti" and ask children to make movies in their minds of the text and then turn and tell their partners what they see. Don't worry that you are revisiting "Spaghetti" over and over—rereading is crucial! You might end this minilesson by saying something like, "When we make a little movie in our minds as we read and specifically when we create the world of the story, this helps us understand what the character is feeling and thinking because we have similar thoughts and feelings." As you send children off, remind them to play the movie in their minds . . . writing down what they see, think, feel . . . so they can connect with the characters and places in their story.

If your children worked through this unit during a previous year and they are ready for the minilesson to be a bit more challenging . . . you'll want your touchstone text to be more complex than "Spaghetti." I recommend that you and your colleagues choose a short story or a picture book and work with it together, using the repertoire of strategies conveyed in these minilessons to help you talk and write about the text you select. As you do this work, you'll find yourself deepening the lessons in this book and inventing new ones. A group of teachers in a school I know well decided to work with Eve Bunting's picture book, *Fly Away Home*. Julia Mooney, one of the teachers at that school, read bits of the text and then envisioned the world of the story. Below you'll see the portion of the text that preceded her envisioning, and then what she wrote in her reading log:

> *Fly Away Home* (an excerpt)
>
> My dad and I live in an airport. That's because we don't have a home and the airport is better than the streets. We are careful not to get caught.
>
> Mr. Slocum and Mr. Vail were caught last night.
>
> "Ten green bottles on the wall," they sang. They were as loud as two moose bellowing.
>
> Dad says they broke the first rule of living here. Don't get noticed.

Dad and I try not to get noticed. We stay among the crowds. We change airlines.

Julia wrote (although when teaching this, she might say this aloud):

> I'm picturing Andrew and his dad walking slowly through an airport with fluorescent lighting and people rushing all around them. They're trying not to get caught so they act like everyone else, pretending to be going on a trip or returning from one. Sometimes they wait in front of the conveyor belt, looking for bags that aren't actually coming. Other times they browse in the airport shops, reading magazines and admiring souvenirs.
>
> I see Andrew looking a little sad as he thinks about Mr. Slocum and Mr. Vail. Andrew feels bad for them, for their being caught. He's relieved that he and his dad are so good at keeping a low profile. But part of him is envious of Mr. Slocum and Mr. Vail. Part of him longs to be noticed, too.

Julia continued to read from *Fly Away Home*.

> Everything in the airport is on the move—passengers, pilots, flight attendants, cleaners with their brooms. Jets roar in close to the windows.

Julia wrote:

> Everything and everyone whirs past dad and me. Sometimes I wonder what all that rushing is about—where people are going and what they'll do when they get there. I wonder what it would feel like to have something to do, somewhere to be. Other times I don't even notice.

You and your colleagues can do similar work, and then mine this work for minilessons you could teach. For example, in one minilesson, you could point out that you (like Julia) brought your own ideas to the text.

If some of your children are envisioning the text by repeating the exact words of the text . . . you might want to explain that making a movie in your mind as you read includes more than simply repeating the story. I might say, "When I read, I am using *all* of my senses to help me make the movie."

In a minilesson or a strategy lesson, I might say, "I'm going to reread the part of 'Spaghetti' we looked at yesterday and help you get a picture of Gabriel. Close your eyes and listen to the text. Do what I say, and this will help you get a clear picture." Then I'd reread an excerpt:

> It was evening . . .

After pausing, I'd say quietly, "See the sky . . . add the colors to your picture in your mind." Then I'd pause and continue reading:

> It was evening, and people sat outside, talking quietly
> among themselves.

"Add the people to your picture. Where are they sitting? What are they sitting on?" I'd pause. Then, "See their faces. What expressions are on their faces?"

Then I'd read on:

> On a stoop of a tall building of crumbling bricks and rotting wood
> sat a boy. His name was Gabriel and he wished for some company.

"See Gabriel. What's he wearing?" (Pause.) "What does he look like?" (Pause.) "Look closely at his face. How is he sitting? (Pause.) Right now, be Gabriel and show me what he looks like as he sits on the steps in front of his building. Sit like Gabriel's sitting."

Then I say, "Let's all look at Sabrina acting like Gabriel. Let's write in the air by putting words to what we see her doing. Turn to your partner and write in the air."

By this time, I'd want to debrief. "Writers," I might say. "Did you notice how I read a tiny bit and we worked on getting a picture in our minds by using our senses as we read? As you read today, pause and write what you are picturing."

COLLABORATING WITH COLLEAGUES

You and your colleagues can invent other ways to help children read deeply by identifying with characters. Notice what your students are doing pertaining to characters, for example, and think about how you can nudge them toward deeper work. If you want your children to identify with characters, to walk in their shoes, then it should concern you if you hear many children in your class dismissing and judging the protagonists in their books, saying things like, "*Why'd* he do that? I would *never* act like that." In these instances, you may want children to take their own questions more seriously, pausing to really consider why the character *did* do something. You might help children to ask themselves, "What is it about the character that makes him do this?" Usually, in a well-written story, a character's actions are motivated. This means that although a child may not have done the same things, hopefully the child will be able to read what the character has done and say, "I can understand where this character was coming from."

Alternatively, you and your colleagues may decide to show children that writing about reading can be an opportunity for envisioning. Instead of asking partners to talk, you could have them write: "I can see it, can't you? Stop and jot what you see in your mind." Following are entries that two third graders wrote during a pause in the middle of a read-aloud from Gary Paulsen's book *The Monument*. [Figs. I-5 and I-6]

Entry 1, Writing in response to *The Monument*:

> Light, light, light is everything. All you need is a dry room and light. While he talked on about light and a dry room and how much light really is, very strange thing happened. Python walked over to him and put his jaw against the leg. Then he bent down and stroked Python's silky fur but Python did not mind at all. This was the first time he had let anybody touch him . . . .

Entry 2, Writing in response to *The Monument*:

> "Look at the light coming down from the old wall! See how it comes down, gold and across your face! Oh god, see the light? It comes down like a blessing, like a kiss from the gods. I've got to get it. Don't move. Stay there." He sketched fast with his head bent over and sweat coming down his head. I still think, "What is he sketching?"

An extension of this would be to suggest that during independent reading, children put sticky notes on places in their independent reading books where they make movies in their minds. Then, after reading silently for a half hour or so, children could meet with partners to share their notes and their mental movies.

Another day you could convey the thin line between envisioning and predicting, again doing this first in the read-aloud. As you read aloud, pause at key moments to speculate over what the character will probably do next. The character reaches into his wallet and finds no money there; the good reader is one step ahead, expecting the character to turn the wallet upside down and shake it. The reader expects the character to progress to checking his pockets, trying to recall the last time he saw that ten-dollar bill. In this way you can demonstrate that reading is an intricate weave of envisionment, prediction, and revision.

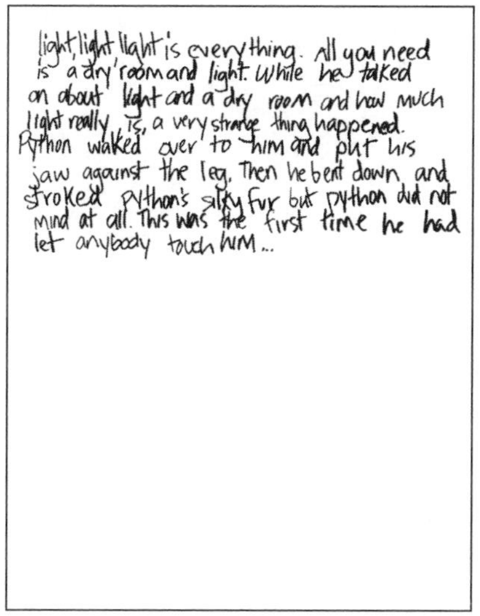

> light, light light is everything. All you need is a dry room and light. While he talked on about light and a dry room and how much light really is, a very strange thing happened. Python walked over to him and put his jaw against the leg. Then he bent down, and stroked Python's silky fur but python did not mind at all. This was the first time he had let anybody touch him...

Fig. I-5 Amelia envisions and writes in response to Paulsen's *The Monument*.

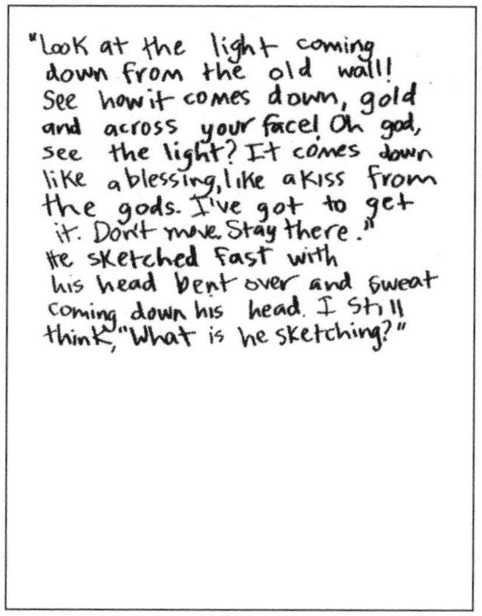

> "Look at the light coming down from the old wall! See how it comes down, gold and across your face! Oh god, see the light? It comes down like a blessing, like a kiss from the gods. I've got to get it. Don't move. Stay there." He sketched fast with his head bent over and sweat coming down his head. I still think, "What is he sketching?"

Fig. I-6 Annie envisions, seeing through the artist, Mick's, eyes.

Later, you and your colleagues may want to talk together about ways in which this session can affect teaching and learning throughout the day.

For example, during your *reading* workshop, you could invite children to walk in the shoes of the main character in a story. You'd probably begin by demonstrating this in your read-aloud. Before you read aloud, read the text silently and note places where you find yourself picturing a character, a scene. The first two or three of those places can become places where you demonstrate for children.

In class, convene the children and read aloud. Pause at the first place you've marked and say something like, "I can just see this. She's . . . ." After

saying aloud what you envision, read on. Your initial picture may be altered by incoming information, which is fine. Just say "Oops!" and make a quick alteration. Within a few minutes, you'll read a section in the text where you want children to do as you've done. Pause in the reading to say, "I can see it, can't you? See it in your mind." You might repeat a phrase or two. Then say, "Partner 1, tell partner 2 what you see." After a minute, interject by reading on. Don't stop and talk as a class. Read on, dream on!

GATHERING WRITING ABOUT THE STORY BY CLOSE READING

I recently watched a child come to the end of his novel, snap it shut, and sling it onto the bookshelf. "I'm done," he said. "I've read sixteen books. I've got to put another star by my name." Before Derrick raced off I asked what he thought of the book. "Umm . . . ," Derrick said. He hastened to reassure me. "I read it, I promise," he said. "I just don't remember it."

Too many children are growing up believing that comprehension is an optional "bonus" to reading. I hasten to tell them that if they have neither a memory of the text nor new ideas as a result of their reading, then they haven't really read the book at all. "Reading," I tell them, "is thinking, guided by print. Reading is response. Reading is your mind at work." We teach children that readers envision, synthesize, question, categorize, connect, and so forth, and then we give them tools for externalizing this brain work—we ask them to write what we hope they will later think. They may use notebook entries or sticky notes or graphic organizers or sketches: In all these cases, readers use tools to make invisible thoughts visible, to render fleeting thoughts lasting.

This session invites children to shift from the writing that helps the reader enter the story toward writing to develop ideas about stories. In the personal essay unit, writers learned that essayists observe the world, then push themselves to have thoughts about what they see. In this session, however, you'll invite your children to "observe" the texts and the worlds these texts represent, then push themselves to have thoughts about what they "see."

You'll teach children that literary essayists notice details to spark big ideas. Often, children either focus on the details of the text or make sweeping generalizations. As a result, their "thinking" amounts to little more than recapitulating the text or writing empty generalities. In this session, you'll tell children that when we read (or live) with a wide-awake attention to details, we are in the best position to grow big, compelling ideas.

IN THIS SESSION, YOU'LL REMIND CHILDREN THAT WRITERS READ WITH AN ATTENTIVENESS TO DETAIL THAT CAN SPARK LARGER IDEAS. YOU'LL SHOW AGAIN HOW WRITERS CAN USE CONVERSATIONAL PROMPTS TO EXTEND THEIR THINKING AND THEIR WRITING ABOUT A TEXT.

GETTING READY

- "Spaghetti," by Cynthia Rylant, or other touchstone text, copied onto chart paper
- Idea for an entry you can use to demonstrate writing about a detail from the touchstone text, then having a larger thought about it
- Start of a chart, Strategies for Writing in Response to Reading
- Story you can tell about a child who initially had trouble making observations, then found lots to notice
- See CD-ROM for resources

MINILESSON

Gathering Writing About the Story by Close Reading

CONNECTION

Contextualize today's teaching by reminding children of strategies they used earlier in the year to generate writing for their personal essays. Tell them they'll follow a similar process to write literary essays.

"Yesterday, when we began our new unit, you learned one strategy for writing in response to reading. The writing we did yesterday helped us get lost in stories, seeing through the character's eyes and feeling all the character feels."

"Today, we will start writing to help us generate ideas about the texts we are studying. Remember back to when we wrote our personal essays? Remember how we generated writing for those projects? What you already know about writing personal essays can help you write literary essays. Writers grow like those little nested Russian dolls, carrying our past experiences as writers inside us as we move forward. In that unit, we learned that writers get big ideas by paying close attention to the details of our lives, to details like cicada bugs shedding their skin. Then we push ourselves to have thoughts about what we see and experience."

Remind children that when writing big ideas about a text, just as they do when writing big ideas about their lives, they must begin by paying close attention.

"Similarly, I want to teach you that when essayists want to grow big ideas about texts, we don't stare up into the heavens and wait for Big Ideas to descend on us. Instead we pay close attention to the details of what we see and hear and notice inside the story."

"If we can live wide-awake lives as readers, paying attention to the little details—to the cicada bugs—of texts, and letting those details lead us to develop fresh, provocative ideas, then we'll be well on our way toward writing powerful literary essays."

COACHING

Not surprisingly, I begin this unit by teaching a repertoire of strategies for generating the new kind of writing that children are studying.

In Session I, children brought a narrative frame of mind to their writing about reading. They wrote within the frame of the author's story. Today, the writing I'm teaching is more similar to the traditional expository writing one might expect in a unit designed to help children write literary essays.

You will see that the strategies children learn in this unit parallel those they learned in the previous personal essay unit. This time, their essays will be about texts rather than about their lives. Our most powerful teaching gathers up all the instruction that has preceded it, using that instruction and taking it just a little bit farther.

The reason I suggest students look closely at the text to grow new insights is that I'm convinced writers are more apt to develop fresh ideas when we begin by attending to detail, rather than generalizing and then supplying details to illustrate those generalizations.

Name your teaching point. Specifically, tell children that to write well about reading, essayists need to be alert to details.

"Today I hope you'll learn that to write well about reading, you need to be wide-awake readers. Some people say they read themselves to sleep, but because you and I are writers, we read ourselves awake! We use writing to help us become especially wide-awake as we read, noticing little details that others would probably pass by."

TEACHING

Demonstrate by rereading the touchstone text. Highlight the fact that you pause to attend closely to what's in the text, saying or writing what you notice.

"I want you to notice how I read 'Spaghetti,' paying attention to little details that some might pass by."

"Watch me as I read, trying to pay close attention to the details of what I see in the text. Notice that I see little details, and then push myself to have a thought about what I see."

> It was evening, and people sat outside, talking quietly among themselves. On the stoop of a tall building of crumbling bricks and rotting wood sat a boy. His name was Gabriel, and he wished for some company. (1998)

"Okay, I could read on. Nothing stands out to me. But I am going to force myself to pause, and to notice details that I could just zoom past. I've learned that there is always something to see, if we have the eyes to see it, so let me look more closely."

I looked at the text, and then I looked up, dramatizing that I had shifted from reading aloud to voicing what was on my mind: "I see that people are sitting outside in the evening, talking among themselves. They are sitting close to each other, talking quietly." Then I said to the observing children, "Now watch," and I shifted into thinking aloud about the text: "The thought I have about this is that Gabriel seems to be sitting far away from others. I wonder, Does he purposely sit far away? Or do his neighbors choose to sit away from him?"

I have come to believe that the sequence of our instruction in writing is incredibly important, because once skills have become automatic, learners can use those skills effortlessly to tackle new and more complex mental operations. This session assumes children have already learned to write entries in which they observe, then shift into reflecting on what they observe. The session also assumes that children already know how to work with conversational prompts, using these to extend their first thoughts. They are already accustomed to letting phrases such as I think *or* This makes me realize that *lead them to write new ideas. All of this was taught during the personal essay unit and in reading workshop.*

When I say that I hope readers notice that I pay attention to the little details in texts, I'm choosing those words carefully because I want children to transfer strategies they learned in the personal essay unit, where I also used that phrase, to this new unit. For this reason, I try to preserve my vocabulary from one unit to the next.

Notice that I role-play the fact that I'm tempted to read on, to say, "There's nothing noteworthy here." Over and over you'll see me role-play the very thing I hope children will not do, correcting myself in ways that I hope will also help them. I use role playing as a way to dramatize what not to do, as well as what to do.

When I first wrote this entry about "Spaghetti," I bypassed the actual words I see *and* The thought I have about this is, *but when I revised I added them. It is important that our demonstrations match what we say. This means that during a demonstration I don't try to dazzle children with my prowess. Instead, I illustrate what I have just explicitly taught in a manner that provides a model. For now I'm asking children to structure their responses to stories so they take in (or see) details in the text, then to think and write the thoughts they have about whatever they see. Therefore, I do likewise.*

Shifting out of the role of reader into the role of teacher, I leaned close toward the children and said, "You already know how to shift between *recording* what you see into your notebook, on the one hand, and on the other hand, *thinking about what you see*. It is important to do this even when you're not sure that you *do* have a thought! Something magical often happens when you write or say, 'The thought I have about this is . . .' or 'I realize that . . .' or 'To add on . . .' Brand-new thoughts sometimes spill out."

"Now I'm going to record what I am thinking and push my brain to have more thoughts about this, like we did when we wrote essays before. Watch." I picked up a marker pen, scrawled on chart paper what I'd already thought aloud, and then said "Umm . . . ," pausing for a moment before adding on:

> I <u>see</u> that people are sitting outside in the evening, talking among themselves. They are sitting close to each other, talking quietly.
>
> <u>The thought I have about this is</u> that Gabriel seems to be sitting far away from others. I wonder, Does he purposely sit far away? Or do his neighbors choose to sit away from him?
>
> <u>To add on</u>, the lead shows a friendly place, full of people who know each other. I think Gabriel feels especially alone because everyone else has friends. Loneliness is hardest when you are alone in a group. <u>This reminds me of</u> riding the school bus, as a kid; everyone else sat with a best friend, I sat alone.

Resume reading, again pausing to notice aloud what's in the text and again writing in response to what you see.

I resumed reading:

> Gabriel was thinking about things. He remembered being the only boy in class with the right answer that day, and he remembered the butter sandwich he had had for lunch. Gabriel was thinking he would like to live outside all the time. He imagined himself carrying a pack of food and a few tools and a heavy cloth to erect a hasty tent. Gabriel saw himself sleeping among the coyotes. But next he saw himself sleeping beneath the glittering lights of a movie theater, near the bus stop.
>
> Gabriel was a boy who thought about things so seriously, so fully, that on this evening he nearly missed hearing a cry from the street. (1998)

This unit begins by asking children to spend a week or two writing about reading in their notebooks. One reason I do this is to teach children that writing is a vehicle not only for communicating but also for growing ideas. You will see, then, that I encourage children to write about ideas that are not yet fully formed in their minds, to let ideas come out of the tips of their pencils, fresh and surprising.

The most important word that I've said might be the umm. It's crucial for us to show children that ideas don't come to any of us right away. We wait for them to nibble, like a fisherman waits for the fish to bite. So often children expect ideas to be right there, fully articulated, in their minds, and they don't understand the experience of fishing for, waiting for, an idea to nibble.

Keep your writing as brief as possible. Minilessons become cumbersome and we overwhelm children if we allow ourselves to read or write too extensively. Students don't need dazzling and extensive demonstrations to grasp the teaching point.

You'll notice that when I name what I see in the text, I focus on the main thing. I don't advise skirting past the main drama of the story to point out a tiny quirk that catches your eye. Instead, read aloud just a paragraph and write (and think aloud) in a way that shows children that you noticed what most readers in your class probably noticed.

This time I said, "The story tells that Gabriel was thinking about things so intently that he almost didn't hear the cat," and as I spoke, I underlined the line that conveyed this.

"But the story doesn't come right out and say *why* he doesn't hear things around him. I think readers are supposed to figure out why Gabriel doesn't hear the cat's cry. It's the same in my life—recently my mother has been acting cranky. She doesn't come right out and tell me that her back hurts her, but I can draw on everything I know and fill in that part of the story. In the same way, we all need to fill in when we read. Although the story doesn't come right out and say why Gabriel is lost in his thoughts, we, as readers, can fill that in."

Explain that you underline or mark with a sticky note what you see, and then write what you think.

"So now I'll try writing an entry to think about what I noticed in that section of 'Spaghetti,'" I said, and I wrote:

> My idea is that Gabriel is alone so often that he has built a wall around himself. He doesn't even listen for people to talk with him. He doesn't expect anyone on the stoop will speak to him. He has tuned everyone out, and he is lost in his thoughts, oblivious. That's why he almost doesn't hear the cat's cry.

I underline the lines from the story that ground what I say and think, because I want this physical way to remind children that our ideas are grounded in a close reading of the story. Often children glance at a text and then spin out ideas that are only tangentially related to the text. Ideally, I will have made an enlarged, laminated copy of the entire text to use throughout this unit, but, if not, I can simply copy the first portion of it onto chart paper. I could also just underline or use a sticky note to mark my own personal copy of the story, demonstrating how I do this without actually showing the text on which I write.

You'll of course teach children during the reading workshop that bits of a story can be windows to a character. Children need to learn that when they notice what a character does, for example, they might also reflect on how the character could have acted differently. What do the character's actions reveal about the person? Children can attend not only to what a character does, but how he or she acts, because this too is a window to the character's traits.

I decided to write this particular insight because I want children to notice really important aspects of a story. A character's changes are almost always worth consideration. It is no accident, then, that I'm thinking about how the protagonist, Gabriel, changes across the text. Specifically, I see Gabriel changing from the well-defended, stalwart (but lonely) child at the start of the text to a child who eventually lets a kitten through his wall of defenses. I decided to highlight the "before" version of this change in Gabriel now, because doing so will pay off for me later when I want to contrast the "before" with the "after." I am setting myself up for later minilessons.

Debrief. Remind writers that when using this strategy to generate writing about texts, you note details in the text, then write your thoughts about those details.

"Writers, do you see that after I read a bit, I look back at the story, noticing details? If I own the book, I underline the details—otherwise I leave a sticky note to mark what I notice. Then I pick up my pen and push myself to write. I could write what I actually saw in the text—in the personal essay unit we usually recorded what we saw in life—but when writing literary essays, I usually just *point at* what I saw in the text and then write the thoughts I have about whatever I've noticed. I write, 'I think . . .' or 'My idea is . . .'. As I write those words, I'm often not sure quite what I will end up thinking, but ideas come to my pen."

ACTIVE ENGAGEMENT
Set children up to read and scrutinize the upcoming passage in the touchstone text, then to share their thoughts by writing in the air.

"If I hadn't been writing about 'Spaghetti,' I would have zoomed right past the fact that other people were chatting in a friendly fashion on the stoop while Gabriel sat there alone. Writers see more, notice more; we live more wide-awake lives. So let's try writing to see more and think more. Partner 1, will you read aloud a bit more of 'Spaghetti,' and then pause. At that pause, partner 2, try to really pay attention to the text. Point at and reread details that matter. You *could* just glance at the text and say some generalization like 'Gabriel's outside,' but good readers look more closely, expecting that the details will be worth noticing. Then, partner 2, write in the air, saying what you see when you really look closely at the details of the text."

"After a tiny bit, partner 1, remind your partner to say something like, 'And the idea I have about this is . . .' or 'I'm realizing . . .' or 'I think . . .'. Okay? Partner 1, start by reading a paragraph aloud." I listened to a few of the partnerships.

Celebrate. Perhaps tell the story of a child who underlined what he noticed in the text and then composed ideas.

After a few minutes, I called for attention: "Writers, eyes on me, please." Once I had everyone's attention, I said, "I want to share with you what Tony just said and did. He first listened to Marie read aloud this bit of the story":

> Gabriel was a boy who thought about things so seriously, so fully,
> that on this evening he nearly missed hearing a cry from the street.
> The cry was so weak and faraway in his mind that, for him, it could
> have been the slow lifting of a stubborn window. (1998)

Many of the subordinate points that I tuck into this minilesson come from previous units in the writing workshop, or, for this unit, from previous units in the reading workshop. Just as we want children to hold a whole text in their heads, not just the chapter they have just read, we also want to them to hold all of our past teaching in their heads. Tucking lessons from previous teaching into our new minilessons, as subordinate points, is one way to do that.

The lilt with which you say, "And the idea I have about this . . ." is important. You hope that partner 1 tucks this into partner 2's sentence in a way that puts words into partner 2's thoughts, words that shift this child from observing to mulling over, growing meaning around those observations.

"Then Tony pointed to the section that said that Gabriel nearly missed the cry, it seemed so weak and faraway. He also went back and pointed to a line from earlier in the text in which Gabriel thought that he'd like to live outside, and saw himself sleeping in a homemade tent surrounded by coyotes. Tony said, 'I notice Gabriel is sort of alone. He sleeps with the coyotes and he doesn't hear stuff around him.'"

"When Marie wisely nudged Tony by saying, 'The thought I have about this is . . . ,' Tony added, 'I think Gabriel is brave. He isn't afraid to sleep outside.' Then he said something really smart: 'He's sort of tough. To add on, it's like he has gotten hardened and toughened so he almost doesn't hear the weak cry.'"

LINK

Reveal a chart showing the two strategies you've now taught for generating writing in response to reading. Invite children to draw on both strategies today and always.

"Today, writers, you learned a second strategy for writing as you read. You now have two strategies you can use anytime, for the rest of your life, when you write about reading":

> ### Strategies for Writing in Response to Reading
> - Find a significant moment from the story. Copy the start of it into your notebook; envision it; fill in details, sounds, actions, thoughts, feelings.
> - Be a wide-awake reader. Notice and underline details others might pass by. Then write a thought about what you notice.

"For today, you will again read as well as write during our writing workshop, drawing on all the stories in your packet. You will probably want to reread the stories you read yesterday. You'll probably shift back and forth: reading, jotting, reading, jotting. And from this day on, remember that if you want to write about your reading, you can use either of these strategies—or others you invent."

You won't report on Tony's thinking, of course, but about what a child in your own class says. As you listen to partners talk, find or help a child to say an idea about Gabriel (or the character in whatever text you read) that you believe is worth revisiting. Record the child's exact words on chart paper. You'll see that I return to what Tony has said in tomorrow's small-group work, when I teach children that as we read further in a story, we revise our first-draft ideas of it.

You'll notice that I'm not making the chart in front of children, as I would have done earlier in the year. By now, the minilessons already verge on being too long, and children grasp the relationship between what we say and demonstrate and what is recorded on the chart. Notice, however, that a new item is recorded each day, even if this happens offstage.

When I talk to children about a strategy, I am less apt to make global comments about the strategy and more apt to articulate the steps that comprise the strategy. Notice the chart captures those small steps.

As Vladimir Nabokov advises readers, "There is nothing wrong about the moonshine of generalization after the sunny trifles of the book have been lovingly collected. If one begins a reading by making generalizations, one begins at the wrong end and travels away from the book before one has started to understand it." This is the message of today's session.

WRITING AND CONFERRING

Celebrating Successes, Anticipating Struggles

Expect that children will encounter challenges in this unit, and welcome these challenges as opportunities to teach. That is, if you find yourself saying, "This is hard for my kids," don't assume hard is bad. At this point in the year, your children are probably game to do a bit of ambitious work. They'll learn all the more because the work stretches them. But of course it will be important to find triumphs to celebrate. Assign yourself the job of reading student writing, looking for bits to celebrate.

Point out places where a child has written powerfully. Let children know when one of them has come up with an insight that stops you in your tracks and makes you go, "Wow." For example, perhaps you will decide to simply circulate the room, making little check marks beside instances in which a child's writing is more insightful than usual. "Bravo!" you can whisper. "That's such a fresh, original idea!" In this way, you can let a child know when she has used a powerful word or image or insight. Sari wrote that Zachary, a child in a divorce story, feels *hopeless*. Sari's teacher pointed to the term and said, "That is such a powerful word! You've said something really strong here." Sari was so fueled by her teacher's recognition of what she had done that she ended up rereading her entire entry, erasing some of her other words and substituting more powerful synonyms. Sari's teacher could have taken this a step further and taught the whole class the importance of selecting precise terms. One could say a character is friendly, but is the character outgoing? Empathetic? Loyal? Supportive? Gregarious? Steadfast? Precision in word choice matters, because each word has a different nuance.

Watch as a child uses a conversational prompt to extend his thinking, and help the child really comprehend the power of the transitional phrase he has just written. If you watch as a child writes, "Jenny lies in bed thinking about the boar, loose in the woods. I *realize* . . . ," point to the phrase I *realize* and say, "Wow! I can't wait to read what new thought comes to you, what the idea is that you realize. It is so

> **MID-WORKSHOP TEACHING POINT** **Noticing Language** "Writers, can I have your eyes and your attention? You learned today that to write about texts, essayists read with wide-awake attention, noticing the details in texts and then growing ideas about those details. And as I worked with you today, I found that many of you especially noticed what your characters do or want. This is wise, especially if you then push yourself to have a thought about this. Remember earlier we noticed that Tony, for example, wrote, 'Gabriel wants to sleep with the coyotes.' Then he pushed himself to have a thought and wrote, 'I think Gabriel is brave. He isn't afraid.'"
>
> "Another really important way you can grow an idea about a text is to notice how the author has written the story—the words she has chosen. Max noticed in 'Spaghetti' that Cynthia Rylant used the word *so* before the word *seriously* (and again before *fully*): 'Gabriel was a boy who thought about things so seriously, so fully.' Max was struck by the repetition of the word, deciding it might be important that instead of writing that Gabriel thought about things 'seriously and fully,' she wrote, '*so* seriously and *so* fully.' He wrote down his observation on the author's craft and began to grow a thought about it. Max wrote, 'I think Cynthia Rylant wanted us to realize something important about Gabriel … he's a very, very serious, thoughtful boy.' I was impressed that Max got all that from the repetition of the word *so*. Keep in mind that you can always get ideas from studying the language an author has chosen—even a tiny word like *so*!"

exciting to see brand-new ideas emerge!" In that way, you can help the child understand the meaning of a phrase that he could otherwise use in a rote fashion. React similarly if a child writes, "The important thing about this is . . . ." Tell the child you can't wait to see what it is she selects as the most important thing, and act as if that choice is a weighty one!

When I praise the strong aspects of what a child has done, I try to be very specific and to name what works in a way that can provide guidance for another day when the child is writing about another topic. For example, Ali wrote this about "The Marble Champ":

> I see that Lupe is laying on her bed and she is flicking marbles, eyes droopy. I think she is so into this she is like a magnet getting pulled into this game. I think she is determined to win and play as if it is her destiny.

I pointed out to her and to others that Ali had used a strategy that could help all of us as readers. "I absolutely love the way you brought your own ideas to this," I said to Ali. "The text does not come right out and tell you that Lupe worked so long that her eyes were droopy, but you figured this out, you brought that detail to the text. Wise move. And it is even smarter that you deduced that Lupe has a magnetic relationship to marbles; she's drawn to them as if with a magnetic force. That is a really smart theory, grounded in the text *but made up in your mind!* Brilliant."

With this support to goad her on, Ali continued working with zeal. Not surprisingly, she continued to shift between writing what she saw and writing the significance she attached to what she saw and thought. You'll notice in these few pages from her writer's notebook (*Figs. II-1 and II-2; emphasis is my own*) that Ali is writing a hybrid sort of entry, one that merges some writing to envision the gaps of a story with thoughts about what she envisions in those gaps:

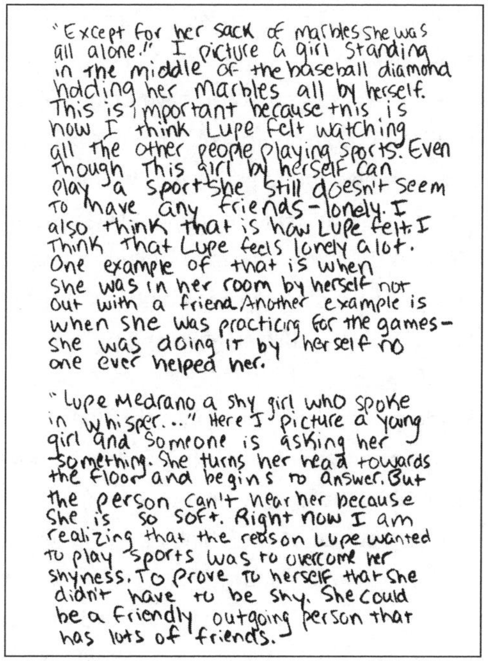

> "Except for her sack of marbles, she was all alone." I picture a girl standing in the middle of the baseball diamond holding her marbles all by herself. This is important because this is how I think Lupe felt watching all the other people playing sports. Even though this girl by herself can play a sport she still doesn't seem to have any friends—lonely. I also think that is how Lupe felt. I think that Lupe feels lonely a lot. One example of that is when she was in her room by herself not out with a friend. Another example is when she was practicing for the games—she was doing it by herself, no one ever helped her.
>
> "Lupe Medrano a shy girl who spoke in whisper . . ." Here I picture a young girl and someone is asking her something. She turns her head towards the floor and begins to answer. But

Fig. II-1 Ali shifts between envisioning, looking closely at the text, and reflecting.

the person can't hear her because she is so soft. Right now <u>I am realizing</u> that the reason Lupe wanted to play sports was to overcome her shyness. To prove to herself that she didn't have to be shy. She could be a friendly outgoing person that has lots of friends.

<u>I find it interesting</u> that Lupe does all the really great things and wins awards, yet she is really shy. Usually when I think of a person like Lupe I would think that she would be outgoing and not shy. <u>I wonder</u> if she thinks if she played sports she would become more outgoing and not shy. I think that does happen. When she wins her first game against Rachel and she asks her to join them. I think that when she began playing marbles, she began having confidence. <u>I think</u> it was when she became more like other people, kids, girls. I think that she kind of wanted to be able to compare herself to other kids. Because she could do all of these things you have to be very talented to do.

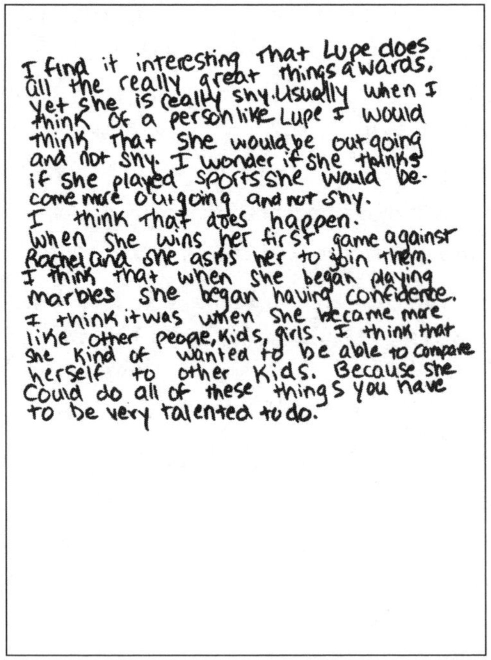
I find it interesting that Lupe does all the really great things & awards, yet she is really shy. Usually when I think of a person like Lupe I would think that she would be outgoing and not shy. I wonder if she thinks if she played sports she would be-come more outgoing and not shy. I think that does happen. When she wins her first game against Rachel and she asks her to join them. I think that when she began playing marbles she began having confidence. I think it was when she became more like other people, kids, girls. I think that she kind of wanted to be able to compare herself to other kids. Because she could do all of these things you have to be very talented to do.

Fig. II-2 Ali's response to "The Marble Champ" page 2

This kind of writing is very fertile ground for essay writing about literature—there is plenty to celebrate here. Ali will have rich material to draw from as she begins her literary essay.

You can enter today's teaching ready not only to notice and fuss about children's successes, but also to scaffold children to use the new strategies you have taught. You can predict that a surprisingly large number of children will have difficulties coming up with thoughts about books. These children are apt to restate facts rather than invent their own new thoughts. So they'll write, "I think Gabriel wants company" or "I think Gabriel goes looking for what is making the sound." Neither of those is a new idea—both are stated outright in the text. To help children understand the difference, I sometimes tell them that their ideas won't be *right there* on the page of the story. If I can point to the section of the text that comes right out and says what the child has stated, then the child is retelling the story, not growing an idea. I also sometimes tell children that ideas are often debatable.

If children are recording facts about the story rather than writing ideas, I find it helps to teach them that ideas hide inside facts. For example, it's a fact that Gabriel thought about a *butter* sandwich. To grow a thought, I need to linger with that for a fraction of a minute, asking myself, "And what do I think about that?" Sometimes a child's first instinct is to think by asking a question, which I believe often reflects timidity. The child might think, "Why a butter sandwich, not peanut butter and jelly?" Nudge the child to speculate on an answer. "Maybe Gabriel remembers his butter sandwich because he's poor and it's basically just bread."

If children struggle to generate ideas about texts, you may want to teach them the kinds of topics that many readers find fruitful. For example, you could share any combination of these topics, remembering that usually we are more thoughtful when we think extensively about one topic rather than race from one to the next.

> Characters: What kind of person is this? What does this character want? Struggle with? What do these characters get from and give to each other? What is the nature of the relationships in this story?

> Connections to other works of literature: How does the meaning in this text fit with the meaning in another related text?

> Craft: Why might the author have made the decisions he or she made? Why did the author title the text this way? Start this way? Use this emphasis? Choose this setting? End this way?

> Significance: What does the text teach us? What is the text *really* trying to say?

> Genre: What kind of text is this? How does the text seem like, or unlike, other texts of this genre?

But the most important thing you can do to help children develop their thoughts about texts is to devote more time to helping them have grand conversations about texts. I write about this elsewhere in this book and in *The Art of Teaching Reading.*

SHARE

Developing the Eyes to See What Others Overlook

Tell the story of a child who looked at a text and couldn't find much of interest in it. Use a metaphor or anecdote to explain how one can learn to see with new eyes.

"I want to tell you about Raffi. When I came to him, he was reading the short story 'The Marble Champ.' He looked up at me and shrugged, like this, and said, 'There's not that much to see in here.'"

"But I said, 'Raffi, remember when you dipped your cup into the pond, then looked at your water? You said, "I didn't get any bugs or anything," and you almost threw your water back? But instead you looked more closely, then studied the water through a magnifying lens, and you found your water was swarming with creatures!'" Shifting away from reenacting my conversation with Raffi, I looked out at the class and said, "So Raffi looked again at Soto's story, and this time, he saw a whole lot and wrote all this." I held up his notebook to illustrate that he'd filled more than a page with observations.

"Writers, if some of you read a story and then think 'What's there to see?' remember Raffi. And remember that Cynthia Rylant once said that a writer walks the aisles of Woolworth's and has relatives over to supper and goes fishing *as a writer*. Raffi and I realized that we can add to Cynthia Rylant's list. Writers walk the aisles of Woolworth's and have relatives over for supper and go fishing and *read books* as writers. Like writers the world over, we see more, hear more, notice more, and, most of all, we *think more* because we are reading like writers."

Ask children to look again at a text, this time with a partner, and see it with new eyes.

"Would you get with your partner, put a story you've both read between you—it may be 'Spaghetti' if that's the only story you have both read so far—and this time, try to *really see* what's there! Point out intriguing things you notice and talk about what you see. Especially talk about what you think about what you see. Grow ideas together!"

I find that when I want to teach a lesson, it often helps to do so through an anecdote. Notice that my stories of children are written in a manner that illustrates the tips I share about how to write stories. When I tuck an anecdote into a minilesson, I try to recall qualities of effective stories. For example, I generally make characters speak. In this instance, for example, I didn't really recall Raffi's exact words, so I supplied the words I suspected he probably said. Like a good Small Moment story, the episode starts close to the heart of the problem. After I tell the story, I unpack it, or debrief, just as I ask children to do after they cite an anecdote from literature in a literary essay.

I find that it can be tricky to talk a lot about the mental work that readers do, because that work is invisible. Often, then, I'll describe a more concrete kind of work, then I'll say, "Isn't reading similar?" I did this in the anecdote about Raffi looking at pond water.

HOMEWORK *Reading with Passionate Attentiveness* A friend of mine, Bess, lost her mother to cancer last spring. Her mother was dearer to her than you can possibly imagine, and the loss was devastating. Bess wondered how she'd face life—summer days at the beach, her thirtieth birthday, the first autumn colors—without sharing all this with her mother. Bess' thirtieth birthday came, and with it a giant feeling of loneliness. Bess walked to the mailbox that day, remembering the previous birthday and her mother's presence. In the mailbox, there were the usual magazines and letters. And there was a package. Turning it over, Bess' heart stopped. The front of the package had her mother's handwriting. In place of a return address, there was a heart. How could this be?

Once inside the kitchen, Bess sat down with the package. She held it and for a moment imagined the impossible. Finally, she loosened the tape, letting the paper fall open. And there, before her, was a letter from her mother and a scrapbook. "Bess," the letter began. "You can't imagine how much I wanted to be with you today. Knowing it wasn't in the stars, I made this gift for you, wrote this letter, and asked Dr. Marcus to be sure you received it."

Imagine the miracle of that letter—those words, coming to Bess like a letter in a bottle, one that had traveled across the sea of time. The books you and I read are all, like Bess' message, miracles. Consider how extraordinary it is that Patricia MacLachlan sat at her desk in Amherst, Massachusetts, remembering her son in Africa, her childhood on the prairie, and wrote *Baby*. Now, years later, in an utterly different place, you and I can pick up the book, read her words, and dream the dream of that story.

Mortimer Adler, a reading researcher, once said, "There is only one situation I can think of in which men and women make an effort to read better than they usually do. When they are in love and reading a love letter, they read for all they are worth. They read every word three ways; they read between the lines and in the margins . . . they even take the punctuation into account. Then, if never before or after, they read."

Tonight, would you read one of the stories we've chosen to study? Read it as if that story came as a message in a bottle, thrown across the seas of time. Read it as if it were a gift from someone you love who is now gone. Read it as if this were a love letter. And write about whatever you notice, whatever it makes you think and feel and wonder and remember. Write this in a long entry.

If your children have already experienced this unit in a previous year and if, therefore, you've decided to ratchet up the complexity of the lesson . . . you'll want to do the work you're asking children to do, and to pay attention to what skills you find yourself needing to use. Julia Mooney and her colleagues worked with Bunting's picture book, *Fly Away Home*. In a minilesson, Julia pointed out that she first observes the text and then pushes herself to have a thought about it. She read aloud this section of the book:

> "Delta, TWA, Northwest, we love them all," Dad says. He and I wear blue jeans and blue T-shirts and blue jackets. We each have a blue zippered bag with a change of blue clothes. Not to be noticed is to look like nobody at all.

Then, thinking aloud, she said:

> I <u>see</u> that Andrew and his dad dress alike, all in blue, and that they carry matching blue bags. <u>The thought I have about this is</u> that they are trying to blend in by not standing out. I wonder if the author picked the color blue to show that Andrew and his dad are sad—that they're blue. <u>To add on to this</u>, the blue clothes and bag seem like a mirror of how Andrew feels: "like nobody at all." <u>This is giving me the idea</u> that the blue clothes are a symbol of this feeling. I think Andrew is blue because he feels unimportant, almost invisible. This reminds me of how I felt when I moved to this country at age six. I didn't speak English yet, so I couldn't talk to anyone except my parents. I felt like I was invisible.

Then she returned to reading:

> Once we saw a woman pushing a metal cart full of stuff. She wore a long, dirty coat and she lay down across a row of seats in front of the Continental Gate 6. The cart, the dirty coat, the lying down were all noticeable. Security moved her out real fast.

This time when Julia paused to think aloud, she said:

> Here the story says that Andrew observes a homeless woman being removed by security because of the things that make her noticeable (that distinguish her as homeless): the cart, the dirty coat, the lying down.
>
> This is just one of the many observations Andrew makes about being noticeable as a homeless person.

Debriefing, Julia pointed out to the children, "Do you see how I come up with ideas that the author doesn't come right out and say? The story doesn't come right out and say *why* Andrew collects ways homeless people are noticeable. Readers are supposed to figure out why he does this all the time. It's the same in life. I have a friend who sometimes doesn't return phone calls. She doesn't have to tell me this is because she's feeling sad over her husband's recent death. I can take what I know about her and her life and fill that part of the story in."

Then Julia said, "So now I'll try to write an entry to think about what I noticed in this section of the text."

> My idea is that Andrew is a boy who understands the dangers of being noticed when you're homeless. He's found ways <u>not</u> to be noticed (or caught) out of the need to survive. This is why he makes so many observations about those homeless people who stand out.
>
> Another thing I notice in *Fly Away Home* is how many times and ways Andrew says that he and his dad are careful not to get noticed, that it's dangerous to be noticed, what makes you noticed and what doesn't. There are mentions of being noticed on many of the pages in this story.

COLLABORATING WITH COLLEAGUES

In this unit, as in every unit, your teaching will be exponentially enriched if you and your colleagues give these lessons to yourselves, doing the same reading and writing that you ask children to do, while maintaining a researcher's awareness. This unit is an especially rich and provocative one, full of nooks and crannies that have not yet been explored. I hope you are especially eager as you teach this unit, ready to add your own ideas, gleaned from your own research.

One fruitful source of insight will be this. Take ten minutes in a staff meeting to read one of the texts your children are reading and then record the thinking you do as you read the text. I call this mirror writing, because the goal is to look at the marginalia you wrote as a way to make visible the invisible work you did as a reader.

With a colleague, look at your writing. Ask first, "What was I trying to do as I wrote about my reading?" You may see that you are still acting as if you are in a classroom, reading to write to convince a teacher that you did do the assigned reading! If your writing about reading seems wooden, if it feels as if it simply records facts to prove that you read, then read a bit more, and in your notes try to really capture your fleeting thoughts.

Look at writing that conveys your thoughts and notice that this writing, when done well, does not resemble finished literary essays. The goal is not full sentences, or ideas that are spelled out and carefully supported with evidence. The characteristics of effective writing to learn are very different from those of finished expository essays.

Try looking at the writing you do as you read as a reflection of your *reading,* not your writing. Which qualities of good reading do you practice a lot? Do you predict? Envision? Ask questions? See ways in which one section of a text is linked to another section of the text? Consider what the author's message might be? Question why the author wrote the text as he or she did, and how these decisions relate to the author's message?

If you contrast your own writing about reading with that of your colleagues, you'll probably learn a few very interesting things. First, you'll probably notice that each one of you has one or two things you tend to do as you read, and you do those things often. One of you may respond personally to texts, another may notice the author's craftsmanship, yet a third may judge and talk-back-to the character. You will probably find that the lens you use a lot is one you already model for children. If you find that you often predict as you read, you'll probably see that your children are doing this as well. It helps to deliberately decide that you can take on a new lens for reading and thinking, borrowing one of your colleagues' ways of seeing a text.

Of course, you'd want to process this work together with your colleagues by naming what it is you all have done together. You may decide that the repertoire of ways you have to read is limited, that you usually lean on one or two qualities of good reading, and you may decide to expand your repertoire by reading with a lens which is not your usual. When you expand your repertoire by deliberately borrowing a lens that your colleague uses, you'll want to let your students know that you are doing this so they can emulate you and expand theirs as well. It is very powerful to give ourselves and our children new lenses for seeing a text. If a reader rarely pauses to think, "What is this author's view of the world? Do I agree? Disagree?" then learning to read critically will lift the level of that person's reading and thinking.

If you are really serious about teaching children that writing can be a tool for thinking, you'll need to invest more time and attention in this instruction. You may invite children to look over past writing about reading that they've done, coding that writing so that it is divided into two piles—one for the writing that represents powerful thinking, the other for the writing that represents recording a rather obvious thought. Help children understand

that the latter form of writing won't help their reading or their writing! Then you and your class could launch an inquiry into the characteristics of writing when it is meant as a tool for thought. My hunch is, your community will find that this writing:

- Is often written in incomplete notes full of abbreviations, diagrams, lists

- Raises and then entertains (or lingers with) questions

- Looks chaotic and all-over-the-place

- Can be unclear and confusing. Thoughts don't come to us in a succinct fashion.

- Is dense. That is, it has a high number of what I refer to as TPWs (thoughts per word).

You can teach children to watch themselves as they write about reading, keeping in mind the purpose of this kind of writing. If the purpose is to grow ideas and the writer is merely repeating the facts of a text or recording the obvious, help writers know they can stop mid-sentence, so as to shift to writing in ways that contain ideas. You or your children can reread the writing about reading and make a check alongside entries that are insightful—remember, the entry may be a sentence in length! Now you may want children to reread any writing they've done all year in response to reading, giving themselves pats on the back when that writing was a tool for thought. Encourage your children not to be writers who fill up pages and pages with words which, in the end, say very little.

GETTING READY

- "The Marble Champ," by Gary Soto, and "Spaghetti," by Cynthia Rylant (or other touchstone texts)
- Thinking About Characters chart
- Strategies for Writing in Response to Reading chart, updated with tips from previous session
- See CD-ROM for resources

GATHERING WRITING BY STUDYING CHARACTERS

My son began his college application essay like this:

> When I enter the class of 2009, I will bring my experiences of trekking through the mountains of Viet Nam and my memories of a 227-day stint in a lifeboat, accompanied by a Bengal tiger. When I attend freshman classes, my role will bear the imprint of my tortuous hours standing above the town square, a scarlet letter emblazoned on my chest. Reading has given me the water I swim in, the heroes I emulate, and the imagination to believe that I can make the world a better place.

I often say that as an educator, I want to give all children what I want for my own sons. I can think of few gifts that have mattered more to my sons than the gift of Nathaniel Hawthorne's Hester Prynne, Katherine Patterson's Gilly Hopkins, A. A. Milne's Eeyore, Brian Jacques' mouse, Martin, and all the other characters who have enriched their lives. In this world that we live in today, it's not easy finding heroes in the newspapers. But our children can find heroes in the books they read, and, better still, they can become these characters, standing for a time in their shoes.

I want all children to empathize with and think deeply about characters—just as I want them to think deeply about one another. Helping children write well about literature, then, involves helping them to care about characters, and to understand what makes characters tick. This session encourages readers to think about characters' traits, motivations, struggles, and changes. These terms are easy to list, but they are potent. They hold unbelievable potential for revealing insight.

This session continues where the last one leaves off—teaching children another way to find and develop interesting, original, true ideas about texts. Those who analyze and write about texts know to pay close attention to characters.

MINILESSON

Gathering Writing by Studying Characters

CONNECTION
Remind children of the strategies for generating writing about reading that they've already learned.

"Over the past two days, you've learned a few strategies for thinking and writing in response to reading. You've learned that you can pause as you read, make a movie in your mind of what's going on, and fill in gaps in the text, thinking and writing about what the main character is seeing, hearing, and feeling."

"You also learned you can use writing to grow ideas about texts. Just as during the personal essay unit you observed on the playground, in the cafeteria, and at your family's dinner table, you now observe in the text that you are reading. Then, after noticing details others might pass by, you write an entry in which you ponder over what you've seen. You might start by writing, 'The thought I have about this is . . . .'"

Name your teaching point. Specifically, tell children that skilled readers pay attention to characters.

"Today, I want to teach you that skilled readers of fiction pay special attention to the characters in a story to unlock the secrets the text holds for the reader."

TEACHING
Remind children that experts on any subject know the features of that subject that merit attention. Illustrate with subjects you know well.

"I've been reading a best-selling book, *Blink*. Malcolm Gladwell, the author of this book, suggests that experts on a subject can gather a small amount of data and from it deduce important and surprisingly accurate insights about a larger subject. For example, an expert can listen and observe an hour of a conversation between a married couple and can predict with 95% accuracy whether the couple will still be married fifteen years later" (2005, p. 21).

"Of course, the secret is that the person who makes those observations is an expert, and therefore he or she knows which aspects of the interactions between married people are especially noteworthy."

"I've noticed something similar when I watch the Westminster Kennel Club dog show on television. I love to put myself in the judge's place, eyeing the Welsh corgis, cairn terriers,

COACHING

Early on in a minilesson, I know that I need to heighten children's interest, grab their attention. Sometimes I try to do this in my Connections, making those segments rich and elaborate; other times (as in this instance) I recruit children's interest in the Teaching component of the minilesson, allowing me to settle for a more commonplace Connection.

Draw from whatever you are reading, doing, learning to make your point clear to children. If I'd been reading about glaciers, I'm sure I could have used that as a metaphor to make my point!

and wire-haired dachshunds. But inevitably, I am still checking out the dog's coat, ears, and shape when suddenly the judge signals, 'Take him around.' Then, before I've had a chance to really take in all that new data, the judge moves on to the next dog! Expert dog watchers, like expert marriage analysts, make judgments in the blink of an eye!"

"*Blink* reveals the secrets. Malcolm Gladwell, the author, says that a good part of the secret lies in the fact that experts on a subject know which features merit our attention. The same is true for good readers. Good readers know that when reading fiction, it pays to think about characters in general and specifically, it pays to think about a character's traits, motivations, struggles, and changes."

Tell students that expert readers know it pays off to attend to specific aspects of a story. Discuss these and demonstrate how you read, attending to these aspects—in this case, character.

"It's easier to say this than to do it, because authors don't come right out and say, 'Lupe's character traits are . . . , she yearns for . . . , but the hard part for her is . . .' Instead, readers read, paying close attention to details (as I mentioned in the preceding session). We know that the details of a story will reveal a character's traits, motivations, struggles, and changes."

"When I mention Lupe, I'm referencing one of the stories that will be central to this unit, 'The Marble Champ.' Right now, I'm going to look back at that story and think about Lupe. Watch how my observations and thoughts about Lupe are guided by my sense of what matters to expert readers of fiction. I notice, for example, that the story says that Lupe's thumb was swollen from practicing marbles. That detail wouldn't be here if it weren't important. I need to think about what this suggests about Lupe, about her traits, motivations, struggles, and changes. Hmm . . . I think it shows that she is really persistent. She doesn't give up, even when her thumb is sore."

"Do you see that the story often gives us concrete details, and then we need to fill in what these details probably suggest about the character? We read on, looking either for confirmation or for those initial ideas to be revised."

"The truth is, all of you do this all the time. Yesterday you had a new substitute teacher. I just bet that when you came in yesterday morning and saw you had a new substitute teacher, you looked for signs that would suggest what sort of person he would be. You probably watched Mr. Harrison closely, knowing that his actions could give you clues. That's exactly what it is like for me when I meet a new character in a story. I watch that character, thinking to myself, 'Oh! Now I get it! He's *that* kind of a person.'"

By now you must realize that I'm a fan of dogs. But dogs may be the last thing on your list of loves! I'm sure that a connoisseur of yarn knows what features of yarn merit attention. Bring your loves into your teaching, and the passion you feel for your subject will come into your teaching as well!

This list of what stories reveal about character is a weighty one, so I say each term slowly, giving time for each term to sink in.

You'll notice that although "Spaghetti" is the text that weaves through most of my minilessons, I deliberately reference other texts as well. I think a steady drumbeat of references to "Spaghetti" could be dull—but for some classes of children, that'd be preferable. You'll need to decide. In any case, I try to refer to stories that children already know, because children can more easily focus on the particular point I'm hoping to make if the text itself is not new to them.

Watch how I extract particular pointers from my demonstration. It's not enough to simply say, "Watch me," and then hope the children will be enthralled by simply watching me read and think aloud.

"Of course, every detail in the story won't be of equal interest to me. If I go for a walk in the woods to think about trees, I don't pay attention to the dirt granules on the trail, but I *do* notice the shapes of leaves. When I want to learn from stories, I know that I'll probably learn something significant from paying attention to the pressures that a character feels, the struggles that he or she experiences, the choices the character makes and how they play out. When you and I read, we can see moments of courage and strength in the lives of characters and learn from those moments, just as we can learn from people and events in our own lives."

Although there are advantages to using demonstration as a teaching method, this can be a slow way to convey information. By tucking bits of information into demonstration minilessons, we keep these minilessons jam-packed with helpful tips and also make them more multilevel. Some children scarf up everything we mention, while others tend to hear only the main teaching point.

ACTIVE ENGAGEMENT

Set children up to try the work you've demonstrated and discussed. In this instance, ask children to look for a character's motivations, traits, and so on.

"We've talked a lot about the ideas we developed about Gabriel at the *beginning* of 'Spaghetti.' We noticed that Gabriel separates himself from other people, and we decided that he is a tough, brave, lonely boy who has learned to build a wall around himself. But Gabriel changes, doesn't he, as the story continues? Listen to another part of the story, later on, and notice what you learn about Gabriel's traits and motivations at this point. Remember to be a wide-awake reader, paying close attention to the details of the text."

> Gabriel was amazed. He had never imagined he would be lucky enough one day to find a kitten. He walked into the street and lifted the kitten into his hands.

> Gabriel sat on the sidewalk with the kitten next to his cheek and thought. The kitten smelled of pasta noodles, and he wondered if it belonged to a friendly Italian man somewhere in the city. Gabriel called the kitten Spaghetti. (1998)

"Turn and tell your partner the ideas you have about Gabriel's character—his traits and motivations—at this later point in the story."

Notice that I don't suggest children pull out copies of one of the stories they've been reading during the workshop and think about the character in that story. Had my children needed lots of support, I would have chosen that option. Instead, I imagine they'll do this during the workshop itself. I don't usually want the work of the workshop to be launched (and I certainly don't want it to be compressed) during the Active Engagement section of a minilesson, leaving students little new to try once I say, "Off you go." However, when working with high-need groups of children, I do want to launch the day's work during the minilessons, and therefore I'd adjust my teaching accordingly.

LINK

Remind children that expert readers know which features of a story are usually worth studying. In this case, remind them that readers generally find meaning in studying a character's traits, motivations, relationships, struggles, and changes.

"So readers, today, and whenever you want to grow ideas about stories, it helps to remember that expert readers know the features of stories that are worth our attention. Among other things, expert readers pay attention to the main character's traits, motivations, relationships, struggles, and changes. We read, asking and writing in response to questions like these." I pointed to the list I had prepared on chart paper.

Thinking About Characters

- What kind of person is this character?
- What does this character long for? Fear?
- What is the character struggling against? What gets in the character's way?
- What relationships does the character have and how do these relationships play a significant role in the story?
- How does the character change over the course of the story?
- Does the character learn lessons or come to realizations?

"Today, continue reading and rereading your file of short texts and jotting entries containing your thoughts. Remember, you can draw on any strategy to help you think well about these texts." I pointed to the updated chart on the wall:

Strategies for Writing in Response to Reading

- Find a significant moment from the story. Copy the start of it into your notebook; envision it; fill in details, sounds, actions, thoughts, feelings.
- Be a wide-awake reader. Notice and underline details others might pass by. Then write a thought about what you notice.
- Think about an author's language choices, even in small words like "so."
- Pay special attention to aspects of texts that are noteworthy, including a character's actions, motivations, struggles, and changes.

WRITING AND CONFERRING

Revising Initial Theories

You may decide to convene a small group of children to give them supported practice drafting and revising their ideas as they read. With one group, I said, "Once you form an idea about a character, it is important to read on, expecting you'll probably revise that idea. Let me show you what I mean. Remember yesterday, when Tony (who was a member of this small group) read 'Spaghetti,' he had this idea." I gestured to where I'd written Tony's idea on chart paper:

> I notice Gabriel is sort of alone. He sleeps with the coyotes and he doesn't hear stuff around him. The thought I have about this is I think Gabriel is brave. He isn't afraid to sleep outside. He's sort of tough. To add on, it's like he has gotten hardened and toughened so he almost doesn't hear the weak cry.

I decided to return to Tony's idea, because I knew that if children kept track of Gabriel's toughness, it would pay off for them. Some of my decisions are calculated ones! I knew that in this story the little scrawny kitten pierces Gabriel's armor of toughness. In most stories, the protagonist undergoes a change, and in this small group I subtly set kids up to watch for the very part of Gabriel that I knew would undergo a change.

I passed out copies of "Spaghetti" and continued, "I'm going to read on in the story while you follow along in your copy. Let's all keep Tony's idea in mind as we read. That's what readers do. We form an idea, then carry it along with us as we read further. When I pause as I read, would you underline sections of the story that add on to or clarify or challenge Tony's claim that Gabriel wants to be alone and that he is tough? Read with me, thinking, 'Does what I see and hear confirm the idea that Gabriel is tough? Could the story be saying something more complicated than that? Could Gabriel be changing?'"

I read more of the story, and paused a bit after the passage that said Gabriel's "ears tingled" as he walked the street, searching for the source of the cry. The children underlined and then talked about this section with partners; some of them proposed that he followed the cry because he was looking for someone or something, which suggested that at least deep down, he didn't want to be alone. Then Gabriel finds the tiny gray kitten, and I read:

MID-WORKSHOP TEACHING POINT

Revising Theories About Characters "Writers, can I have your eyes and your attention? Many of you have been paying attention to characters, noticing their actions and speculating on what those actions reveal about the characters as people. I want to remind you that the ideas you develop about characters start as rough drafts. Once we have drafted an idea about a character, scrawling our idea on the page, we can hold that idea in our hands and say to ourselves, 'I'm going to continue to read, and see if upcoming sections of the text push me to *add on to* this idea or to *revise* it.' Often when we read more, we learn that our first idea was only partly warranted, and so we discard half of it. Often our ideas change in the light of new information. Our ideas need to undergo constant revision as we read more of the story, and also as we reread and rethink the story."

continued on next page

> Gabriel was amazed. He had never imagined he would be lucky
> enough one day to find a kitten. He walked into the street and lifted
> the kitten into his hands.

To me, this section of the text is very revealing: Gabriel could never have imagined he'd be lucky enough to one day find a scrawny, stray kitten! I'm not suggesting that this section will resonate for every reader, but it is really important to bring the things that speak to us into our teaching. You may want to highlight an entirely different section of this story.

"What are you thinking now about Gabriel's toughness?" I asked. I again gave children a few seconds to underline relevant sections of the text as a way to prepare for conversation. Then they talked.

Raffi said, "I think this shows that Gabriel isn't tough. He feels like the luckiest boy in the world to have found a kitten. That means he doesn't have a wall around him, or how come he feels so lucky?"

"So do the rest of you agree?" I asked. Then, upping the ante, I pushed on, gesturing to Tony's entry. "When Tony suggested at the start of the story that Gabriel was tough, that he almost wanted to be alone and had built a wall around himself—do you think that the evidence *wasn't* really there to support that claim? Or what do you think is going on? Could Gabriel be changing?" Then I added, "Right now, each of you, reread the story and try to figure out your position on this. Do you think Tony will need to revise his initial thought, or do you agree with Raffi's conclusion that Gabriel has let a kitten into his heart—or what? Underline sections of the text that help you think about this." After a minute or two of silence, I said, "Tell your partner your thinking."

Frankly, I was hoping to bring out the fact that Tony's idea and Raffi's idea could both be true. At first Gabriel had a wall around his emotions; now the cat is getting through that wall.

Soon Tony spoke. "I still say Gabriel *was* tough because he wanted to live outside, all by himself, with just the tent and the wolves, and he doesn't even hear people 'round him and almost doesn't hear the kitten. But I think Raffi's right, too, at the end. The kitten got through his wall. The kitten changed him."

Wanting to extrapolate the lessons that pertain to other days and other texts, I said, "This is the work that readers who write do all the time. We read, we notice things in texts, we push ourselves to grow tentative ideas and we talk about those ideas, and then we read on, knowing our first ideas will be revised. Sometimes we can make our ideas more specific. Sometimes we cross them out. And sometimes we can

---

continued from previous page

"Let me show you what I mean. You already know that after I read that Gabriel sat on the stoop of a tall building of crumbling bricks and rotting wood, I theorized that Gabriel is poor. I wrote that down in my writer's notebook," I said, and pointed to chart paper where I'd copied the entry. "After I wrote my idea, I put it beside me as I continued to read, knowing new data would confirm or challenge this initial idea." I picked up "Spaghetti" and resumed reading:

> Gabriel was thinking about things. He remembered being the only boy in class with
> the right answer that day . . .

"'Does this relate in any way to my idea that Gabriel is poor? No.' I continued to read:

> . . . and he remembered the butter sandwich he had had for lunch.

"Again I ask myself, 'Does *this* relate to my idea that Gabriel is poor?' I'm not exactly sure of the answer. Gabriel could conceivably just *like* butter sandwiches, but I am pretty sure that Rylant wouldn't add that detail (or describe the crumbling bricks and the rotting wood) if she hadn't wanted to suggest that Gabriel is poor, and didn't have anything else to put in his sandwich. Probably the detail about the butter sandwiches supports my theory that Gabriel is poor."

follow a story and see that the events in characters' lives lead them to change over time. Characters make decisions, they confront their problems, they resolve tensions—and they change."

"You'll probably want to crystallize ideas *you* have fashioned about a particular story and then reread that story with that idea beside you, seeing if further rereading helps you revise that initial idea. You can, if you want, use the left-hand side of your writer's notebook to rethink what you've written on the right-hand side. [I opened a notebook and gestured to the blank left side of an open page.] Or just write additional thoughts that address earlier ones."

"I hope you noticed that because I've written my idea about 'Spaghetti,' I can keep it beside me as I read, and check it as I keep reading. If the upcoming text challenges my idea, I'll need to decide whether my initial idea was wrong, or if the character is changing. Either way, I'll write my thoughts. As you continue reading, expect that your story may lead you to revise your initial ideas. If your ideas turn out to be partly right or partly wrong, fix them. If your ideas suggest the characters in the story are changing, note that. As you read on, your ideas can become more specific or more precise."

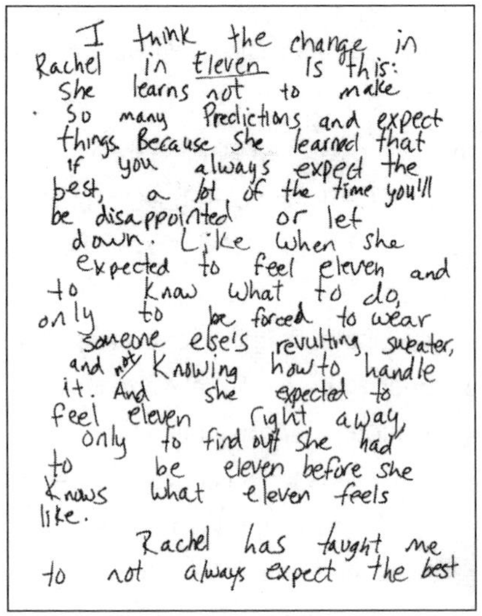
I think the change in Rachel in Eleven is this: She learns not to make so many predictions and expect things because she learned that if you always expect the best, a lot of the time you'll be disappointed or let down. Like when she expected to feel eleven and to Knaw what to do, only to be forced to wear someone else's revulting sweater, and not Knowing how to handle it. And she expected to feel eleven right away only to find out she had to be eleven before she Knows what eleven feels like.
Rachel has taught me to not always expect the best

Fig. III-1 Max writes about the change he sees in "Eleven".

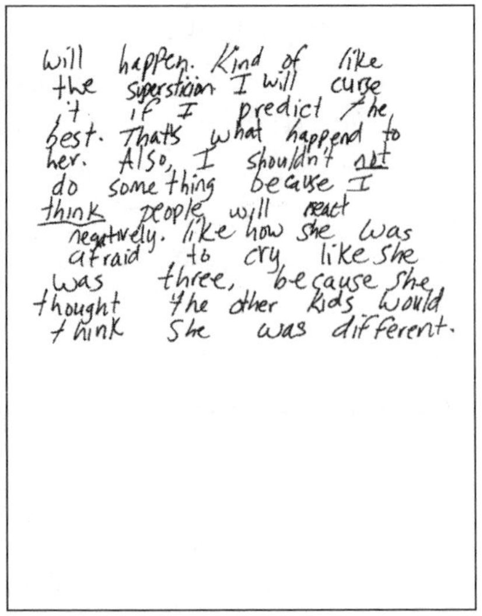
will happen. Kind of like the superstition I will curse it if I predict the best. Thats what happend to her. Also, I shouldn't not do something because I think people will react negatively. like how she was afraid to cry like she was three, because she thought the other kids would think she was different.

Fig. III-2 Max's entry page 2

SHARE

Writing to Know Characters

Tell children that when we read fiction, we live with a character and see the world through that character's eyes.

"A friend of mine, Ralph Fletcher, once said, 'If you want to get to know a person, don't go out to dinner with that person—instead have a flat tire together, get caught in a rainstorm together.' When we read, we're caught in rainstorms—or in whatever happens in the story—with the characters we meet on the pages. By living through the storms of life together, we form relationships with characters in books—and we learn not only *about* them, but also *from* them."

"So, readers, remember that to develop ideas about characters, it helps to first live with that character through the storms of life. If you want to grow ideas about Rachel in 'Eleven,' then you first need to be Rachel. Imagine that *your* teacher has told you, 'Put that sweater on,' and *you* are looking at it, knowing it's not yours. As you read, you should be practically cringing at that sweater that's hanging over the corner of *your* desk. When you are climbing inside a story and experience the story within the skin of a character, you should find that the character's reactions make sense to you."

"Another time you could read differently, asking, 'Do I agree with this character?' and 'Would I see the world as this character does?' But during some of your journeys through a text, try to take on the character's point of view and empathize. If you read with this amount of empathy, perhaps writing to envision or perhaps just envisioning as you read, *then* you'll be able to come to smart, new insights about the character—about people in life! And *that's* your goal!"

Ask children to reflect with a partner about what they've written about literature so far, checking whether they've empathized with a character.

"Right now, would you share what you've written with your partner, checking to see if you have stood in the shoes of a character? If not, that's okay, but sometime try reading with empathy, as Judah and Max both did in reflections on 'Boar Out There,' a story from your packet. Judah actually empathized with the wild boar. She wrote": *[Fig. III-3]*

> My big idea is: you need to think of everyone in the
> situation's feelings. I think this might be the moral of

When I was at college, I had a poster on my wall that said, "Love does not come from gazing into each other's eyes, but from gazing together in the same direction." When we read, we and the character gaze together in the same direction. We encounter storms, predicaments, heartaches together—and because we live through life side by side, we bond with characters.

Notice that this Share essentially reminds readers of the first minilesson in this unit. You'll often want your teaching to hark back to earlier instruction; the larger lesson here is that readers and writers share a repertoire of strategies.

> my big idea is: You need to think of
> everyone in the situation's feelings. I
> think this might be the moral of the
> story... I felt sorry for the boar
> because nobody paid him any mind
> other than Jenny. I would be hurt
> if someone treated me that way.

Fig. III-3 Judah's notebook entry

the story . . . I felt sorry for the boar because nobody paid him any mind other than Jenny. I would be hurt if someone treated me that way.

"Max, like Judah, read 'Boar Out There' with a wide-open heart, and he let himself feel for both Jenny and the boar—which is good reading and good living!" *[Fig. III-4]*

> I think that Jenny is lonely. Maybe she goes out to find the boar to either befriend him or to show everyone she is brave. Which she is. She is brave to go find the boar. The boar is also brave because he stays there with Jenny without attacking. But he is not all brave because he gets scared when he sees or knows that someone is after him. Also Jenny knows that there is more inside the boar than most people think. Even a wild boar can have a true kind heart inside. People pre-judge him, but Jenny knows not to.

"Share your entries with your partner, especially entries in which you (like Judah and Max) have empathized with your characters."

Remind children that their talk about texts will be clearer if they refer to characters by name and try to use precise language.

"Writers, can I stop you? I can see that many of you are excited about ideas that you are growing, but when I try to learn about your ideas, I'm having a hard time understanding you. I want to give you a few tips on how to be clear:"

- "When you speak of a character, use his or her name. If you say, 'This kid, he . . .' and then say, 'Then he . . . ,' I am often unclear what person your pronouns are referencing."
- "Try to avoid talk that sounds like this: 'Well, you know, he likes all that stuff, you know.' Assume your listeners *don't* know what you are getting at. Say outright what you mean!"

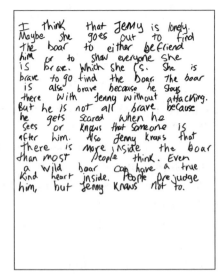

Fig. III-4 Max's notebook entry

Notice that whenever we send children off to do some work, we listen and watch to be sure they are on the right track. If we see indications that they need further channeling, we intervene, as in this example.

When children try to describe characters, some of them will reach for sweeping, generic terms, describing characters as "nice" or "friendly" or "happy." When the opportunity arises, either in conferences or in discussions about books, encourage precise language. Show children that words differ by nuance. Help children brainstorm webs of related but different words. Is a character proud? Haughty? Arrogant? Imperious? Outspoken? Condescending? Each term connotes a different quality. You'll want to teach children that writers search for the precise term. Some words have positive or negative connotations. For example, "outspoken" and "verbose" differ in that one term is more positive than the other.

HOMEWORK *Studying How a Mentor Author Portrays a Character* In a few days, you will each reread your notebook to select a seed idea that you can develop into a literary essay about one of the stories you've been reading. Tonight, select a story from your packet that speaks to you. This will be the text you write and think and talk about during writing workshop for the next few days. Tonight, spend some time thinking about the protagonist, the main character, in the story you've chosen.

It is often helpful to study the ways in which people who write book reviews and literary essays capture the essence of a character. The famous author, Eudora Welty, wrote a review of a book you know, *Charlotte's Web*. In her review, Welty describes the pig, Wilbur, this way:

> Wilbur is of sweet nature—he is a spring pig—affectionate, responsive to the moods of weather and the song of the crickets, has long eyelashes, is hopeful, partially willing to try anything, brave, subject to faints from bashfulness, is loyal to friends, enjoys a good appetite and a soft bed, and is a little likely to be overwhelmed by the sudden chance for complete freedom. (*New York Times*, October 19, 1952)

There are dozens of lessons to be learned from this. Tonight, jot a list of lessons you can learn from what Eudora Welty has done. For example, on my list I'll record that I notice that when Welty wants to convey what a character is like, she lifts tiny, emblematic details about the character's actions from the story, condensing these to create a collage that represents the character in all his or her idiosyncrasies. But you'll make your own list of observations.

After you've thought about what Eudora Welty has done to describe Wilbur in her book review, write an entry in which you use similar techniques to describe the protagonist in the story you have selected.

TAILORING YOUR TEACHING There is no question but that children will need more time and help learning to pay attention to what characters do—to their actions, their dialogue, their choices—and they'll need help regarding what's written about a character as windows to the person. You may want to read *The Art of Teaching Reading*, paying special attention to chapters twelve, fifteen, and eighteen.

If your students are ready for further study of character . . . you may want to teach them to ask whether a particular character represents an archetype. For example, in *Cinderella*, the stepmother definitely fits the archetype of the mean stepmother. Cinderella also fits into a kind-of-character that one meets often in stories. Children will enjoy thinking about possible archetypes. Fairy tales are full of these. In many fairy tales, one character fits the

It is very important to ask children to focus their efforts on one text. Although this work is lodged in a homework assignment, it is not expendable.

stereotype of the youngest son, the one whom everyone underestimates, who rises to the challenge in the end. Many stories contain a scheming, wily, fox-like character who outsmarts the others (and in the end is outsmarted)!

When readers recognize that a character fits into an archetype, this helps the reader anticipate the role the character may play in the book. Of course, you may want to teach children that there can be a thin line between archetypes and stereotypes. Wise readers sometimes resist an author's way of conveying characters. Such a reader may say, "I question why the author needed to write one more story about the handsome boy who gets the lovely girl," or "I resist the idea that the father has a job and the mother in this book bakes cookies and drives her children from place to place."

If your students are ready for further study of character . . . you may want to teach them that narrators often merit special attention. The narrator's voice may not necessarily be one which the wise reader trusts as a universally true perspective. For example, in John Steptoe's picture book, *Stevie*, the eight-year-old narrator calls young Stevie a crybaby, but the reader is meant to bear in mind that this is the older child's jealousy speaking and as such, the word choice says as much about the narrator as it says about Stevie.

If your students are ready for additional study of character . . . you may want to teach them that there is a saying: "When you go over the bumps, what's inside spills out," telling them that this is true for characters in books as well. When a character struggles, what's inside spills out . . . and for this reason, experienced readers pay special attention to what a character does in the face of difficulties. Often when characters struggle, they end up finding strengths inside themselves that they never knew existed, and this is one force which accounts for the way a character changes.

If you'd like to help students eventually form sound thesis statements about characters . . . you might help steer them toward opinions about characters even now. In the end, when children write literary essays, they'll each need to develop a thesis statement (or a claim about the text). You'll steer children toward choosing a thesis which relates to the whole story, not just to one small part of it. Many of your children are apt to write a thesis like this: "With persistence and hard work, Lupe learns that she can succeed in sports as well as in academics." You can prepare children for writing thesis statements about characters by teaching them to pay attention to the difficulties their protagonist faces and the resources she relies on to meet those difficulties. Don't mention the upcoming search for a thesis statement yet, but teach children strategies writers use to grow entries about characters that will yield the ideas that can eventually be central to an essay.

ASSESSMENT

As you move among your children, assessing their work to help plan your one-to-one, small-, and whole-group instruction, remember that you've asked children to use writing to grow new ideas. The measuring stick a writer uses to assess writing differs based on the goals the writer brings to a piece of writing. You may, for example, show children that when they write to grow ideas, they'll reread their writing in a special way. They won't ask, "Is this a well-organized text?" or "Is my writing correctly punctuated?" Instead, they might ask, "Have I written ideas that seem true and interesting?"

When I pulled my chair alongside Adam, he'd already written this entry. Read it closely, as I did, and see if you can follow his logic (and lack thereof): [Figs III-5, III-6, and III-7]

> "Because the way you grow old is kind of like an onion or like the rings inside a tree or like my wooden dolls that fit one inside another, each year inside the next one. That's how being eleven is." —quotation from "Eleven"
>
> I think that Rachel feels that being eleven is a big turning point for her where she feels like she is supposed to be very mature, because in the next part she says, "Today I wish I was one hundred and two" so she feels the older she is, the smarter you are.
>
> I think Rachel isn't enjoying being a kid as much as she should be, because she is wishing she is older than she really is. That is basically stereotyping that kids aren't ever as smart as grown-ups. This leads me to the idea that Rachel is a push-over to all her friends because her friends think they're smarter than her. I think this because Rachel calls the two girls stupid.

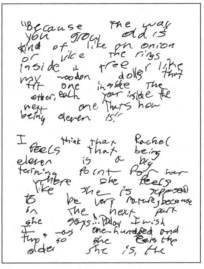

Fig. III-5 Adam's notebook entry

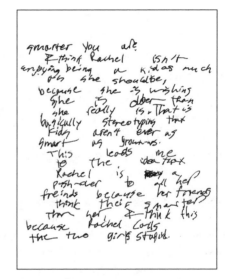

Fig. III-6 Adam's entry page 2

Using Rachel as a mentor, I have learned to respect adults but also respect my friends and my self. I also learned that it is okay to cry when you feel like it. It taught me to not care what other people think about you and only what you think matters. Rachel also taught me that sometimes you have to be tough and strong while other times you just have to cry and that is alright because you can be tough and still cry.

I told Adam that the writing he'd done was meant to grow ideas, and that he'd done half the work: He'd written a thoughtful entry, using thought prompts to develop ideas. But he still needed to

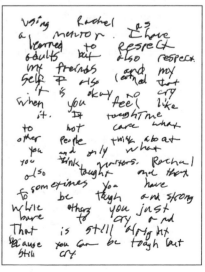

Fig. III-7 Adam's entry page 3

harvest the thoughts that he valued from his own entry. I told him that to harvest our own best ideas, we reread our musings, stopping at the end of each chunk, each bit of thinking. At the end of each bit, it is helpful to paraphrase what we just said, and think, "Is this *really* true?" As we do this, we keep in mind that often we find we've written ideas that are close to true but not *exactly* true. Giving our own ideas the truth test is one way to clarify what we really think.

I showed Adam what I meant by rereading a chunk of his text and then scrutinizing, with him, what his text said:

> I think that Rachel feels that being eleven is a big turning point for her where she feels like she is supposed to be very mature, because in the next part she says, "Today I wish I was one hundred and two" so she feels the older she is, the smarter you are.

Then I said, "So this first part says that Rachel thinks that growing older is a big deal because she believes that grown-ups are smarter than kids. You'll need to weigh whether you really believe that the evidence shows Rachel believes this." (I jotted a note reminding Adam to double-check on this claim.) "For now, let's read on."

"Let's find the next chunk of your text." I gestured for Adam to reread the next part of his entry:

> I think Rachel isn't enjoying being a kid as much as she should be, because she is wishing she is older than she really is. That is basically stereotyping that kids aren't ever as smart as grown-ups. This leads me to the idea that Rachel is a push-over to all her friends because her friends think they're smarter than her. I think this because Rachel calls the two girls stupid.

Adam said, "This says Rachel's friends think they are smarter than she is."

I intervened, "Adam, it does say that Rachel's friends think they are smarter than she is—but you need to read your own writing more slowly and carefully, because your evidence only says Rachel calls them stupid!" Then I said, "It's so wise to reread your writing and realize there are places in your entry where your ideas aren't clear or aren't warranted by the text. You do say Rachel's friends think they are smarter than she is, but as evidence you point out that *Rachel* calls her friends stupid! You never back up the idea that Rachel's friends think they are smarter than she is. When you reread your writing, you need to pause and think, 'What did I just say? Is it what I want to say? Do my different points go together?' There *may* be some connection between Rachel calling her classmates stupid and your earlier claim that she believes grown-ups are smarter than kids, but you'll need to figure that out."

Then I said, "When you reread your own entries, you'll often see that your ideas are at first a bit confusing and contradictory. That's how people grow new ideas—because they often *are* tangled at first. It can be really helpful to box out places where you've expressed an idea in a confusing fashion and rewrite that idea, this time aiming to really capture exactly what you think. Often the places where your entries are confusing are the places where really smart ideas are hiding under the surface."

"After I go, there are two things you can do—and these are things you can do *whenever* you write about reading. First, continue reading your entry, giving each chunk of it the truth test. And second, revisit sections where you have made claims you need to check or written ideas that seem confusing. Try to rewrite those sections, seeing if you can name exactly what you really do think."

In this fashion, assessment will feed into your conferences.

ELABORATING ON WRITTEN IDEAS USING CONVERSATIONAL PROMPTS

IN THIS SESSION, YOU WILL TEACH CHILDREN ONE WAY WRITERS ELABORATE ON THEIR IDEAS—IN THIS CASE, IDEAS ABOUT CHARACTER. YOU'LL GUIDE CHILDREN THROUGH A DISCUSSION THAT HAS THE SAME FEATURES AS A WRITTEN ANALYSIS OF A TEXT, REMINDING CHILDREN THAT THE CONVERSATIONAL PROMPTS THEY KNOW ARE ALSO USEFUL AS WRITING PROMPTS.

GETTING READY

- Pushing Our Thinking chart from personal essay unit

- Sample of student work from personal essay unit showing use of conversational prompts from the Pushing Our Thinking chart

- Prompts for Pushing Our Thinking About Reading chart, prepared as a handout

- Transcript of teachers' book talk that uses conversational prompts

- "Spaghetti," by Cynthia Rylant, and "The Marble Champ," by Gary Soto (or other touchstone texts)

- Student notebook entry that shows observations about the text and responses to those observations, prepared as handout for homework

See CD-ROM for resources

When we write a narrative, the sequence of events is usually determined by chronology. We can record events in the order in which they happen, making it very easy for us to say more. We recall the first thing that happened, then the next, then the next thing, and as long as we are taking small steps through the sequence of events, we don't quickly run out of things to say.

When we write expository texts, however, and especially when the expository text conveys our ideas, it is no easy matter to say more. To say more, to elaborate, the writer needs not only to recall what happened, but also to think more. This requires that the writer have not only stuff to say but also a plan, a structure, that determines the sequence of what he will say. Many students have enormous trouble with elaboration when writing expository texts, and as a result, their writing ends up with "a muddle in the middle." We worked through this challenge first in the personal essay unit, and of course will work through it again in the current unit.

Your job today will be to lure your students into learning how to elaborate upon their first thoughts—in this lesson, their first ideas about character. You'll help children to do this in writing by first encouraging them to elaborate in conversation. If children can talk well about a text they have read, making and defending and elaborating upon their ideas, then it is not difficult to teach them to write well about the text. But the first goal is not a small one! In this unit, you need to value talking well in addition to writing well about texts.

Schools often treat talk as if it's to be avoided. If a principal says to a teacher, "I passed your classroom and your children were talking," the teacher doesn't generally regard this as positive feedback. If we describe a child as "a real talker," we don't usually intend this as a compliment. Yet in our own adult lives, we recognize that talking is a way to grow. If we need help working through an issue, we meet with someone to "talk things through." If we want to imagine possible ways to teach, we're apt to "talk over our options" or "talk out a plan."

Today you'll encourage children to tap the power of talk as a tool for thinking. Moreover, you'll help children realize that the features of a probing, generative discussion are also the features of probing, generative writing.

MINILESSON

Elaborating on Written Ideas Using Conversational Prompts

CONNECTION

Remind children that when writing personal essays, conversational prompts can serve as thought prompts, helping them extend their first ideas.

"You'll remember that when we were writing essays, we found that at first we wrote only very briefly about our ideas. We'd write our idea—say, 'soccer teaches sportsmanship'— and then we weren't sure what else to say, so our entries were often short. But we came to realize that we could rely on the conversational prompts we use in book talks to help us talk back to our own ideas as they emerge on the page. Remember?" I refer to the "Pushing Our Thinking" chart.

"I won't forget, for example, when Ellie wrote this entry during the personal essay unit; she used our conversational prompts to help her get more good ideas."

> I hate it when I am doing something important and then I get interrupted.
>
> For example, when I'm reading a book and my mom calls, "Ellie, it's time to go to sleep" but I really want to finish the book because that's what I am into. I realize that this happens a lot to me, like when I'm watching TV or having fun with my friends. What surprises me is I always have a lot of time and no one interrupts me when I am doing things I don't like, like homework or practicing my oboe or other things.

Name the teaching point. In this case, tell children that they can use the same—and some new—thought prompts to extend their thinking about reading.

"Today I want to teach you that when we write about our reading—and specifically about a character—we can use the same prompts we use in conversation and in our other essay writing to help us grow ideas. I will also teach you a few new prompts that readers often use to help us talk and think more about our reading."

COACHING

Notice the way that one minilesson stands on the shoulders of an earlier one, and in this way brings children toward more sophisticated work. We strive to do this as much as we can.

Usually in a teaching point I lay out more precisely what I will teach, but in this instance, I couldn't tuck the Prompts for Pushing Our Thinking About Reading *chart into a teaching point.*

TEACHING

Dramatize a discussion between you and a few colleagues about a text that is familiar to your class. Set children up to notice that you incorporated "thought prompts" into your conversation.

"Yesterday at lunch the other teachers and I decided to read and talk about a story that you know: 'Spaghetti.' We transcribed a bit of our book talk so you could see how we used 'thought prompts' to help us grow ideas. We realized afterward that there are a few thought prompts we use specifically when we talk about reading, and so I've made a big list for each of you." I handed out this list.

Prompts for Pushing Our Thinking About Reading

For example . . .

Another example is . . .

To add on . . .

This makes me realize . . .

This is important because . . .

This is giving me the idea that . . .

The reason for this is . . .

Another reason is . . .

This connects with . . .

On the other hand . . .

I partly agree but . . . because . . .

Could it also be that . . .

Might the reason for this be . . .

This is similar to . . .

This is different from . . .

I think this is important because . . .

I noticed that section, too . . . and I think this connects to the whole story because . . .

I see (the item you are discussing), and then a similar thing happens (in this place); I think this is repeated because . . .

There is one thing in the story that doesn't "fit" for me, and it's . . .

This might be present because . . .

In the beginning . . . then later . . . finally . . .

In the beginning . . . in the middle . . . at the end . . .

Many people think . . . but I think . . .

I used to think . . . but now I'm realizing . . .

Notice that there is a general progression in these prompts towards increasing sophistication. It is easier to add another example, and it is more complex to compare and contract them. Usually a reader first uses one of the earlier prompts and then moves up the level of abstract thinking towards one of the later responses.

This list is too long to actually use with your class. Cull from it, saving some of these suggestions for another year.

"Instead of just reading you the transcript of our book talk, I'm going to help you imagine it by asking four of you—you and you and you and you—to come up and take a role, helping me reenact how that book talk went."

We organized this simulation of a book talk among teachers, giving each child the role of one teacher. I gave away my role as well. "We'll reenact a little bit of the teachers' book talk. I want the rest of you to notice (and underline) the thought prompts that the other teachers and I used in our conversation about 'Spaghetti.' You'll see that these prompts helped us extend and revise our first ideas."

"As you listen, would you also notice the number of times we go back to the text, reading specific bits of it to illustrate our points? You'll see that we don't just talk and think generally, in the abstract, about the text; we instead attach our ideas to specific parts of the text. After you listen to a bit of the book talk, I am going to give you and your partner a chance to take our places and continue the conversation."

Ms. Errico: I think Gabriel chooses to be alone. <u>For example</u>, when Gabriel is outside on the stoop, there are many neighbors sitting around talking, but he chooses not to join their conversation.

Mr. Nineteman: I agree. <u>Another example</u> of Gabriel choosing to be alone is in the second paragraph:

> Gabriel was thinking he would like to live outside all the time. He imagined himself carrying a pack of food and a few tools and a heavy cloth to erect a hasty tent. Gabriel saw himself sleeping among the coyotes. (1998)

Ms. Boland: <u>I used to think Gabriel was lonely, but now I am realizing that</u> maybe Gabriel chooses to not be with *people*. But maybe he likes being with animals. In the example Mr. Nineteman just gave, Gabriel imagines that he will be sleeping among the coyotes. <u>I think this is important because</u> later, when Gabriel finds Spaghetti, he starts to feel less lonely. He likes getting company from animals.

Ms. Errico: So are you saying that Gabriel feels more comfortable with animals?

Ms. Boland: Yes, some people are that way. They can communicate with animals better than with people. <u>So in the beginning</u>, Gabriel wants to sleep with coyotes and <u>then at the end</u>, with a cat.

Ms. Errico: <u>There's one thing that doesn't fit for me:</u> coyotes. If the author was saying Gabriel liked being with animals, why wouldn't she pick a more warm-fuzzy animal? 'Cause I think of coyotes as being in the distance, howling, and to me they are all about loneliness.

Sometimes we refer to this as fishbowling. *It is great to find new ways to demonstrate, because novelty ignites interest. The sheer fact that this is a new configuration will draw kids' attention. You or your colleagues may want to take on the topic "Developing New Methods for Teaching Within Our Minilessons." You can certainly use fishbowling a lot more often, with people reading or talking in front of the class.*

Notice that here and nearly always, before we ask children to observe something instructional, we highlight what it is we hope they notice and set them up for the work they will soon be doing in response to what they see.

Notice that we tend to begin with the conversational prompts that come earlier in the list. It is easier to say and think in associative ways (Another example of this is . . .) than in analytical ways (I am realizing . . . I think this is important because . . .).

Of course, instead of bringing in a conversation among teachers, I could have simply demonstrated how I go from reading and having a thought to developing that thought, and do so using conversational prompts and repeated references to the text. For example, I could have reread the opening paragraph of "Spaghetti" and then paused, pointing out (in an aside), "Sometimes I almost force myself to pause, to pause and to look and to think." Musing to myself, I would reread one line of it aloud, " . . . he remembered <u>*the butter sandwich*</u> *he had had for lunch," and then say, "Gabriel's sandwich contained just butter. It wasn't a ham sandwich, it wasn't roast beef. It was just a butter sandwich."*

Debrief. Tell children that when they use thought prompts to talk or write about an idea, the idea deepens.

"Readers, I hope you saw that we used this list of prompts to push our thinking about reading, to help us talk longer and deeper about our first ideas. We also referred to and read particular passages in the midst of our discussion. When we do these things, we end up growing thoughts that surprise even ourselves! The conversations we had let us extend and revise our first ideas, and made them more powerful, more specific, more true."

ACTIVE ENGAGEMENT
Set children up to carry on the book talk with their partners, using thought prompts to refer specifically to the story. Then have them continue this work in writing.

"So that's a fragment of our book talk. Instead of analyzing it, pretend you are part of the conversation and continue it—only you'll be talking just with your partner. Continue to use the thought prompts and refer specifically to the story, just as we were doing." I listened in on one set of partners:

Jessica: <u>This is giving me the idea that</u> being alone is different than being lonely. Being alone is just being by yourself. It's not lonely; it's just doing something without anyone there.

Alex: <u>To add on</u>, sometimes being alone is fun. <u>For example</u>, when you're part of a big family. Then it's kind of nice to be alone for a change.

Jessica: Yeah, yeah, I agree.

Alex: <u>This makes me realize that</u> sometimes people think they want to be alone, but then they really don't. <u>For example</u>, <u>in the beginning</u> Gabriel kept to himself and got used to being without people. He didn't try to make friends. But in the middle, when he heard the kitten crying, he was curious, and then when he found the kitten he really wanted to be around it. <u>At the end</u>, he made the kitten his friend.

"Can I stop you?" I asked, and waited until I had everyone's attention. "Remember that these conversational prompts also work for writing! Once you've written one idea, you can extend it using one of these prompts."

Then I would look up at the class, cueing them to notice what I would do next. <u>"The thought I have about this is</u> that Gabriel's sandwich is only butter because his family can't afford fancy sandwiches. <u>To add on</u>, even though Gabriel's sandwich isn't much, it hit the spot. He still remembers it, hours later. He probably ate that butter sandwich in tiny little bites, wanting it to last as long as possible, and then he probably used his finger to scoop up the crumbs and ate those too. <u>This connects to</u> times when I was a kid; I remember looking longingly at the pink marshmallow snowballs that Susan Downer had in her lunch box, wanting to heave my bruised pear into the trash. When kids open our lunch boxes, the stuff we find there feels like a letter from home. Gabriel is lonely; I'm not sure if he has a mom or a dad who packs his lunch."

Children may ask you whether they should speak and write about characters from books in the past or present tense. They will wonder whether it is better to say, "Gabriel was lonely" or "Gabriel is lonely." Generally, when writing about character traits, readers use the present tense. In the story "Spaghetti," Gabriel is a lonely boy.

LINK

Remind children of the teaching point. In this case, remind them that they can always use conversational prompts to extend their thinking when they talk or write.

"So readers, today and always, when you say your first thoughts about a story or put them onto the page, it is important to push yourselves to revise those first thoughts. One way to do this is to use thought prompts to nudge yourself to say (and think) more. Keep the thought prompts with you during the writing workshop this month, and whenever you write or talk about texts you've read, use these to extend and revise your first thoughts. Soon you'll use them just from habit. It's more fun and interesting to talk and write in ways that dig deep, so I'm pretty sure you'll end up using these prompts as you talk on the phone at night. You'll invent other thought prompts too."

WRITING AND CONFERRING

Elaborating on Theories About Characters

When you and your colleagues plan for today's (and every day's) teaching, be sure you plan for the conferences and small-group work as well as for your minilesson. Today, you can expect that some children will list rather than describe their ideas about a character, and many of them, like Sophia, will merely name one character trait after another. [Fig. IV-1]

Peter's Chair

My character is Peter
He is very jealous
He loves his baby sister
He likes toys
He tries to help the baby

Eleven

My character is Rachel
She feels weird (not eleven)
She feels bad when she wore the sweater
She hates her teacher

You'll probably want to carry a short text with you and to be prepared to demonstrate thinking hard about how to find words that precisely describe a character's trait. Sophia, in the example here, has said that Rachel, the main character in "Eleven," feels "weird." Then Sophia clarifies this by saying that Rachel "doesn't feel eleven." What *does* she feel? Encourage children to speak in whole sentences and to be explicit. Once children have made their claims—about, say, a character's traits—you'll want to show them that writers then choose ways to elaborate. It often works for children to provide examples of this trait while using transitional phrases such as *In the beginning of the story; then in the middle; finally, at the end of the story; for example;* and *another example of this is . . . .*

<u>MID-WORKSHOP</u> <u>TEACHING POINT</u> ***Developing Powerful Thoughts*** "Writers, can I have your eyes and your attention? Right now, if you haven't done so already, reread what you've written. Find a thought that seems powerful, and make a box around it. After you find one, look for another or help someone near you recognize power on his or her page." I circulated, helping children find powerful thoughts. "Sometimes, writers, the way you've written a thought is *almost* powerful, but not quite. You can rewrite your thought to make it more powerful."

"Once you've boxed off a powerful idea, use your thought prompts to elaborate on it. If you are having trouble using the conversational prompts to grow your ideas on paper, then remember you can also talk about your ideas. I sometimes take my ideas to a friend, and say, 'Will you listen to my thoughts about this?' and we talk about my idea. The other person listens, saying, 'Can you explain that more to me?' or 'Why do you think the text does this?' Writing and talking should fire you up so that you're able to put more ideas and insights onto the page. Then you can go back and write some more."

Peter's Chair
my Character is Peter
He is very Jealous
He loves his baby sister
He likes toys.
He tries to help the baby

Eleven
my Character is Rachel
She feels weird (not eleven)
She feels bad when She wore the sweater
She hates her teacher.

Fig. IV-1 Sophia's entry merely lists character traits

In the following notebook entry, Ali makes a claim about Lupe. In the entry, Ali seems to brainstorm a host of possible terms that could possibly be apt ones for Lupe. *[Fig. IV-2]*

> I think Lupe had, before, put herself down. But now, she will try to prove herself wrong. This is important because she was insecure. She thought badly of herself. She thought she was only a brainy person. But she was good at things. It doesn't matter if you can't do it, it matters what's on the inside. Even though she wasn't good, she was nice and good on the inside. "She tried again and again." This shows that she doesn't give up. She works and works at a goal. She won't disappoint herself. This takes a lot of self-confidence and courage. She tries to believe in herself.

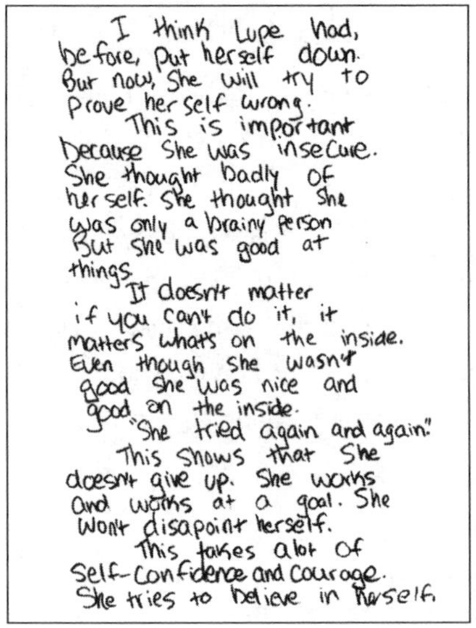
I think Lupe had, before, put herself down. But now, She will try to prove herself wrong. This is important because She was insecure. She thought badly of herself. She thought She was only a brainy person But She was good at things. It doesn't matter if you can't do it, it matters whats on the inside. Even though she wasn't good She was nice and good on the inside. "She tried again and again." This Shows that She doesn't give up. She works and works at a goal. She wont disapoint herself. This takes a lot of Self-confidence and courage. She tries to believe in herself.

Fig. IV-2 Ali reaches for the words to capture Lupe.

When I conferred with Ali, I showed her that characters can't always be shoehorned into a single description, so her effort to locate the one precisely right term could actually be doomed from the start. I suggested that Ali might have more success if she tried for sentences that capture Lupe. For example, Ali might say, "Lupe was full of contradictions. Although she had rows of trophies and awards that showed her academic prowess, her inabilities at athletics made her insecure."

Angelina begins her entry by summing up Clover, a character in Jacqueline Woodson's *The Other Side*, in a single term. Clover, Angelina suggests, is courageous. Although this is a short entry, Angelina not only advances her idea, she also tries to convince others of it. She cites a particular passage from the text to support her point and returns to her claim at the end of this entry. But what I find most impressive is that at the end of her entry, Angelina comes to a rather remarkable insight: Clover is a courageous person because she dares to bend the rules. Writing, for Angelina, has been a tool for thought. *[Fig. IV-3]*

> **The Other Side**
>
> Clover is a very, very courageous person. Because in the book, I could tell that she is courageous since she would dare to bend rules. Clover was not supposed to go over the fence that separates the town of whites and blacks. But she instead sits on the fence with a white girl named Annie. "My momma never said anything about sitting on the fence," said Clover. She knew better than to sit on the fence or even go near it. This is why to me Clover is a courageous person. Because she dares to bend rules that were actually laws in her time.

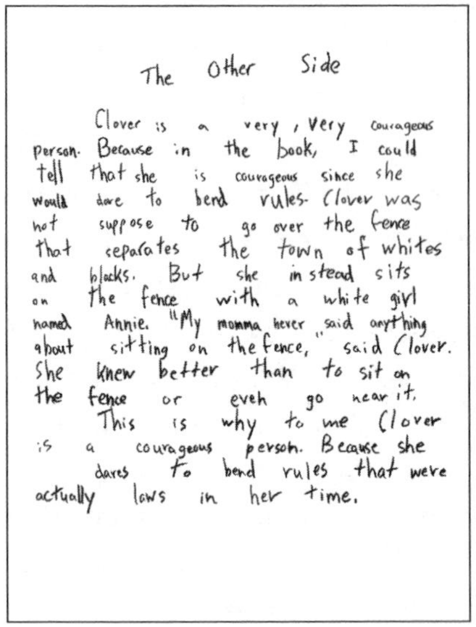
The Other Side

Clover is a very, very courageous person. Because in the book, I could tell that she is courageous since she would dare to bend rules. Clover was not suppose to go over the fence that separates the town of whites and blacks. But she instead sits on the fence with a white girl named Annie. "My momma never said anything about sitting on the fence," said Clover. She knew better than to sit on the fence or even go near it. This is why to me Clover is a courageous person. Because she dares to bend rules that were actually laws in her time.

Fig. IV-3 Angelina advocates for her claim, then grows a further idea!

After I saw Angelina's work, I stopped the class and said, "Eyes on me." I waited until I had their attention. "Class, I want to show you the smart work Angelina just did. In her entry, she doesn't ramble from one idea to another idea to another. Instead, Angelina puts forth one idea, one claim, and then she takes the time to develop that idea. This is really smart. When writing ideas about characters or texts, it is helpful to focus, to zoom in. Only this time you'll zoom in on a single idea you want to advance, and then you'll develop that idea across the text as Angelina has done. But best of all, as she says more about her idea, she actually *thinks* more—and comes to a better idea! Listen," I said, and read Angelina's entry.

SHARE

Discussing Texts Aloud to Prepare for Discussing Them in Writing

Invite children into a book talk. Coach them to brainstorm ideas and select one that is especially provocative and important to the story as a starting point for discussion. Explain that essayists proceed in the same fashion.

"Readers, can you gather for today's Share?" I said, and waited until they'd convened in the meeting area. "You have been talking a lot with your partners—I am dying to hear some of your ideas! Today, let's let our Share be a bit longer than usual so we can have a whole-class book talk about 'The Marble Champ.'"

"This story talk is going to help you with your literary essays. Over these weeks, as you work toward a literary essay, you'll first brainstorm ideas as we've been doing, Then you'll select one that will make a great essay and you'll develop that one idea. For now, we'll do a miniature version of the same process. We'll brainstorm ideas and select one that will lead to a great discussion (instead of a great essay). The ways we make a great discussion and the ways we make a great essay are often very similar."

"We need to start by laying out a bunch of thoughts about the story. First, look back at the story and your writing about it, and think of a provocative or interesting claim, an idea, about the story we could use to get us started talking; we'll list several of them." I gave them a moment to think. "So what ideas do you have about this story?"

As children spoke, I listed the ideas on chart paper quickly:

> Lupe shouldn't be so competitive.
>
> Lupe learns that with hard work you can accomplish anything.
>
> Lupe really, really wants to be good at some sport and so she doesn't give up. She's got a good attitude so that changes her from being a poor marble player into a champion.
>
> Lupe's father encourages her.

"Let's think about which of these ideas might spark an especially great talk. That's what writers of literary essays do. We know we'll be writing about an idea, and we want to choose an idea that'll be worth pursuing. It's the same for people who want to have a good book talk. We need to choose an idea that'll pay off. To do this we choose an idea that feels close to the heart of the story, and one that is grounded in the whole text. We also want an idea that is interesting: I choose an idea that gets me excited to think more about it. Would you join me in looking over our list of possible ideas, asking yourself, 'Which of these ideas might start a really provocative story talk, one that will get to the best and most important parts of the story?'"

"Which idea do you think is provocative enough to initiate a great talk, and is also central to the whole text?" We discussed this for a minute, chose one, and then talked together as a class about that idea. I reminded kids to use thought prompts when they talk back to each other's ideas.

Debrief. Retell the sequence of work the class just did, and tell readers they'll follow a similar sequence of work when they set out to write literary essays.

After the talk about the text continued for ten minutes, I intervened. "Readers, I am hoping that every one of you noticed that we began this talk by generating a bunch of possible ideas; then we asked, 'Which one of these is central to the story? Which is provocative?' Then we selected an idea that we expected would generate a great book talk. When you write about reading, you need to view your possible ideas with the same lens, asking, 'If I write about this idea, will it generate some interesting writing? Will my writing address something that is central to the story?'"

The work that I describe here could easily happen almost every day in reading workshop or in response to your read-aloud. Try it. Read, then ask children to talk in pairs to get their ideas flowing. Then elicit a bunch of ideas. Then ask the class to select one idea, using the criteria I've just described. Once an idea has been agreed upon, I find it helps to give children a moment to either jot thoughts about that idea or to talk with a partner. Then you can convene a whole-class talk in response to the idea. Encourage children to use the thought prompts to grow and talk back to the idea, and to gather new ideas.

You will see that when children talk with each other, they often say, "I agree with that." Ask children to restate the exact part of the idea they agree with. This gives them practice talking about ideas and allows them to listen for and work together to find the words that carry ideas. It also helps children feel comfortable disagreeing a bit, as debate sparks great conversation. Give them words for such discussion, such as on the other hand, could it be that . . . or I partly agree but in one way, I think differently because . . .

⊙ ⎡HOMEWORK⎤ *Bringing More of the Text to Reading Response* Writers, I wonder if any of you have ever taken a photograph and decided one portion of that photograph was really important. If a photographer looks at a picture and decides that the tree in the upper-right-hand corner is important, he can zoom in on just that one tree. In the same way, literary essayists look over all that they have written about a text and ask, "Is one portion of this writing especially provocative and central to the text?" We did this in our Share today. We generated lots of ideas about "The Marble Champ" and then we chose one idea and spent a while talking about just that one idea. When we write about texts, we often reread all we've written and box a line or a passage that feels to us to have potential. Then we copy that onto the top of a fresh sheet of paper, and assign ourselves the job of expanding our first idea.

There are many ways to expand ideas. Of course we use thought prompts, and I know you each have a list of them that you've taped into your notebook. But another thing writers do is we reread the text, looking much more closely at it, listening much more closely to it. If we look really closely, if we listen really carefully, we can generally find more places that help us think in new ways about our original idea. Logan Pearsall Smith has said, "What I like in a good author is not what he says, but what he whispers" (Burke, p. 89). Literary essayists learn to listen for ways in which a text whispers.

So tonight, before you write just anything, select an idea that is worth expanding about the short text you selected as the focus for your work this month. Try to stay with that idea for a little while—write lots and lots about it. Reread the text and find more sections that connect with your idea, then write about them. Give examples of your idea. Use thought prompts to nudge yourself to say more. Then, I challenge you to also ask, "What part of the story *doesn't* fit with this idea?" You may find that all of this leads you to revise your original idea, and that'd be incredibly exciting.

I'm sending home an entry that Judah wrote, which I think can serve as an example of the sort of writing and thinking you can aim toward doing tonight: *[Fig IV-4]*

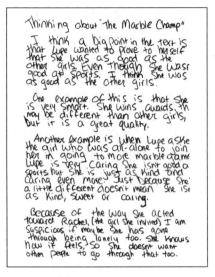

Fig. IV-4 Judah's entry

Thinking about "The Marble Champ"

I think a big part in the text is that Lupe wanted to prove to herself that she was as good as the other girls. Even though she wasn't good at sports, I think she was as good as the other girls. One example of this is that she is very smart. She wins awards.

Another example is when Lupe asked the girl who was all alone to join her in going to more marble games. Lupe is very caring. She isn't good at sports but she is just as kind and caring, even more. Just because she's a little different doesn't mean she isn't as kind, sweet, or caring. Because of the way she acted toward Rachel, (the girl she invited) I am suspicious if maybe she has gone through being lonely too. She knows how it feels, so she doesn't want other people to go through that too.

This part doesn't "fit" for me: I can't tell if Lupe has or doesn't have self-confidence. She does for going to play marbles and being so brave and courageous. She doesn't for having to prove to herself that she was as good as the other girls. I think she does and doesn't have self-confidence. No matter if she does or doesn't, she is caring and sweet and kind on the inside. That's what matters the most.

You'll notice that Judah's entry is shaped a bit like an essay, and some of you will probably find that the same thing sometimes happens to your writing when you make a point of staying with and elaborating upon an idea before jumping to the next one.

TAILORING YOUR TEACHING

If you are teaching a class of children who are revisiting this unit for the second year . . . you will probably want to remind them of the important lessons they've already learned about the way conversational prompts can help talkers and writers grow our own ideas. But you'll also want to teach them other strategies that can help accomplish this purpose. Here are a few:

- Teach children to monitor what they say and write, asking, "Will this contribution take the thinking further?" Some children—some adults, too—act as if it's not a problem if one person after another says the same thing in a conversation, and similarly, some children seem to not feel that there's any problem with repeating themselves over and over in a piece of writing. Coach children to be able to listen to a group conversation, notice when the talk recycles over the same terrain for long enough, and say, "So we have established that . . . Can we move on to a further point?" Children can also learn how to find further points. Sometimes it works to think, "If this *is* true, then what are the implications for . . . ?" Then again, sometimes it works to stand back and imagine that an idea which feels resolved and finished could be regarded as tentative. "Could it be otherwise?" one can ask.

- Teach children that if they find themselves saying (writing) what everyone else is apt to think, it can help to ask, "What ideas might I have about this that are uniquely mine?"

- Teach children that one way to take a conversation deeper is to ask questions. It can help to generate several questions, then to look back on them and select one which stands a chance of yielding productive thought. It's important to build on the question, just as one builds on an idea. Let the question snowball. Then, once it is a question that fires up the child's mind, it is wise to entertain the question rather than to simply answer it. Nothing closes an inquiry down faster than a hasty answer.

MECHANICS

You and your colleagues will want to look at children's entries through a variety of lenses. When you do this, use a lens that allows you to notice the demands this unit places on their syntax.

When children talk and write about contemporary (or at least familiar) objects or events, they can rely on what some refer to as the register of social English. This is the sort of English we use during everyday interactions. If children are instead speaking about times and places that are distant and unfamiliar (especially if they are speaking about language itself), then they must use what some call academic English. This is the register that children must use when writing literary essays.

The linguistic demands on children who attempt to write literary essays are high. This is especially true for English language learners. Sometimes this struggle is evident because children write their thoughts only in a very brief, bare-bones fashion. Other times, a child's struggle with syntax results in the child restating the same thing over and over. Still other times, the child may write in garbled prose: "The influence shown by the character on his interactions with others shows the relationships and the tensions and the feelings that are important to all." If a teacher presses for more clarity and explicitness, the child's language can become even more tangled. Usually, the tangled prose represents a child's efforts to sound impersonal, objective, and scholarly, relying on passive tense and strings of noun phrases. Be forgiving; it's impressive that the child is trying to take on a new role and a new way of using language. All of us need support when we take the great risk of outgrowing ourselves!

Still, it is crucial to let children know that getting an idea across to the reader is more important than a scholarly tone. If a child says or writes something you sense is important, but you can't discern the message because of the convoluted syntax, tell her! Don't think for a moment that you do the child a favor by neglecting to mention that the message is confusing to you. You might say, "I'm trying to follow what you are saying, but I don't understand." If the child tries to explain by making unwarranted assumptions, such as saying "you know" when in fact you don't know, then let the child know you are not exactly sure what she means. "I don't know what you are getting at," you could say, "but I want to understand. Can you try again to explain it and let me see if I can follow you?"

As in the personal essay unit, you'll probably find that children struggle with pronoun references. It may be helpful to remind them that readers must always know the person to whom a pronoun refers. Children make dramatic progress toward this goal when they learn and use characters' names—often they make vague references to "this guy" and "that other guy" because they neither learn the character's name nor look back at the text as they talk, think, and write about it. Children need to become accustomed to rereading their own work and detecting places where a reader won't be sure which character is being referenced. Ask children to exchange their notebooks and to observe their partners' efforts to comprehend their entries. You may suggest that partners read each other's writing aloud quietly, adding (in oral parentheses) the proper name referenced by each pronoun. If the reader is unclear of the antecedent, the writer then needs to use the proper name or a more precise reference. By the way, you can ask children to do this without teaching complex, long lessons on parts of speech—simply list pronouns (he, she, me, etc.) and tell your children that readers need to know who is signified by each of these words. To help children specify pronoun references, teach them to include modifying clauses (again, without using that term) in their writing so that when they introduce a character, they give themselves more than one way to reference that character. If a child writes, "Gabriel, the protagonist in this story, is a lonely boy," then she can later refer to Gabriel not only by his name but also as "the protagonist" or "the lonely boy."

Of course, there are many reasons to use modifying clauses apart from having additional ways to refer to a character. Descriptive clauses also enable the writer to tuck tiny bits of information about a character immediately after mentioning what the character has done or said. The added information often allows readers to picture not only what is being done, but also how that action occurs. Watch meanings become more specific as sentences become more complex:

Gabriel picked up the kitten.

Gabriel, the main character in this story, picked up the kitten.

Gabriel, bursting with pleasure, picked up the kitten.

Gabriel, bursting with pleasure, picked up the kitten, putting it close to his cheek.

Or

Gabriel ate his sandwich.

Gabriel, ravenously hungry, ate his sandwich.

Gabriel, sitting alone on the stoop, ate his sandwich, savoring the thin layer of mayonnaise between two slices of Wonder bread.

You can use examples such as these in conferences or in a minilesson to help children learn how to use subordinate phrases to make their writing more clear and nuanced.

IN THIS SESSION, YOU WILL
TEACH CHILDREN THAT LITERARY
ESSAYISTS ASK, "WHAT'S THIS
STORY REALLY ABOUT?" AND THEN
ANALYZE THE WAYS THE AUTHOR
DELIBERATELY CRAFTS THE STORY
TO CONVEY THIS MEANING.

GETTING READY

- List of provocative questions—
  Interpretation: What Is This Story
  Really About?—prepared on
  chart paper
- Passage from "Spaghetti,"
  by Cynthia Rylant (or other
  touchstone text), copied onto
  chart paper
- Strategies for Writing in Response
  to Reading chart, updated with
  bullet points from today's lesson
- See CD-ROM for resources

DEVELOPING PROVOCATIVE IDEAS:
"WHAT IS THIS STORY *REALLY* ABOUT?"

This session stands on the shoulders of Session III, *in which you taught children that expertise in any field involves knowing what does and does not merit attention, and that skilled readers know it pays to think about character. You will now teach them that skilled readers also know it pays to read with an interpretive lens, thinking, "What's this story really about?"*

The lesson for today links also to your earlier instruction on narrative writing. Many times this year, you've called children's attention to the fact that when writing both personal narratives and short fiction, it is important to ask, "What's this story really about?" You helped children understand that a story about riding the Ferris wheel could really be a story about how, when one grows older, childish thrills aren't the same, or about how the author conquered fears. In those earlier units, children learned that deciding what their story was really about influenced their choice of a lead and an ending as well as which sections of the story deserved to be stretched out and which could be less elaborated upon. Children learned that all details aren't equally important to a story, and that once a writer has decided what her story is really about, the writer can add the details that support her meaning.

Now the tables have turned. Now you will help children read someone else's narrative, asking the same question: "What is this text really about?" You'll help children examine the way in which the text has been crafted, recognizing that the meaning in a story is often conveyed by the craftsmanship. You'll teach children that just as they worked hard to write leads that were linked to the heart of their stories, now they'll examine the lead that another author has written, thinking, "Why might the author have chosen this particular way to start this story?" Similarly, readers can consider why some parts of a story are told in detail, have been stretched out, asking, "Why might this author have decided that this particular moment of the story was such an important one?" Implicit in these questions is the understanding that as authors we make deliberate choices as to how we will write, and those choices reflect what it is we want to say.

MINILESSON

Developing Provocative Ideas: "What Is This Story *Really* About?"

CONNECTION

Rally your children's commitment to thinking deeply about texts by suggesting that as we read, we can learn life lessons from characters just as we do from people in our lives.

"Writers, earlier this year you wrote essays conveying lessons you've learned in your lives. In those essays you mostly wrote about people who have helped you learn things about the world and about yourselves. In this unit, you'll again write about life lessons, but these will mostly be lessons you learn from characters in books."

"There is a psychologist who says kids grow strong based on the number of people they have in their lives from whom they can learn. Her theory is that kids are lucky if they have a grandparent, a coach, a preacher or rabbi, an older cousin, a big sister or brother, a camp counselor, a friend—people who can act as mentors."

"I agree that learning relationships make kids (also grown-ups) strong, but I don't agree that we need to just sit around and *hope* that we luck out and get people in our lives who can teach us. The good news is that when we read, each of us can give ourselves our own learning relationships. When we read, we can let people into our lives and our hearts and we can learn from them. Just as we learn from our moms, our grandparents, and even our pets, we can bring characters into our lives and learn from them."

"You already know how to write personal essays in which you hold tight to what you learn from your life relationships. I want to propose that we work for the next couple of weeks to become the kind of people who can learn from the characters in stories. Are you game for that?" The kids indicated they were.

"In another day or two, you will each reread your writer's notebooks, searching for an idea that can become the seed idea for your literary essay. You'll want to find an idea that not only matters to you, but that is also central to the story."

Name the teaching point. In this case, teach readers that important ideas about stories often reside in the question, "What's this story *really* about?"

"Specifically, today, I want to teach you that many readers find important ideas in stories when we reread, asking, 'What is this story *really* about?' We may ask more specific questions, such as, 'What is the character learning in this story? Is this a lesson that pertains also to my life?'"

COACHING

When I teach minilessons, my goal is not simply to follow the architecture of good minilessons. I'm also hoping that my minilessons illustrate the qualities of good teaching. To me, this means that my minilessons need to be memorable. I use a variety of techniques to achieve this, but few are as effective as the use of metaphor.

When I describe literary essays in this way, saying that children will be learning life lessons from the characters in stories, I am angling children toward writing interpretive essays. By channeling them to look for messages in stories, I'm directing them toward the work that high-school educators refer to as literary interpretation. For the past few years, I've felt as if I have been attending high school along with my sons, trying to learn from their teachers' instruction. One thing I've learned is that the standard secondary-school essay assignment asks students to identify a theme in a work of literature and show the ways in which the author used literary devices to support that theme. I've also learned that when they assign writing tasks, secondary-school teachers rarely teach students what they need to know to be successful. This unit of study is my attempt to give kids the foundational skills they will need to fare well under the regimen of secondary-school English classrooms!

I don't summarize the sorts of questions I hope readers ask; instead I literally put words in their mouths. This is true across the entire series. I'm hoping to put words not only in my students' mouths, but also in their minds.

TEACHING

Remind children that earlier in the year, they learned that once they, as writers, asked, "What is my story really about?" their choice of lead, details, places to elaborate, and so forth all reflected their answer.

"Earlier this year, we learned that a writer could angle a story about riding on the Ferris wheel so it is really about how that writer looks for occasions to be alone. Alternatively, written another way, it could become the story of how he wants to cling to the joys of childhood. Then again, it could highlight his relationship with his father. We learned that writers need to ask, 'What is my story *really* about?' and the answer then influences our lead, our points of emphasis, the thoughts the character reveals, which actions are told in detail versus which are quickly summarized, and many other aspects of the story."

"There is a reciprocal truth. When we read stories *others* have written, we can ask, 'What is the significance this author wanted to highlight?' We can notice the craft decisions an author made and think, 'How does the author's decision to title the story like this, to start it at this point or to elaborate on this section, convey a meaning that resonates in us, long after we've completed the story?'"

Show children that readers have a repertoire of questions to ask to develop interpretive ideas about a text.

"What I am suggesting is that readers don't just finish reading a text, close the book, look up in the air, and think, 'What was that story really about?' Instead, we study the way a text was written and we develop a tentative idea about a story's central meaning. For example, when we want to know what a story is really about, we often use these subordinate questions as stepping stones." I gestured to the chart I had prepared.

Interpretation: What Is This Story Really About?

What single section—or which two related sections—best capture(s) the story's meaning?

Is there one object or one moment from the story that symbolizes the whole message of this story? How does this object or moment convey the overall meaning?

What does the <u>character</u> learn in this story? Is this a life lesson that readers are also meant to learn?

What life lesson can I draw from this story? How does this story teach me a lesson that can help me live my life differently?

How might all the elements of this story contribute to the message of the story? How does the title contribute? The beginning? The setting? The way the character changes? The form? The end?

ACTIVE ENGAGEMENT

Demonstrate reading with interpretation, asking questions about a well-known text. Have children make silent observations of the moves you make with this story, noticing these are moves they could also make with the stories they're studying.

"So watch me as I start to bring these questions to 'Spaghetti,' and then I'll ask you to name what I've done, and to step in where I leave off and continue doing this work."

"I'm going to reread the list of questions and choose one that'll get me started. Um . . . I think I'll ask, 'What did the character—Gabriel—learn?' Let me look back at the story with that in mind." I turned to the text that was written on chart paper, then reread and mused aloud as I did so. "I better tell the before and the after," I muttered to myself. "At the start of the story, Gabriel wears a tough shell that keeps him from feeling how lonely he really is. But in the story, he learns—" Abruptly, I paused.

Reenact what you've just done, asking children to list with their partners the steps you took to apply an interpretive question to the text.

Shifting out of the role of being a reader, I leaned toward the children and said, "Let me stop. I'm going to rewind and replay what I just did. As I do this, would you list across your fingers particular moves that I make with this story that you could later make with your own story." Quickly, I reread the questions from the interpretation chart (gesturing with an upraised finger to show this was the first step I took) and then I chose one question—What did the character learn? (When I chose the question, I gestured that this was my second step.) Next I looked over the story with the question in mind, thinking about what specifically I needed to find to answer the question. I realized that I needed to notice the before and after in order to illustrate how a character changes. This, then, was the third thing I did, and I gestured to a third finger to indicate I'd made another move that the children, too, could take with their texts. Then I asked the children to list with their partners the steps I had taken. After a few minutes, I convened the class' attention. I could have reiterated what they said, but instead moved on to make my larger point.

Sometimes we, as teachers, listen to children talk about texts and we despair. "They're always jumping away from the text," we say. "They veer off to their own lives so often," we complain. If we're not happy with what children do, then we need to teach them what we'd like them to do. This session teaches children how to generate questions that keep them close to the central issues of a text.

I often pause very early on to process what I'm doing. There's not much reason to postpone this move.

Instead of asking children to name what I did, I could have asked them to look at another text, asking, "What's this really about?" I might have encouraged students to notice unusual craft moves the author made and think, "How might this bit of craftsmanship support the meaning the author was trying to convey?" For example, children are apt to say that Gwendolyn Brooks' poem 'We Real Cool' is really about the futility and pain that teenagers experience when they try to be cool. It is productive, then, to look at Brooks' odd use of white space. One can speculate why her lines end with a jagged edge, as in this example: "We real cool. We . . . ." I did not look at craft moves at this point, however, because I know this is something I will invite children to do later.

LINK

Remind children of the strategies they can draw upon when writing about reading.

"So writers, from this day on when you want to write about texts, remember that you have lots of options." I showed the chart that I had updated with the latest strategies.

"I can't wait to see the choices you make today as you continue to use writing to help you think in deep, smart ways about the text you've selected."

Strategies for Writing in Response to Reading

Find a significant moment from the story. Copy the start of it into your notebook; envision it; fill in details, sounds, actions, thoughts, feelings.

Be a wide-awake reader. Notice and underline details others might pass by. Then write a thought about what you notice.

Think about an author's language choices, even in small words like "<u>so</u>."

Pay special attention to aspects of texts that are noteworthy, including a character's actions, motivations, struggles, changes.

We ask, "What is this story <u>really</u> about?" More specifically, we look at:

- the section(s) that best capture the whole story's meaning
- what the character learns in the story
- how all elements of the story contribute to the story's message

As you help children interpret texts, it is important to remember there are different schools of thought in the world of literary criticism. Some people argue that by close reading, a student can detect the author's message. Others, and I count myself among them, believe that texts do not carry a single message. Texts aren't fortune cookies that can be cracked open to reveal a single moral. I believe that by close and responsive reading, readers coconstruct meanings. I'm convinced that readers will not (and should not) all arrive at the same meaning for a text, because reading involves integrating all that we know from the text and all we know from our own prior reading and prior experiences. Although I do not believe there is any single message encoded into a story, I am not uncomfortable suggesting that children read closely, trying to ascertain what an author has tried to convey. With older children, I reword this, asking them to attend to what the text says, because often the author is not accessible. But with upper-elementary children, I try to help them reach toward an understanding of what the author might be saying; in doing so, I avoid channeling them toward a single consensus about "the author's meaning," because this can close down conversation and thoughtfulness.

Whichever school of thought you represent, it is important that children learn to read closely and to bring their own constructive minds to the job of asking, "What's this story really about?"

WRITING AND CONFERRING

Choosing a Tone

When I drew my chair alongside children, I found that the questions about the themes of the texts seemed to have nudged some children, including Emily, to believe they should give definitive responses and assume the authoritative stance of a literary expert. Many of these children seemed to feign confidence in their entries, but at the same time seemed insecure over their conclusions. In one entry and then another, Emily had taken a stab at crystallizing the message of "Eleven." *[Fig. V-1]*

> In the story "Eleven" by Sandra Cisneros, Rachel is a girl who has confidence on her birthday, but when is singled out it causes her to lose confidence.
>
> Rachel does not act old as eleven should. Rachel is stuck in her childish ways. Rachel is older but old habits of her being young aren't completely hidden.
>
> Rachel has no power in the story "Eleven." Sylvia and Mrs. Price are the ones with power. Without the power, Rachel had to take more responsibility.

I began my conference by asking Emily how her writing was going. She said, "It's hard because I am not sure what to say." She expected that next she'd try to write about a different story. When I asked if she'd write differently or in a similar way, she wasn't sure what the question meant, but seemed to suggest she'd again try to pinpoint the text's "real meaning."

I nodded, feeling like I'd grasped enough information to be able to help, and then made a double-decker compliment. "Emily, I love the fact that after you asked a giant question like, 'What is this story really about?' you didn't just point to what's right there in the story as the response. You didn't say: 'It's about a girl whose teacher makes her wear someone else's red sweater.' Instead you read between the lines and talked about meanings that are *suggested* but not *stated*. That's brave work because you are adding your own ideas to the text—and, as a result, you've said things that are really interesting!"

"For example, I think it is fascinating that you think Rachel is stuck in her childish ways. I'm also so interested that you think she has no power, and that Sylvia and the teacher have all the power. We could

continued on next page

MID-WORKSHOP TEACHING POINT ***Entertaining, Rather Than Answering, Questions*** "Writers, can I have your eyes and your attention? The questions that I posed today are big and difficult questions. They are meant to make a person think; they are meant to be puzzling. So, in this instance, you probably won't ask yourself one of these questions and then just pop out with an answer. Instead, you will take one of the questions and then muse about possible responses. If you come to a quick answer, you may want to force yourself to say, 'So that's one idea. How else could I respond to this question?'"

"The writing you do when you are musing over something difficult (and when you don't want to become clear too quickly) has a different quality to it than the writing you do once you are sure of your ideas."

> In the story 'Eleven' by Sandra Cisneros, Rachel is a girl who has confidence on her birthday, but when is singled out it causes her to lose confidence.
>
> Rachel does not act old as eleven should. Rachel is stuck in her childish ways. Rachel is older but old habits of her being younger aren't completely hidden.
>
> Rachel has no power in the story 'Eleven'. Sylvia and Mrs. Price are the ones with power. Without the power Rachel had to take more resposibility.

Fig. V-1 Emily assumes an authoritative tone in her entry about "Eleven."

definitely gather the class together and have a grand conversation over your ideas. They are provocative; they stir up thoughts! So congratulations for doing that."

Then I shifted. "I have one thing I'd like to teach you, if that's okay." Emily nodded, and I pressed on. "What I realize is that when we talk or write about our big ideas about texts, we need to make several choices. We need to choose not just the strategy we'll use to generate our ideas. (You decided to think about 'What's the story really about?' and to think about the character, too.) We also need to choose what role we want to play as we talk and write about the text."

"You have a choice when you write about a text. You can talk and write as if you are a professor, teaching others the smart theory that you've settled upon. If you decide to play this role, you'd probably talk a bit like an announcer, using a strong, declarative voice." (I illustrated the tone by altering my own voice to match what I was describing.) "You'd talk like this":

> In the story, such and such happens. This is evident from . . . Clearly, . . . It is important to notice . . . Furthermore . . . In conclusion . . . .

"On the other hand, you could decide to talk and write about the text as if you are an explorer, a wanderer. In that case, your voice would be tentative and exploratory. For example, if I were writing about 'Spaghetti' in that voice I might write":

> Spaghetti is a story about a boy who learns to love. He learns this from a cat. Some people might say it's not really love he felt. He just held the cat and his heart opened. Or was it already open? Would he have picked up the cat and put it by his cheek if he was so hardened? I don't think so. He maybe learns love from his own life, not just from the cat, but I'm not sure.

"Do you hear how I used a wondering, thinking voice?"

"I'm saying this to you, Emily, because the ideas you've recorded are really smart, but you seem to be struggling, and therefore you want to hop to the next text. I'm thinking that you may have been pushing yourself not only to take on Big Questions, but *also* to write in a professor voice, and perhaps you've pushed yourself to do so before you were ready for that voice. You have a choice as a writer about literature. You can write or talk in a professor voice or you can write or talk in a tentative, exploratory voice."

continued from previous page

"Listen to Max's writing about 'Eleven' and notice its musing, explorative, unsure quality." *[Fig. V-2]*

> At the beginning of the story, I thought that she was kind of immature, but a kid. Because of the way she talks about the sweater and they all yell "not mine."
>
> Then I thought she was kind of sensitive, or she gets a little more upset at things or people then she should. Like when Sylvia just said "I think it's Rachel's" and she got all upset and called her stupid.
>
> Then I thought she was the sort of person who held in her anger without expressing it. I think this because of all her closing her eyes shut tight and big.
>
> I have been thinking that Rachel's expectations are too high. That's because she expected to feel eleven when she woke up on her birthday. Also, when she expected the kids in her class not to know about the different ages. Now I am thinking, and maybe, it is not that she expects things to happen a certain way. Maybe she thinks these things because that is the way someone taught her to think. Maybe she is just naïve. I think that she thinks that everything will go as she thinks it will. This makes me think that maybe she has to think for herself sometimes. And maybe what happened in the class will teach her to make her own decisions. Or, to work it out and see.

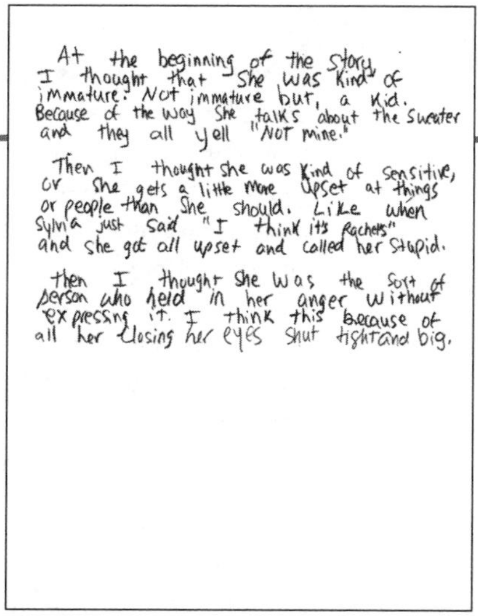
At the beginning of the story I thought that she was kind of immature. Not immature but, a kid. Because of the way she talks about the sweater and they all yell "NOT mine."

Then I thought she was kind of sensitive, or she gets a little more upset at things or people than she should. Like when Sylvia just said "I think it's Rachels" and she got all upset and called her stupid.

then I thought she was the sort of person who held in her anger without expressing it. I think this because of all her closing her eyes shut tightand big.

Fig.V-2 Max's entry reflects his exploration of "Eleven."

Later I came back to Emily and she had written this: *[Figs. V-3 and V-4]*

> Rachel wants to grow up and she's still young. Maybe she's not very nice because she called Sylvia stupid or maybe that's the reason she said it was Rachel's. Why does Mrs. Price believe Sylvia? It's interesting how she says "because she's older and the teacher, she's right and I'm not." That could be another reason why she doesn't want to be eleven and younger than Mrs. Price. She doesn't want the sweater. Rachel tries to cheer herself up. If she doesn't feel eleven why would she be one hundred two, even older.
>
> This is true because if she was one hundred two then she would be older than Mrs. Price and be right. This is important because if she was older she would have been right and she wouldn't have to wear the sweater, or cry. This connects to fairness because it's not fair she's only eleven.

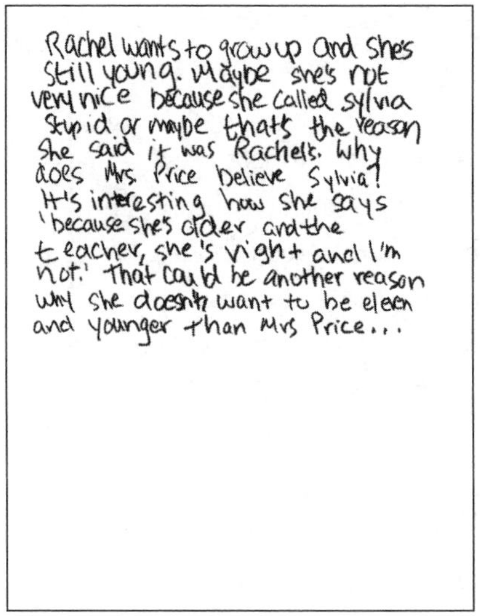
Rachel wants to grow up and she's still young. Maybe she's not very nice because she called Sylvia Stupid or maybe thats the reason she said it was Rachel's. Why does Mrs. Price believe Sylvia? It's interesting how she says 'because she's older and the teacher, she's right and I'm not.' That could be another reason why she doesn't want to be eleen and younger than Mrs Price...

Fig. V-3 Emily tries to write in the voice of an explorer.

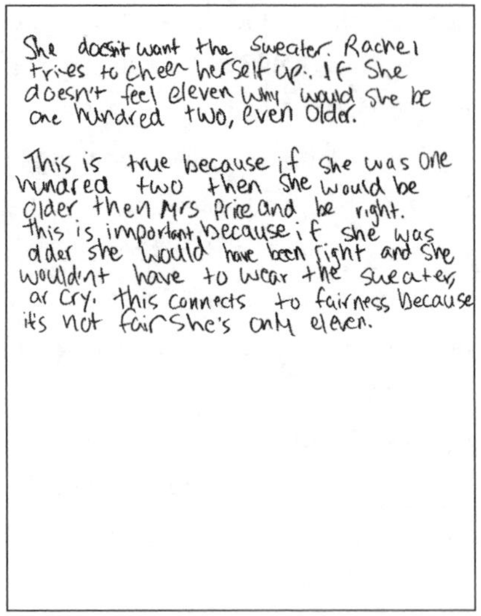
She doesnt want the sweater. Rachel tries to cheer herself up. If She doesn't feel eleven why would she be one hundred two, even Older.

This is true because if she was one hundred two then She would be older then Mrs Price and be right. this is important because if she was older she would have been right and she wouldn't have to wear the sweater, or cry. this connects to fairness because it's not fair she's only eleven.

Fig. V-4 Emily page 2

Other children showed that they needed very different instruction. When I pulled my chair alongside Adam, I found that in his effort to pinpoint the main idea of the story and then "write long" about it, he ended up writing about a host of very tangentially related subjects. Within the space of a brief entry, he crystallized what he regarded as the main idea of "Eleven" and then related it to Iraq, Osama bin Laden, to school bullies, and to Jenny from "Boar Out There." *[Fig. V-5]*

> I think that this is a social issue and if it isn't a social issue then it connects to each social issue. If we all thought of everyone's feelings, this world would be twice as nice. Almost half of the reason we are in Iraq is because we don't think about their feelings or even thoughts.
>
> If Osama bin Laden cared about what we think or what the families who lost someone would think he may not have done this. Everyone is mean from school bullies to evil dictators. They don't think of others' thoughts like Jenny does.

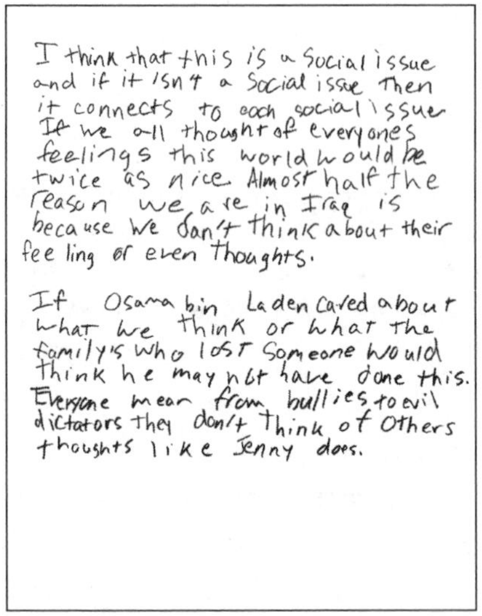
I think that this is a social issue and if it isn't a social issue then it connects to each social issue. If we all thought of everyones feelings this world would be twice as nice. Almost half the reason we are in Iraq is because we don't think about their feeling or even thoughts.

If Osama bin Laden cared about what we think or what the family's who lost Someone would think he may not have done this. Everyone mean from bullies to evil dictators they don't think of Others thoughts like Jenny does.

Fig. V-5 Adam's writing could profit from focus!

It was not hard for me to point out to Adam that the lessons he learned during the personal essay unit of writing still pertain to his entries. "When you write, keep in mind that each time you shift from one idea or one topic to another, you need to indent and start a new paragraph. And you don't want paragraphs that are one or two sentences long! When you see yourself writing in two-sentence paragraphs, ask, 'Am I jumping too quickly from one topic to another? Should I spend a bit longer elaborating on whichever idea I put forward?' The answer will probably be yes."

As you move among children, conferring with them, you'll probably see that today's session led many children to talk about their ideas about texts. Often they'll try to name an idea with just a single word. It's not enough to say that "Spaghetti" is about loneliness. Try saying to kids, "Can you use more words to say that idea?" This can help readers phrase ideas as propositions or claims, rather than as topics.

You'll find that many times young readers develop an overall interpretation of the text, and then they want to paint the entire text with that one idea. So if a child thinks the story is about loneliness, he decides that everyone in the story is depressed because of loneliness—and overlooks all evidence to the contrary. You may want to teach readers that if a story addresses an idea, the characters in the story will probably take different stands on that idea, and some may well alter their relationship to the idea over the course of the story. For example, in Jacqueline Woodson's *The Other Side*, the narrator longs to be friends with a girl "from the other side," while both her mother and her friend, Sandra, hold people who live on the opposite side of the fence at a distance. They are cautious about keeping the worlds—and the people who inhabit them—separate. But by the end of the story, when the narrator has eased the tension by befriending the girl from the other side, sitting with her on the fence that serves as a barrier, both her mother and her friend soften to the possibility of a time when the two worlds can come together.

"I hope you are realizing that there are some times in life when we answer a question crisply and clearly. There are other times when we take a question and we 'entertain' it. Have you ever entertained a guest in your home? You know how you say, 'Have a seat, stay awhile'? You may ask, 'Can I get you something to eat?' You try to make the guest feel at home. In a similar way, when we *entertain a question*, we try to be sure that question lingers, that it stays a while. We make the question feel at home; we chat back and forth with it."

"For a second, let's practice responding to questions in two very different ways. Here's a question for you *to answer* (to your partner): What happens most days during writing workshop? (Before you answer, get your mind clear. You want to answer in a crisp, clear, direct style.) Here's a question for you *to entertain*: What is one moment from this year that best encapsulates the writing workshop for you? (Before you answer, think through different possibilities, and different lenses you could use to approach the question. Remember, this time you don't want to *answer* the question, you want to entertain it, to linger with it and grow thoughtful insights.) To entertain this question, you'll use phrases such as *it might be . . .*, *it could be that . . .*, *on the other hand . . .*, and *one way to think of this is . . . .*"

"Writers, get back to your work. Try, as you proceed, to *entertain* rather than to answer questions."

SHARE

Finding and Developing Provocative Ideas

Invite children into a book talk. Coach them to brainstorm ideas and to select one that is especially provocative and important to the story as a starting place for discussion.

"I am dying to hear some of your ideas! Let's have a whole-class story talk about 'Spaghetti.' Would one of you who has written about this story share an entry in which you've advanced an idea (made a claim) about the story." A few children indicated they could start a conversation.

Speaking to just these children, I said, "Before you read your entry or say your thought, would each of you share your entry or your thought with the group of kids sitting near you? Then would that group talk together about whether the idea feels provocative enough to initiate a great talk, and whether it is also central to the whole text?"

Ask children to select one entry as the discussion starter, and let the discussion begin. At times, invite children to write to grow their ideas from the conversation.

After children talked in these informal small groups, I asked for a group to nominate a child's entry as starting material for a class conversation.

Adam read aloud this entry:

> Gabriel is brave, but not very smart. The reason he can be brave is because no one told him how dangerous picking up a stray cat is. We never heard about a guardian or anything. So I think there was something sad that made Gabriel brave. The cat is like Gabriel.

"Would you talk in partners about Adam's entry, just to get your thoughts going?" I said. After they talked for a few minutes, I said, "Keep 'talking' over Adam's idea, but now *jot* your next thoughts instead of saying them. That is, each of you write down your thoughts. Then exchange notebooks, and reread your partner's idea and jot a further thought into your partner's notebook. You'll be passing notebooks back and forth among yourselves."

After another few minutes, I asked, "Jill, would you get us started in a conversation?"

"I am thinking about the difference between tough and brave. Tough means brave to some people."

I nodded, repeated what she'd said, and asked everyone to think about it and be ready to talk about it. "You can be tough on the inside or on the outside," Tyler said first.

The work that I describe here could easily happen almost every day in response to your read-aloud. Try it. Read, then ask children to jot their thoughts, then to talk in pairs or small groups to sift through their ideas and find some that are worth pursuing, and then begin to pursue them. Then elicit either a small bunch of ideas (which you'd then narrow) or just one idea. Invite children to help assess whether the idea is provocative enough to generate a good discussion and is central to the text—and then hold a whole-class talk in which everyone uses the thought prompts to grow related ideas.

You'll notice that in the next unit of study, one child—Ali—uses this question to frame a memoir in which she explores the bravery she believed she showed in the face of her father's illness. You'll notice that children—people, actually—do not always invent big ideas. They take a big idea that is floating in the world around us and apply it to a near situation—and voila! Insight!

Max added, "I don't think he's tough here, but he is brave. He needs courage to be himself, to be the only one with the right answer, and to live so alone."

"This connects to what Tyler and I were talking about. There's a tough, mean kind of bravery and there's a caring kind of bravery. We think Gabriel is the second kind of brave. We think he cares about the kitten because he's lonely. He needs the kitten. The kitten has a personality for him," Judah responded.

Emily chimed in, "Gabriel being lonely reminds me of Journey and Bloom. Journey was lonely—'and then the cat came,' Patricia MacLachlan said. Bloom helped cure Journey's loneliness. Bloom also helped connect Journey to the rest of his family. I wonder if Spaghetti will do that for Gabriel."

"To go back to what Judah said, I agree there are lots of types of bravery. A fireman, for example, going into a fire—that's pure bravery," Harrison said.

As the children talked, many of them jotted notes. Here are Adam's jottings during this conversation:

> What does it mean to be tough?
>
> Tough is a thought, brave is what you do.
>
> Gabriel thinks of the NOW, not the "what can happen."

After the conversation, I asked each person to again jot his or her thoughts about the text. "Take a minute and think back over the many ways you talked about Gabriel and his bravery. Look at something you wrote earlier, take that sentence, and write off of it using one of the ideas we grew in this conversation."

Set children up in partnerships to develop ideas about the texts they have selected, just as they have just done as a class.

After the children did this for a bit, I intervened to say, "These are unbelievably powerful ideas that you are growing today! All of these ideas, however, are about 'Spaghetti.' Many of you may find that your mind is especially on fire about 'Eleven' or 'The Marble Champ' or 'Boar Out There' or 'The Birthday Box.' Right now, would you each reread your entries on the text that especially interests you and box out an idea that feels provocative and central enough to that story that you'd like to develop it." I let the children do this for a moment or two. Then I said, "I've regrouped you into partnerships based on the story you are focusing on especially. I'm going to read off some partnerships, and when I finish reading my list, would you meet at the desk of the partner's name I read first (that will be partner 1 in these new groupings), bringing your writer's notebook and your story with you." I then read the list, and let the class regroup.

You'll notice that this is really more like the Active Engagement portion of a minilesson than like a Share. Sometimes more practice with a new way of learning helps children more after the workshop time than making public some of the work they've done, which is more usual for a Share.

"All eyes on me. Partners, I suggest that you discuss one partner's idea only, and talk about it just as we talked about Jill's idea. After you and your partner have agreed on a claim that you want to discuss, take a minute to look back at your chosen short text so that you get yourself ready to talk more about the one idea you select. Mark sections of the text that relate to that idea. Afterwards, try to talk as long as you can about that one idea. You may find other sections of the text that relate to that idea, in which case, talk about them, too."

"You may decide the original idea can be revised so it is more specific and more true. You may find exceptions to the idea. You may talk about whether the idea is true in your own lives or in the lives of characters in other books. Your job will be to talk as long as you can about one person's idea, always referring to the text as often as you can."

HOMEWORK *Finding Elusive Meaning in Texts* For homework tonight, reread the text you have been studying, and this time pay attention to a part of the text where nothing much happens. Ask yourself, "Why is this section of the text here?" Don't settle for "Who knows?" as the answer. There must be a reason—so speculate. Ask, "Could it be . . ." and then say, "On the other hand . . ." Entertain the question!

As you do this, you may find that you come up with several central ideas. Good readers generate lots and lots of ideas about a text's larger meaning.

TAILORING YOUR TEACHING

If children need more practice learning how to use interpretive questions to lead them to interpret . . . you might want to first ask one child to do this, and then use that one child's work as a demonstration text. For example, a fifth grader, Jose, used these questions to reflect on "Boar Out There." He felt that the section which best captured the story's meaning was the one where Jenny sees the boar and cries because he's been hurt. She isn't afraid anymore. It's important to notice that this one section of the text pertains to both the start of the text—to the fearful rumors associated with the boar—and to the turning point in the text, when Jenny develops sympathy for the boar. When reflecting on what object from the story symbolized the message of the story, Jose wrote this:

> The boar's torn ears are the object that symbolizes the whole message of the story. The ears represent the hurt part of the boar, and maybe of all of us. They are also what allow Jenny to sympathize with the boar.

The question which really nudged Jose to do some important work, however, was this one, "How do all the elements in the story contribute to the message?" This question. . . especially following the others . . . scaffolded Jose to make a journey of thought. He wrote this:

> All the elements of this story are about imagining something that isn't really true. Jenny thinks the boar is this really wild, scary beast but in fact he's hurt and scared. So the message is that we shouldn't make assumptions about people. The title, "Boar Out There" shows that the boar isn't a part of Jenny's world; he's "out there," which is why she imagines him to be something he's not.
>
> The beginning of the story shows this, too: "Everyone in Glen Morgan knew there was a wild boar in the woods over by the Miller farm." Right away Cynthia Rylant shows that all the people in the town, not just Jenny, know there's a wild boar. Cynthia goes on to describe the boar that everyone knows exists, but then she says, "No one in Glen Morgan had ever gone past the old back Dodge and beyond, as far as she knew," so we know that what these people think about the boar has nothing to do with the way things actually are.
>
> The setting shows that fear is big in the story. The rail fence that separates the boar from the town is "splintery," the trees are "awful," the leaves are "damp" and "dark" and the air of the woods presses "deep into" Jenny's skin. This isn't a warm friendly place. It's an uncomfortable, heavy, dark place.
>
> Jenny changes from a scared girl to a caring girl. She cries when she sees that the boar is hurt and from then on she doesn't fear him anymore, she just feels bad for him.
>
> The end of this story shows that it's possible to think new things about people or animals. Jenny realizes that the boar has as little to fear about the people of Glen Morgan (the "bluejays and little girls") as the people have to fear about the boar.
>
> From this story I can learn to not judge people too quickly, before getting to know them and I can learn to be more sympathetic to people who are strangers. I hope I'll keep this in mind as I meet new people.

COLLABORATING WITH COLLEAGUES

Today's session opened up the topic of teaching children to interpret texts. For those of you who teach fifth or sixth grade, this should be an especially important topic, because it is a huge priority in secondary-school English courses. I remember when I was in high school, my teacher asked me, "What does the light at the end of the dock mean?" I remember thinking, "It means a lamp, a lantern, at the end of the pier"—but of course I knew from my teacher's penetrating gaze that he wanted a deeper answer. I ventured forth. "Does it mean heaven?" I bravely queried.

"Any other ideas?" my teacher asked, scanning the room. When no one else put forth a hypothesis, my teacher proceeded to explain the deeper meaning of the text. How well I remember sitting at my desk thinking, "How did he get *that* out of *this*?" I learned from that day and others like it that I didn't have what it takes to read literature well—and decided against majoring in English, as I'd always planned.

Too many children come to feel that because they don't see the meanings that the teacher sees in a text, this means their ideas about texts are somehow "wrong." I once sat in on a class discussion where the teacher asked her class to describe the relationship between Frog and Toad in Arnold Lobel's Frog and Toad series.

A child suggested they were adventurous friends—a reasonable thought—but the teacher had a particular answer in mind that she wanted her children to produce. "No," she said. "It begins with *d*."

"Damp?" I thought, wracking my brains for the correct answer (and I was an adult at the time!).

To help the children out, the teacher asked a leading question. "Are Frog and Toad the same, or are they . . . ?"

A child produced the requisite word. They are different. That is a perfectly reasonable (if not very surprising) conclusion about Frog and Toad, but it is not reasonable for us to work so hard to elicit our ideas from children that we silence them.

With your colleagues, talk and think about the role of leading questions in your teaching. Teachers are taught, of course, to ask leading questions. We are taught to elicit information and ideas from children. Basal textbooks tell teachers the questions to ask and the answers to expect.

But I believe this sort of teaching silences children. I often tell my graduate students that as a rule of thumb it is best to aim never to ask a question for which we know the answer. This means that instead of saying, "Are Frog and Toad good friends?" the teacher might ask, "What aspect of their friendship especially interests you?" I hope, then, that today's session invites you to rethink the role of leading questions, and to entertain the notion that it is not important for children to see the same big meanings in a story that you have seen.

What *does* matter is that children grow up to be the kinds of readers who pause in the midst of reading to ask, "What is this really about?" To support children in doing this, be sure that when you read aloud chapter books, you sometimes demonstrate the way in which you pause to think about a book's message. Show children, for example, that when you pause to think about *Because of Winn-Dixie*, you think first that it is the story of a girl, Opal, who goes to the grocery store and ends up adopting a stray dog. To earn money for the dog, she gets a job, and in the process meets lots of people. But then show children that you entertain other ways to think about the book.

If readers ask questions such as "What do the characters want? What choices do they make? Why does this matter?" we read more deeply. Perhaps you might think, "In this book, Opal adopts a stray dog and this matters because she is lonely. The dog helps her make a relationship with her father, she and her father get to talking. The dog also helps her make relationships with people at the pet store, and with a recluse." Or you might think, "This story starts by introducing a girl who is not just an only child. She's also a child who is isolated. In the end, she and her dog are part of a network of relationships."

DEVELOPING PROVOCATIVE IDEAS:

"How Does This Story Intersect with My Life?"

In this session, you will teach children some ways that literary essayists draw on their life experience to understand and develop ideas about texts.

GETTING READY

- Story you can tell of an instance when reading changed a person's life (perhaps your own)
- Example of an important issue from your own life
- "Spaghetti," by Cynthia Rylant (or other touchstone text)
- Idea for a shared life issue children can discuss in relation to a text
- See CD-ROM for resources

My family and I gather every Sunday at 10 p.m. to watch Grey's Anatomy, *a show chronicling the drama experienced by a cluster of surgical interns and the attending surgeons. We all watch the same show at the same time, but when it's over and we share our responses, we invariably find that the story has meant something very different for each of us. I'm a sucker for Meredith: I love her resolute efforts to hold herself together, even when her insides are coming out. My husband admires George, who rarely asks to be in the limelight, but in his quiet way does countless small acts of generosity. Each of my sons has his own favorite character and his reasons for championing that person. Each of us constructs our own meaning of the story. We each construct meaning out of all that we are and long to be. I suspect that a person who knows John and me well would suggest that my affinity for Meredith, and John's for George, mirrors our own life stories. But that's not surprising—after all, we bring ourselves to the books we read and to the shows we watch!*

We read, in part, to know that we are not alone. Who among us has not looked up from the pages of a book and thought, "That's it! That's exactly what I've been feeling." Just as we take exquisite comfort in having a friend who understands us— even the parts of us we don't understand—so, too, do we find solace in opening a book and finding ourselves there on the page.

In this session, you'll provide children with one strategy for making personal connections to a book. You'll suggest that when we approach a book aware of our own issues and struggles, and expect the story to speak to us in a deep and profound manner, the chances are great that it will do just that.

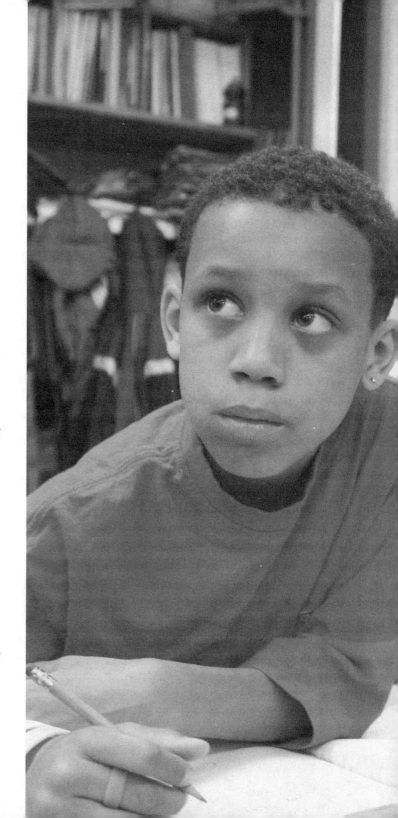

MINILESSON

Developing Provocative Ideas: "How Does This Story Intersect with My Life?"

CONNECTION

Tell your children a story of when reading changed a person's life or your own life. Suggest that by writing about reading, we make it more likely that books will "get through to us."

"I remember last year, one of my students—Ramon—was reading about the author Walter Dean Myers. Ramon brought me a passage in which Myers said, 'The book that changed my life was . . . .' Ramon said to me, 'I don't get this. How could a *book* change someone's life?'"

"I hope that in this unit of study you come to understand that texts can, indeed, change our lives. And I hope you learn that we write about our reading so that it will be more likely that texts get through to us and make a difference."

"Books have definitely changed my life. When I was your age, I read a book about people who lived in an Israeli kibbutz—they were willing to risk their lives to build their promised land, and I was envious of their sense of mission. I remember thinking, 'I wish I were Jewish!' I suspect that I am a teacher today because books taught me that some people don't just have jobs, they have missions—and I wanted a sense of *mission* in my life as well."

"Sometimes I see kids read a book, and when they reach the last page they just throw the book to the side and say, 'I'm done!' They don't seem to understand that we read to be affected by what we experience on the page."

Name your teaching point. In this case, teach children that we write so that stories we read will be more apt to matter to us. Give writers a strategy for connecting personally to the texts they are studying.

"Today I want to teach you that when readers write, we can make it more likely that stories get through to us. One way to be sure that stories speak to us and to the issues in our lives is to think, 'What are the issues in my life?' Then we can read or reread a text, thinking specifically, 'How can this story help me with my issue?'"

COACHING

In this unit of study, I am trying to rally children not only for a particular kind of writing but also for a love of reading. My connections, then, have more work to do than usual. Over and over again, I plead with children for their attention, their dedication.

Shirley Brice Heath has said that one of the most important gifts we can give our students is allowing them to form bonded relationships with richly literate adults. To that end, we need to wear our love of reading and writing on our sleeves. Minilessons provide opportunities not only for teaching but also for preaching.

Notice that my teaching points are often several sentences long. In the first sentence, I name the general goal of the minilesson, and in the second or third sentence I spell out the specific strategy I will teach students so they can reach the goal.

TEACHING

Show children that they can become aware of the issues in their lives by rereading their notebooks, looking for the topics and themes that reoccur.

"Writers, some people can just say, 'Hmm . . . what are the issues in my life?' and those issues pop into their heads. Other writers need to go on a search for those issues. We can find them if we look back through our writer's notebooks, glancing at the personal narrative and personal essay entries we've written, thinking, 'What's this *really* about? Is that a big topic, a big concern in my life?'"

"I did that work at home already, and I'm aware that in my life, one of my big issues is that I am bracing myself to deal with a feeling of emptiness. My son Miles will be going off to college very soon, and there will be a gaping hole in my heart when he is gone."

Demonstrate to children that once a person is aware of an issue, she can reread literature, looking at it through the lens of that concern, asking, "How can this story help me deal with my life issues?"

"So watch me think (and write) about 'Spaghetti,' letting this story help me with my issue."

"How can Rylant's story help me deal with the hole that will be in my life when Miles goes? Let's see . . . at the start of 'Spaghetti,' I get the feeling that Gabriel has a hole in his life too; I'm just going to reread the story again and think about what Gabriel does with that hole in his heart." I did this, and said, in a musing tone, "I think Gabriel had steeled himself to not feel the hole in his heart . . . but as a result, he hardly heard or felt *anything*. I hope that when I need to deal with Miles' departure, I don't wall myself up like Gabriel started to do." As I spoke, I jotted some of this in an entry on chart paper. I continued musing and jotting, "I'm thinking about the fact that Gabriel got himself a kitten, and found a way to fasten his love onto something. This reminds me of how I've always wanted to adopt a little girl from China. I'm tempted to race to China right now! But actually, I've got people at home already waiting for me, and some of them have been as neglected as that kitten."

Debrief. Replay the sequence of work you've done, giving added tips.

"Readers, do you see how I reread my notebook and came upon an issue that was important to me—the hole that will be in my heart when my son leaves for college? Then I reread the story, asking, 'Does this story speak to my issue?' and I wrote about it. I could have looked at 'Spaghetti' and just said, 'No, this isn't about my issue. I'm not poor or homeless. My issue involves my son going to college, and Gabriel's not going to college.' But I think when you look to the root of any issue, often that issue is universal. Sometimes, of course, one particular text won't speak to an issue, but I recommend you don't give up too quickly."

I'm telling the truth when I let children know this is a big issue in my life. Obviously, you'll need to think about your own issues, and to speak the truth of your life. Your children will be much more apt to open their hearts to the stories you are studying together if you do so. I may not initially be moved by "Spaghetti," but if I read this story while thinking also about Miles' upcoming departure, suddenly it all means more to me.

When writing in front of children, you have choices. You can write on chart paper, a white board, an overhead transparency, or in your own notebook (in the latter case, your children won't see your script, but you can voice what you write as you go and/or you can write silently and then reread later). I find that even if I decide to simply write in my own notebook, this has some visual power, and of course writing in my notebook is vastly faster than the other formats because I can use shorthand.

Of course, if need be, you can always think of another issue in your life and see if the text can help with that second issue.

ACTIVE ENGAGEMENT
Ask children to pretend they have a shared life issue and to view the class text through the lens of that problem.

"So let's pretend you've already read over your notebook and found that one of the issues that is huge in your life is the pressure that so many of us feel to fit with the in crowd and to be popular. So now you think, 'How does Rylant's story help me deal with the issue of feeling pressured to fit in and be popular?' I'll give you a minute to think about that."

After some silence, I said, "You could think, 'Rylant's story isn't about a kid and his friends—it doesn't really speak to the issue of peer pressure.' But if you give things a chance, I bet you and your partner can find that Gabriel struggles (in his own way) with some of the same pressures to fit in that many people feel, and he's made some choices that might teach you. Would you turn and talk with your partner about how Gabriel and this story could perhaps help you, or someone else who is struggling with feeling that the only way to be popular is to remake yourself to fit in with everyone else."

LINK
Review optional ways writers can generate entries about the texts they are studying.

"So, writers, by this time in the year you have become skilled at making decisions about the work you need to do. Today you may decide to continue to entertain big questions such as, 'What is this story really about?' You may read, trying to be the kind of reader upon whom nothing is lost. That is, you may read closely, noticing details others would pass by, and then write an entry in which you linger over a description of one thing you see in the story. Afterwards, skip a line and write, 'The thought I have about that is . . . .' If you want to reread your notebook, grasp onto a life issue, and then think, 'How can this story help me with an issue in my life?' that'd be especially great. The important thing is that you read, reread, reread, and do all this as a wide-awake writer. Let your mind be on fire, and write what you think."

Over and over you'll see me making decisions for children so that during the Active Engagement section of a minilesson they are set up to accomplish what I've named and demonstrated. Notice that if I set up the Active Engagement well, children usually waste no time on peripheral or lead-in activities.

You can be sure that I've already thought this through, and I'm pretty convinced this will be in reach for these kids. If I'd felt it was important to be even more supportive, I might have asked them to keep that question in mind while rereading the story, and I would then have selected a particularly relevant part to read aloud, pausing at the most pertinent sections.

Whenever possible, I want to end a minilesson by reminding children of the array of options available to them so they learn to be the job captains of their own writing. In this Link, I list options, but for variety or for engagement's sake I could instead ask children to list across their fingers three different ways they could write about reading.

WRITING AND CONFERRING

Making Personal Connections to a Text

"Adam," I said, "You look very serious."

Adam answered, "I can't find anything in my notebook like in 'Eleven.'" He shook his head, discouraged. "I haven't had a birthday. I haven't had a mean teacher like Mrs. Price. I've never been forced to wear someone else's clothes—or not that I can remember."

"To make personal connections with a story," I said. "I usually *start with my own life*. Remember I suggested you reread your writer's notebook and ask, 'What issues do I talk about a lot?' Let's try that together."

"I looked through my notebook, but there isn't anything in my life about turning eleven or anything."

"Let's just take an entry," I answered. "For example, this one." I pointed to an entry Adam had written about his brother pounding his arm as they rode in the car to his grandparents' house. "So what's the issue here for you?"

"Oooh! I get it. Jon—he's kind of mistreating me like the teacher is mistreating Rachel."

"You are so smart! You see, when we read, we *do* bring our own lives to texts, but it helps to start by reading your notebook or thinking about a specific issue in your life. Then (and only then) look at the story and think, 'How might this story help me with my life issue?' You'll find this works often."

Adam nodded and began to write:

> Whenever we ride in a car with my parents, Jon and I sit together in the back. Sometimes he hits me hard on the shoulder. I tell him it hurts, but he says, "I'm just trying to toughen you up." When Mrs. Price tells Rachel to put on the red sweater that isn't hers, she is mistreating Rachel the way my brother mistreats me when he punches me.

Interrupting the class I said, "Can you give me a thumbs up if you are finding it a bit hard to make significant personal connections with your text?" Half a dozen kids indicated yes, so I rounded up a small group and we huddled together. "I just had a conference with Adam, who was struggling to find important ways to bring his life

MID-WORKSHOP TEACHING POINT *Celebrating* "Writers, can I have your eyes and your attention? I need to tell you that the work you are doing today is blowing me away. I am amazed by the reflective thinking and writing you are doing today! You are combing through your writer's notebooks in search of entries that feel meaningful to you and rereading, asking yourself 'Why does this entry matter to me? What does this reveal about me?' Emily, for example, found an entry in her notebook about how she likes to dress up in grown-up clothes, and now she has realized that there are times in her life when she, like Rachel in 'Eleven,' feels both old and young at the same time! And Dominic found just a sentence in one entry that reminded him of a time when he forced himself to act in brave, tough ways (even though he felt something very different). For him, 'Boar Out There' is a story of a character who has done this same thing. But for Harrison, our animal lover, 'Boar Out There' is instead a story about the fact that animals that act mean are often really just hurt."

"You are pushing past your initial thoughts, and making connections between your life and the text you are reading. This is the work that great readers and writers do, and this enables texts to change our lives. When we read a text together, each one of us brings along our life experiences . . . it is the lens we read through. When I read 'Spaghetti,' I bring the hollow feeling of Miles leaving for college. Oona may bring the lens of loneliness based on her personal essay about being an only child. Zach, after getting a puppy for his birthday, may read through the lens knowing that animals make great company."

to the text he is studying. He did some great work, and I thought maybe you'd be willing to try some similar work—am I right?" The children indicated they were game.

"Take just a second and open your notebook to almost any page—but choose a place where you wrote about something important to you. Reread that page. If it reveals an issue in your life, name that issue. For example, my entry was about my son packing for college, and my issue is that I'm bracing myself for this giant hole I am going to have in my life. Adam's entry was about his brother pounding on his arm, and his issue is that Jon sometimes mistreats him. Usually if you've written about a subject that is important to you, you'll find an issue or a hard part right there. Take just a second to reread your entry and find the issue that is lurking there." After a moment the children looked up, signaling they were done. "It is easier than you think to find issues within your own writing notebook," I said. "The trick is to not spend too much time flipping the pages—settle on one page, and trust that there is definitely an issue on that one page." Then I said, "Zach, tell us the issue you've realized is there in your life," and I motioned to all the children that they should watch what I did to help Zach take the next step.

Zach replied, "Leaving for camp."

I wasn't totally convinced this qualified as an issue, but I tweaked what he'd said a bit so that it would suffice. "That's such an important time, isn't it? Are you saying you have lots of feelings when you are leaving for camp?" I asked.

Then I glanced at all the children. "Once you know an issue that is important in your life, you can pause in the midst of your reading and think, 'How does this text speak to (or help me with) my issue?' So, Zach, in what ways does 'Eleven' speak to the deep issues that are wrapped around your leaving for camp?"

"Because sometimes when I go to camp, I feel like crying like a kid, and Rachel feels like that?" Zach said, his voice tentative.

I nodded. "That's huge, Zach. You know the feeling of being both eleven and three years old, and you know that when you feel like crying, you feel as if you are three." Then I asked, "Does Rachel's struggle to deal with that sweater and with the feelings the episode caused in her help you learn ways you could deal with your feelings?"

"'Cause she should have talked; she should have said something," Zach said.

"You need to write that down. It is really important." To the others, I said, "Do you all see what Zach did here with his entry?" As I spoke, I jotted a list of what Zach had done. "First he reread an entry from his notebook and found an issue in his life. Then he asked, 'How does this text speak to the issue in my life?' and he took his first answer deeper. Finally, he asked, 'How might this text help me think more about or realize some new things pertaining to this issue in my own life?' That's how you can let stories matter in your lives! Can you all do this now? Follow these steps," I said, sliding the list I'd made into the center of the table. "I'm going to go work with some other children, but I'll be back in five minutes to see how you've done. Stay right here and do this work beside each other, okay? I can't wait to see what you do!"

SHARE

Helping Friends Connect Personally with Texts

Share the story of a child who struggled to make a personal connection to the text, and then did with the help of someone else's eyes.

"I want to share something with you that Max did this morning. When I conferred with him, he shook his head and whispered to me, 'I can't . . . I can't do this!'"

"Max," I said, "What's the matter?"

"'There's nothing here that matches my life. I can't see the stuff I noticed in "Eleven" in my life! I tried, but really, my life is not like hers.'"

"I asked Max to show me what he'd tried to write today and he pointed to this entry," I said and read it aloud to the class: [Fig. VI-1]

> I think that people don't understand Rachel. They don't understand her being eleven, ten, nine, eight, seven, six, five, four, three, two, and one. I see this in the text where it says, "I don't know why but I'm feeling sick inside, like the part of me that's three wants to come out of my eyes, only I squeeze them shut tight . . . and try to remember today I'm eleven . . ." This tells you that she is afraid to be three, because other people don't know she is also three. She may be too afraid to be herself because the other people don't know the real her. And they are also probably three, and can cry like they are three, but are too afraid to. Because it's different. And Rachel is different. But she as well as her classmates are afraid to be different.

After I read that, I said to Max, "Sometimes, when we write about a text, issues from our lives leak through into what we notice and think. Sometimes, we're not aware that our lives have affected what we notice in a text until someone else points out possible connections to us."

Then I said to Max, "Do you remember an entry you wrote about how you love to bake—remember we had a huge class discussion about the fact that you don't always share things because you (like many others) get uneasy over what people think? And do you remember the entry you shared with the class about not liking sports and being different in

Fig. VI-1 Max's notebook entry

You may be surprised that I'm willing to talk in this honest way about one writer's struggles. The truth is, writing workshops become intimate places and we do talk about struggles as well as successes. Also, Max is an especially capable writer, so I'm more apt to spotlight his struggles than those of another student. Of course, in an instance such as this, I'll check with the child before using his story as the centerpiece in a lesson!

that way from a lot of kids? Well—look again at what you wrote about Rachel. You said she 'may be too afraid to be herself because the other people don't know the real her.' And you wrote, 'Rachel is different. But she, as well as her classmates, is afraid to be different.'"

"Max's eyes got big behind his glasses and a smile spread across his face when I said that. He knew his issues in his personal life had already leaked into his response to 'Eleven.' *His* life had leaked into his thinking about Rachel."

Point out the ways the one child's struggles and solutions could apply to everyone's. Ask children to work with their partners to explore potential personal connections to the texts in their writing.

Looking around at the class, I said, "Max didn't realize at first that his life issues had leaked into his thinking and writing about Rachel. I bet the same thing has happened in your writing today. I know Ali, for example, has paid a lot of attention to the relationships Lupe had in 'The Marble Champ.' Ali, I'm wondering if you realize you may be noticing Lupe's relationship with her father especially because *your* relationship with your dad has been on your mind a lot lately?"

Then I said to all the children, "My guess is that your lives have been leaking into what you see in texts and that, like Ali and Max, you may not even realize it. Partner 1, tell partner 2 what you have noticed especially in your short text, and share a few entries you have written about the text. Partner 2, listen carefully and give your partner feedback if you see that some of your partner's life issues may have been leaking into your partner's thinking about the text. Then switch so that you both get this sort of help. Think hard—be smart and try to *make* the writing connect to your partner's life."

This may seem to you like a lucky coincidence that Max noticed in "Eleven" what he also deals with in his own life. You may be surprised at how often you notice this "coincidence" of a match between a response to literature and the readers' response to his or her life. Even if at first there appears to be no connection at all, ask children to assume the connection must be there and free write about it until they surprise themselves by finding it really is there. We all share the human experience, and there is always a way to empathize with other people or characters, even those with very different lives.

● HOMEWORK *Learning from Characters* Writers, tonight as you read, instead of focusing on how an overall text speaks to you, think about a single quality of a character you admire—one you'd like to have yourself, or one you have deep inside you but haven't yet found a way to express. You might, for example, notice that someone in your book finds ways to deal with her anger without shouting or losing control. If you're someone who does get heated when angry, you might think about how you could let this character in, learning from her, maybe even finding ways to change yourself. You might find that it isn't always the main character who affects you. Often secondary characters, in their quiet and sometimes quirky ways, touch us more immediately or more deeply. Once you've identified a character who speaks to you in some way, spend some time jotting down your thoughts about the quality you admire in this character, the ways in which he or she demonstrates the quality. What it is about the quality you identify with, long for, or are trying to bring out in yourself? You might use prompts like, "The quality I admire is . . . ," "This quality makes me feel . . . ," "I notice in my own life that . . . ."

TAILORING YOUR TEACHING

If children are making personal connections that veer very far from the text . . . then you'll want to help them deepen this response. Often, a child reads a text, sees a word or passage in the text that reminds the child of her own experience, and suddenly it is as if the text no longer exists. All the child can think about is her own experiences. Reading, then, becomes an orgy of self-expression. Be sure, with these children, that you help them to shuttle back and forth between the text, their lives, and the text. That is, if a child pauses in reading to say, "The same thing happens to me," it is helpful to ask, "So how was this character's experience the same as yours? How was it different? What can you learn from this?" Then too, some children regard personal response as a conversation stopper. You'll hear these children make comments such as, "Well, that is just my own idea," or "There is no one right way to read this." Be sure these children know that responding personally to a text needs to be the beginning, not the end, of conversation.

If your children are having trouble getting started making personal connections with the text . . . you might try teaching them a different way to go about it than the way presented in this session. David Bleich, author of *Readings and Feelings,* suggests a different set of steps to try that can help readers recognize ways in which their own lives and experiences affect what they see in a text. A reader can read a text, and then search for and mark what he believes is the most important sentence, image, or word in the text, the bit that represents what the text is really about for him. If a number of different readers do this work with the same text, it will immediately become apparent that different aspects of a text stand out to different readers. It is helpful, then, for a reader to ask himself, "Why was it this, out of everything else, that stood out for me especially in this text?" "What is there about my own life that can help me understand my experience of this text?"

COLLABORATING WITH COLLEAGUES

I've previously shared with you the wise advice the poet Lucille Clifton gave me and my colleagues when she visited us almost fifteen years ago. "Nurture your imaginations of what's possible," she said. "We cannot create what we cannot imagine."

That advice has been important to me as I help school districts imagine and plan for large-scale reform in the teaching of writing. It's also advice that helps me when I coach teachers in developing units of study. And I think we need to remember this advice when we work with writers.

Children need an image of the sort of thing we hope they will write in a unit of study, so you and your colleagues will need to find or to write exemplar essays. Before you can proceed, you need to clarify for yourself what it is *you* hope your children will write.

Over the year in my community of practice, we've taught toward a variety of templates for literary essays, and no one template is more right than another. You may choose any one of these templates as the one you want to teach toward, or you may invent yet another, or you may spread the array of options before your children and let them know they can sculpt their essays in any of these ways.

The first template described below is the one we taught with the children in this class. The accompanying pieces of student writing are available on the CD-ROM.

I. A claim, with several parallel supporting ideas drawn from the text

- Introductory paragraph which generally begins with a broad statement about literature or life and often (but not always) includes the author, genre, and text summary, which ends by stating a claim about the story. This claim, the thesis statement, overviews two or three subordinate ideas.

- One subordinate idea is restated at the start of body paragraph 1, and that idea is supported with evidence from the text

- A second subordinate idea is restated at the start of body paragraph 2, and supported with evidence from the text

- A third subordinate idea may or may not be restated in body paragraph 3—if it is, then it is also supported with evidence from the text

- In the last paragraph, the claim is reiterated. The writer may make a personal connection or put a new spin on the writer's initial claim.

Literary Essay on "Eleven" by Sandra Cisneros written by Jill

In my life, not everything ends up like a fairytale. I like to read books where characters are like me. They don't live fairytale lives. We have the same kinds of problems. Many people read Sandra Cisneros's essay "Eleven" and think it's

Literary Essay On "Eleven" by Sandra Cisneros written by Jill

In my life, not everything ends up like a fairytale. I like to read books where characters are like me They don't live fairytale lives. We have the same kinds of problems. Many people read Sandra Cisneros's essay "Eleven" and think its about a girl who has to wear a sweater she doesn't want to wear. But I think the story is about a girl who struggles to hold onto herself when she is challenged by people who have power over her.

When Rachel's teacher, Mrs. Price, challenges Rachel, Rachel loses herself. One day Mrs. Price puts a stretched out, itchy, red sweater on Rachel's desk saying "I know this is your I saw you wearing it once" Rachel knows that the sweater isn't hers, and tries to tell Mrs. Price, but Mrs. Price doesn't believe her. Rachel reads to Mrs. Prices actions by losing herself "In my head I'm thinking...How long till lunch time, how long till I can take the red sweater and throw it over the School

yard fence, or leave it hanging on a parking meter, or bunch it up into a little ball and toss it over the alley." This shows that Rachel loses herself because she's not listening to her teacher. She's dreaming about a whole other place. It is also important to see that Rachel has all this good thinking about the sweater but when she wants to say the sweater isn't hers, she squeaks and stammers unable to speak. "But it's not Rachel says. "Now" Mrs Price replies. Rachel loses herself by not finding complete words to say when Mrs Price challenges her.

When Rachel's classmates challenge Rachel, Rachel loses herself. Sylvia Saldivar puts Rachel on the spot light when she says to Mrs. Price, "I think the sweater is Rachel's." Sylvia is challenging Rachel, she is being mean and she makes Rachel feel lost, Rachel cries to let her emotions out. Rachel feels sick from Sylvia. Rachel tries to cover herself up by putting her head in her sleeve. Tears stream down her face. She doesn't feel special like it's her birthday. Instead she feels

Fig. VI-2 Jill page 1   Fig. VI-3 Jill page 2

about a girl who has to wear a sweater she doesn't want to wear. But I think the story is about a girl who struggles to hold onto herself when she is challenged by people who have power over her.

When Rachel's teacher, Mrs. Price, challenges Rachel, Rachel loses herself. One day Mrs. Price puts a stretched out, itchy, red sweater on Rachel's desk saying, "I know this is yours. I saw you wearing it once!!" Rachel knows that the sweater isn't hers and tries to tell Mrs. Price, but Mrs. Price doesn't believe her. Rachel reacts to Mrs. Price's actions by losing herself. "In my head, I'm thinking . . . how long till lunch time, how long till I can take the red sweater and throw it over the school yard fence, or leave it hanging on a parking meter, or bunch it up into a little ball and toss it over the alley?" This shows that Rachel loses herself because she's not listening to her teacher, she's dreaming about a whole other place. It is also important to see that Rachel has all this good thinking about the sweater but when she wants to say the sweater isn't hers, she squeaks and stammers, unable to speak. "But it's not," Rachel says. "Now," Mrs. Price replies. Rachel loses herself by not finding complete words to say when Mrs. Price challenges her.

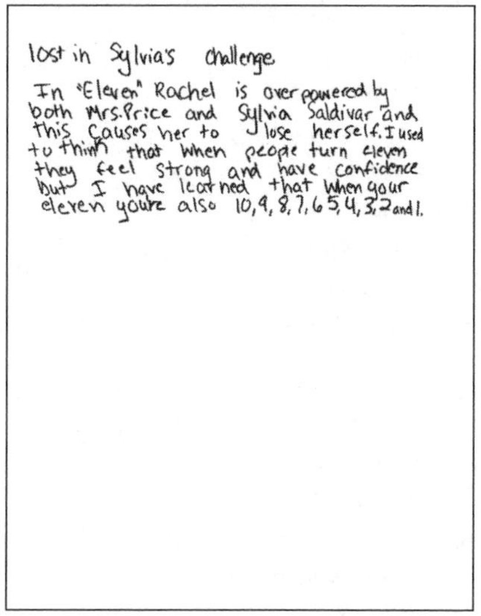

When Rachel's classmates challenge Rachel, Rachel loses herself. Sylvia Saldivar puts Rachel on the spot like when she says to Mrs. Price, "I think the sweater is

Rachel's." Sylvia is challenging Rachel, she is being mean and she makes Rachel feel lost. Rachel cries to let her emotions out. Rachel feels sick from Sylvia. Rachel tries to cover herself up by putting her head in her sleeve. Tears stream down her face. She doesn't feel special like it's her birthday. Instead she feels lost in Sylvia's challenge.

In "Eleven," Rachel is overpowered by both Mrs. Price and Sylvia Saldivar and this causes her to lose herself. I used to think that when people turn eleven they feel strong and have confidence but I have learned that when you're eleven, you're also 10, 9, 8, 7, 6, 5, 4, 3, 2, and 1.

II. A journey of thought: one claim leads to another

- The introductory paragraph may or may not be a summary, but it mentions the title and author and makes a claim.
- The claim is supported, perhaps with subordinate ideas but certainly with examples or instances from the text.
- A secondary claim, one that pushes off from the first or turns a corner from the first, is made.
- The secondary claim is also supported.
- The writer finds a way to end the essay.

Two Sides of Esther
by Miles

The story begins in 1941 in the Polish town of Vilna. Esther Rudomin, the ten-year-old heroine of Esther Hautzig's fictional memoir The Endless Steppe, lives an idyllic life. Esther lives together with her extended family in a mansion encircling an amazing garden. Her father is a successful engineer. She has a summer cottage on the bank of River

lost in Sylvia's challenge

In "Eleven" Rachel is overpowered by both Mrs. Price and Sylvia Saldivar and this causes her to lose herself. I used to think that when people turn eleven they feel strong and have confidence but I have learned that when your eleven youre also 10, 9, 8, 7, 6, 5, 4, 3, 2 and 1.

Fig. VI-4 Jill page 3

Wilja. During the school year her days are full of lessons—piano lessons, dancing class, and trips to the library. Her problems were small ones, she fought with the librarian for grown-ups' books and she fought with her mother for silk underwear that the other girls wore, instead of her white cotton ones that her mother made her wear.

She was happy, carefree, trusting and optimistic. In the early pages of the book you start seeing how optimistic and trusting she really is. Even when her world starts to collapse she still acts as if her life is perfect. Because she is Jewish and this is taking place during World War II the Russians confiscate her father's job and her family's property, but they do not evict her—yet. It was amazing to me that instead of being panicked and depressed she continues to live blissfully on, playing in the garden with her cousin and happily skipping down the street to school. Things get worse and she continues to believe that her life will improve.

When the Russians come to evict her she assumes she can take all her precious belongings as if they were headed to a hotel. When she is on her way to Siberia she is optimistic in thinking of Asia as a land full of men with long beards and turbans and the air heavy with spices.

You could say that Esther is optimistic and trusting. But you could also say she is blind and that she was deluding herself. Two on one coin. Maybes she deludes herself and acts like she does not see how bad things are because of the family custom to share one's joys and hide one's sorrow. Maybe she hides them so well that she hides them from herself.

III. A claim, with support from the text and from the writer's life

- The introductory paragraph usually includes the author, genre, and a summary of the text, and a hook to draw the reader in.

- The author makes a claim or thesis about the story, usually at the end of the introductory paragraph.

- The writer offers a comment about why the text matters to him or her.

- The writer provides one example or instance from the text that supports the claim.

- The writer gives another example or instance from the text that supports the claim.

- A final story, usually contained within a concluding paragraph, shows how the claim pertains to the writer's own life.

Who says you're supposed to be a certain age on your birthday? Eleven, by Sandra Cisneros, is an admirable story. Many people don't know that whatever age you are, you're also all of the ages you've ever been. Those ages are inside of you. In Eleven, it's Rachel's 11th birthday. She can't pull out her other ages and tell her teacher, Mrs. Price, that a certain hideous sweater does not belong to her. I think that a lot of people don't know how to get the other ages out of themselves. Some people don't even know that these ages are there. Mrs. Price thinks she's the best because she has only one age—the oldest one in the class. Also, Rachel doesn't know that she can bring out her younger ages. I'll be 11 in a week and now I know it's okay to be all my ages if I have to.

In Eleven, Mrs. Price thinks she's the best because she's the oldest in the class. She thinks she's always right because she's older and wiser. "Of course[this sweater] is yours," Mrs. Price says when Rachel tries to say that the sweater isn't hers. Just because she thinks that the ugly sweater is Rachel's, she won't let anyone tell her otherwise. Also, Mrs. Price does a good job of getting people to think she's always right. During the sweater situation, Rachel thinks, "Because [Mrs. Price] is older and the teacher, she's right and I'm not." Mrs. Price doesn't know that she's not only the oldest in the class, she's also the same age as everyone else in the class. She doesn't know that she has every age she's ever been inside of her. Therefore, she's not always right, and she's not the best. She's the same as everyone else.

Also in Eleven, Rachel doesn't think she's allowed to bring out her other ages. She knows that she's not only 11, she's also 10, 9, 8, 7, 6, 5, 4, 3, 2, and 1, but she doesn't think she can use those ages. She thinks she always has to "act her age", as people say. Rachel is embarrassed to bawl like she's 3 again, or to have a tantrum like she's 5 again, or to use any of her other ages to let Mrs. Price know that the sweater belongs to someone else. She holds all of the ages in, even though they're practically bursting out of her.

Rachel has just turned 11, and she feels like she has to "act

her age." But her age won't let her do anything about the big heap of red, itchy material that is hanging like a waterfall over the edge of her desk. That's when 10, 9, 8, 7, 6, 5, 4, 3, 2, and 1, come out and she starts crying. All because she can't let herself let her other ages out.

Eleven teaches us that age isn't just a number. Age is what you are. Many people think that everyone is only one age. If this is true, and if age is what you are, then you'd only be one thing, like a one-way street, or a house with nothing inside. This is impossible. A person is like an encyclopedia. There are so many pages, so many chapters, so much information in a person! Mrs. Price doesn't know this. She's missing a page—no, a chapter.

Rachel knows that she is not only 11, she is also 10, 9, 8, 7, 6, 5, 4, 3, 2, and 1, but she is holding these ages in. She learns that you can't hold in something that is a part of you. She can be all her ages at once.

Fig. VI-5 Final draft linking "Eleven" to the writer's life page 1

Fig. VI-6 Final draft page 2

Fig. VI-7 Final draft page 3

Fig. VI-8 Final draft page 4

IV. A universal claim, with support from several texts

- The introductory paragraph makes a claim about literature or life.

- Several subsequent paragraphs each suggest that a different text elucidates this theme/claim.

- An ending paragraph relates back to and resembles the opening paragraph.

If you think about it, people are capturing beautiful things constantly. They do so with memory, and creativity, but before that, they use sight, smell, sound, taste, and touch. But only with wisdom can you realize what you've captured.

In "Morning Assignment," a little girl and a woman capture buttons and ribbons for royalty. Do you think the average eye could have captured that? Or would the eye just see fabric?

In "Window" and the excerpt from "Music," the poet captures something fairly simple. Notes. Light. But when music and brightness are caught by the wise ones, they turn into complex pieces of art.

In the piece from "Living," a salamander is caught with the hand. Using the mind, paper, and a pen, the creature was transformed into the magnificent dragon of the imagination.

Only when a wise one captures something simple can the philosophy be released. Everything has majesty. Everything has one love.

GETTING READY

- "Spaghetti," by Cynthia Rylant
- Your own sample seed ideas from "Spaghetti" you can use to demonstrate choosing and testing possible thesis statements
- Start of a chart: Questions Essayists Ask of a Thesis Statement
- Manila file folders
- Sample of student work where ideas are boxed and bulleted
- Sample thesis statements that illustrate using a template— juxtaposing the internal and external story lines
- See CD-ROM for resources

FINDING AND TESTING A THESIS STATEMENT

I remember well the analytical papers *I was asked to write when I was a young girl. I bought myself several packets of index cards, took the bus into the city of Buffalo, made my way to the library, and spent days recording my data about my assigned author. When children in today's world are asked to write academic papers, the challenge has far less to do with collecting data—that they can do with one click—and far more to do with synthesizing it.*

After this watershed session, children will no longer write assorted ideas about the text they've chosen. Instead, they will invest themselves in shaping, organizing, drafting, and revising entries that elaborate on their claim.

As you approach this session, you and your children bring all that you know from previous cycles through the writing process and specifically from Session VI of Narrative, Session VI of Essays, and Session V of Fiction. You may want to reread those minilessons so that you can help children remember them. Earlier, you reminded children that writers grow like nesting wooden dolls, one inside the other. "When we are in our second unit of study," you said, "we are also in our first, drawing on all we already know as writers." Of course, now you could say, "When we are in our fifth unit of study, we are also in our first, second, third, and fourth units of study."

Hopefully, children will bring to this session an understanding of the relationship between the seed idea (the claim, the thesis) and the subordinate ideas they will develop in their essays. Today, we hope each child not only searches for and selects the best possible thesis statement, but also imagines the categories of support that idea needs and revises that thesis accordingly. That is, you hope children shift between crafting a thesis and imagining the ways they would support that thesis.

In this unit you're asking children to make a claim (that is, to write a thesis) about a short text. The claim needs to be interesting to the writer and defensible with evidence from the text.

MINILESSON

Finding and Testing a Thesis Statement

CONNECTION

Celebrate the writing and thinking your writers have generated thus far in the unit. Remind children of earlier work they did with thesis statements and supporting ideas.

"Writers, your notebooks are brimming with ideas about the short text you've chosen to study. You've each got reams of ideas about 'Eleven,' 'The Marble Champ,' 'Boar Out There,' 'The Birthday Box,' and 'Spaghetti.' Today I want to remind you that in the end you need to decide on *one idea* for your essay. It's never easy to focus on just one idea. Fred Fox, a famous speechwriter for President Dwight Eisenhower, once said, 'You ought to be able to put your bottom-line message on the inside of a matchbook.' He was talking about a speech, but he could have been talking about a literary essay or a short story or a memoir or any text at all."

"A few months ago, you looked over all that you'd written and selected a seed idea for your personal essay. You rewrote it as a thesis statement and then framed your essay using boxes and bullets. Writers do similar work in writing literary essays. We find a main idea that is really important to us—writers call it a claim, or a thesis."

Name your teaching point. In this instance, remind children to reread their notebooks, collecting materials that could become a thesis. Teach them to collect an excess of possible seed ideas.

"Today I want to teach you that when we are writing literary essays, as when we write personal essays, we find our seed ideas (our thesis statements) by first rereading all our related entries and thinking, 'What is the main idea I really want to say?' We often star lines in our notebooks or copy material from our notebooks onto a special page, one we title 'possible seed ideas.' Then writers usually spend time—at least half an hour—drafting and revising a thesis statement and supporting ideas (boxes and bullets) until we settle on something that feels right."

TEACHING

Demonstrate your own process of rereading your entries and starring possible seed ideas.

"So let's pretend it's time for me to write a thesis statement for a literary essay about 'Spaghetti.'" Sitting in the front of the children, I opened up my notebook and skimmed it for a moment, circling a few bits.

Showing children the page on which I'd just worked, I said, "As you can see, I first reread my entries and then I circled or starred sentences that express ideas that especially

For a moment, consider the ways in which your children's ideas on focus have developed across the year. Earlier in the year, your children believed that focusing mainly involved narrowing in on a smaller subject. More specifically, a focused story was one that involved less time. By now, the locus of focus has shifted. A writer could be writing about a very big topic and still write a very focused text. Writers focus by asking, "What is the meaning I am trying to convey?" and by having an answer that one could write on the inside of a matchbook!

Visual cues and props can make a big difference in our minilessons, and I haven't emphasized them enough. In this instance, for example, when I held one of the working folders we'd used from the earlier essay unit so that as I mentioned boxes and bullets, the object—in this case the folder—nudged children to recall the entire process they experienced in that unit.

This teaching point contains mostly reminders, but when the point of my minilesson is to remind children of something they already know, I try to add a new layer of complexity.

It may seem odd to you to sit in front of the class and reread your notebook silently. Don't make the decision to instead read your notebook aloud! This minilesson already contains as much detail as it can hold. Don't convince yourself that children need to hear all your entries and your entire thinking process. And the truth is that it's rather impressive to actually watch someone reading silently at the front of the room! Do this for twenty seconds—it's an important demonstration.

matter to me. I'm looking in my notebook for *ideas*, not for facts. An idea refers to something that occurred to me, something not actually stated in the text. I've circled a couple of sentences from my entries in which I express an idea about 'Spaghetti.'" I copied two of these onto chart paper, saying, "Here are two possible seed ideas":

> Possible Seed Ideas
> Gabriel is a lonely boy who has steeled himself to accept being lonely.
> Gabriel has a hole in his life.

Demonstrate testing your possible thesis statements with questions and revising them based on the answers.

"After I've chosen a few seed ideas, I look these over, think these over, and revise them. I first reread each idea and ask, 'How does this idea relate to the whole story—both the first and the second half?' Often this question leads me to revise my seed idea so that it becomes an umbrella idea—one that stretches over both the beginning and the end of the text."

"Watch how I go about letting this question lead me to revise my seed idea," I said, and pointed to my first possible seed idea:

> Gabriel is a lonely boy who has steeled himself to accept being lonely.

"I'm thinking that this relates to only the start of 'Spaghetti.' Let me try to revise the idea so that it relates also to the ending. Umm . . . "

> Spaghetti is the story of a lonely boy who has steeled himself to accept being lonely but then lets a cat into his life.

"That's awkward," I said, and tried again:

> Spaghetti is the story of a lonely boy who lets a cat into his life and isn't lonely anymore.

Turning back to the children, I said, "That thesis fits the beginning and the end of the story now, doesn't it? So one way I rethink my thesis is to ask, 'Does this relate to both the first and the second halves of the text?'"

"A second way that I rethink my seed idea is to ask, 'How would I support this?' I think about what I might write for my categories, my supporting ideas. Very often, I support a thesis in a literary essay by showing how the thesis is true *at the start of the text*, then *at the end of the text*. But I might alternatively support a thesis by showing how it is true *for one character*, then *for another character*, or *for one reason*, then *for another reason*."

You'll notice that I return often to "Spaghetti." This unit is complex enough that I do not aim for variety in the texts I use. This one short text threads through many minilessons, because the children have enough shared knowledge of the text and our work with it that I do not need to do a lot of reminding and summarizing; instead I can spotlight each new point I want to make.

There are a number of reasons each thesis needs to pertain to the entire text. First of all, when children are writing thesis statements about very short texts, if the thesis pertains to only one portion of the text it will be almost impossible for the child to garner enough support for the claim. The texts are too sparse! Then, too, I am steering children toward writing interpretive essays, and this means I am hoping they consider lessons they can learn or messages they can carry from the text. An effective interpretation of a story requires that the reader take into account the most important features of the complete text, including the first and the second halves of the text, certainly, and including a great many smaller features as well.

Pay especially close attention to this instruction, because helping children write effective thesis statements and supporting ideas is far more complicated than you might imagine. This session and the one that follows it were far and away the most difficult to write in the entire series. Hopefully the teaching seems simple and clear now—but the trail of thought leading to this point has been quite complicated and challenging!

Questions Essayists Ask of a Thesis Statement
- Does this relate to both the 1st and 2nd halves of the text?
- How would I support this?
  - At start of story, then at end of story
  - One character, then another
  - One reason, then another

This is a great deal of important material to convey simply through talk, so at this point I revealed a page of chart paper on which I'd written both the questions I ask of possible thesis statements and those I ask of subordinate questions. Notice that I don't take the time to write these in front of the class.

"Let me think whether I could support the idea 'Gabriel had a hole in his life.' I could write one paragraph that shows how Gabriel had a hole in his life at the start of 'Spaghetti' and another paragraph showing that this is also true at the end of the story." As I spoke, I made notes:

Gabriel, the protagonist of "Spaghetti," had a hole . . .
- in the first half of the story
- in the second half of the story

"But let me just think whether I have the evidence I need to prove my point!" I glanced at "Spaghetti." "The start of the story *does* provide enough details about Gabriel's loneliness, so yes, I could probably write that at the start of the story Gabriel had a hole in his life. But I'm not at all sure I could get enough evidence to make that case for the end of the story! So I have some options. I could change this seed idea so it *is* something I could support with references to both of the beginning and end of the text. Or I could try to find other ways of supporting the idea. For example, I could try to develop the idea by thinking instead of different *reasons*." I wrote this example on chart paper:

Gabriel, the protagonist of "Spaghetti," has a hole in his life. He has this hole because:
- reason 1
- reason 2

I could, alternatively, have shown children how I ask these questions of the thesis statement I'd already been developing. That thesis will not prove to be a very workable one, however, and for now I wanted to show that these questions prompt revisions.

In front of the class, I silently mulled over possibilities for a moment, shaking my head to show that no, nothing was coming to mind. Turning to the class, I said, "If I can't figure out a way to support my thesis, this pushes me to revise it!"

Again, don't convince yourself that the children need a more detailed account of your thinking here. If anything, they may need less detail—you may decide to leave off all reference to the fact that a writer can try out other ways to support a thesis.

ACTIVE ENGAGEMENT

Set children up to work in partners, testing out another possible thesis. Remind them to ask whether the thesis pertains to the whole text and whether it can be supported with references to the text.

"Let's try another one of these possible thesis statements," I said, and gestured toward the first seed idea.

'Spaghetti' is the story of a lonely boy who lets a cat into his life and isn't lonely anymore."

"Right now, working with your partner, would you test out this thesis? Be sure to test it by asking the questions on the chart." I pointed to the chart.

> Questions Essayists Ask of a Thesis Statement
> * Does this relate to both the 1st and 2nd halves of the text?
> * How would I support this?
>   * At start of story, then at end of story
>   * One character, then another
>   * One reason, then another

I listened in as children did this work in pairs, and then asked for their attention. "So many of you found ways to make this thesis statement really work! I can't wait for us all to label folders, one for each supporting paragraph, and to begin collecting evidence in each folder!" I pointed to the place where the materials lay waiting.

LINK

Recap that writers reread entries looking for possible thesis statements, then revise their theses by asking questions of them.

"So writers, today and whenever you write a thesis statement for a literary essay, look over the entries you've collected about the text, and ponder your thoughts about it. Box or star or list the ideas you've written about the text, ideas out of which you will shape your boxes and bullets, your thesis statements and supporting sentences. And then remember that writers ask questions to test out their possible seed ideas." I pointed again to the list of questions.

By now you should realize that if your class brims with struggling or resistant writers, and moving kids through the process of writing anything at all is a big problem, you may need to tweak the Active Engagements throughout the series so that students are working with their own writing while sitting in the meeting area. In this instance, you would need to first give children time to reread their entries, selecting and revising their seed ideas; then you could nudge them to test out their chosen seed ideas while sitting together in the meeting area. This is not ideal, but it does allow you to shepherd kids along.

I did not elaborate on the materials, because for now the children are just at the very start of this work, rereading their notebooks to find seed ideas. I know I will need to work in small groups, reiterating ways to test a possible thesis statement. I have indicated where the materials are for making folders, so that if some children progress quickly they won't create a logjam.

Notice that prior to this point in the minilesson, I've emphasized the final actions children will take at the end of the upcoming workshop. This Link allows me to bring children's attention back to the work they need to do right away.

WRITING AND CONFERRING

Anticipating Predictable Problems

For students to write a great literary essay, it is essential that they start with a strong, clear thesis statement. The thesis is like a car engine—without one that works, a car, or an essay, cannot move forward. You'll need to confer often today and tomorrow!

Encourage your children to make multiple drafts of their boxes and bullets—their thesis statements and supporting ideas—and to regard these as one organic unit. Children often encounter difficulties imagining the paragraphs they could write to support their theses, which should prompt them to revise their theses. Judah, for example, boxed these ideas in her notebook:

> Lupe wanted to prove herself that she was as good as the other girls.

> Lupe was insecure. She had put herself down.

> Even though she wasn't good, she was nice and good on the inside. She tried again and again. This showed that she doesn't give up.

> Lupe is very caring. She is good on the inside. She doesn't need to be on the outside.

> I used to think Lupe was a goody-goody two-shoes. She got all of those awards and seemed so perfect. I realized she isn't perfect. She has to work and practice like everyone.

Then Judah consolidated her efforts, settling for this more modest possible thesis statement:

> Lupe works hard to overcome her difficulties.

I helped her add the expected trimmings to this:

> Lupe, the protagonist in Gary Soto's short story, "The Marble Champ," works hard to overcome her difficulties.

MID-WORKSHOP TEACHING POINT **_Using a Template to Create a Thesis_** "Writers, can I have your eyes and your attention? Many of you have lots of possible thesis statements—you are well on your way. If you are struggling, though, I want to give you a bit of advice to use today or whenever you are stumped in trying to write a literary essay. Usually you can arrive at a pretty solid thesis if you think about the story mountain for the story you've read, and think not only about the external but also about the internal story line. The internal story line shows what happens on the inside of the main character from the beginning, through the turning point, to the end of the story. These two story lines can give you a pattern, a template, for constructing a thesis statement."

continued on next page

Fig. VII-1 Judah's boxed ideas

Then Judah began to imagine how her bullet points might go. She considered whether she wanted to provide *examples* to establish (to prove) that Lupe works hard. Did she want to write about the *kinds of work* Lupe does? To write about the *reasons* Lupe works so hard to become a marble champ? Did she want the fact that Lupe works hard to be one factor and to cite another factor that helps Lupe overcome her difficulties?

The truth is that these ideas are not all equal in sophistication. The simplest way to elaborate upon the claim that Lupe works hard would be to provide two examples of the fact that she does this. If Judah simply provided examples for her point, this would not require her to be analytical. In contrast, to elaborate upon *the kinds* of hard work, or the *reasons for* her work, Judah *would* need to be analytical. This was Judah's next draft of her thesis:

> In the short story, "The Marble Champ," by Gary Soto, Lupe learns to overcome her difficulties by working hard and by believing in herself.

This thesis set up the topic sentences that Judah then developed: Lupe overcomes her difficulties through hard work; Lupe also overcomes her difficulties by believing in herself. Notice that in each of her subordinate points, Judah repeats the stem (as I call it) of her thesis.

Some children will need help finding possible thesis statements in their notebooks. Help them reread their notebooks respectfully, looking for possible thesis statements and paying attention to ideas that resurface often as well as patterns that reoccur across entries. It can sometimes be very productive to take two ideas that may not at first seem connected, and to write in an effort to connect those ideas. Teach children that, from time to time, it helps to ask, "How might these two different ideas go together?"

You'll find that once children have developed an idea that is rooted in one section of the text, they often want to comb that one idea through the entire text—and will do so even if there is no supporting evidence. Help children understand that applying an idea to an entire text does not mean painting the whole text in one monolithic color. The statement that Gabriel is lonely can apply to the whole text without the reader suggesting he is lonely in every paragraph of the story! Perhaps his loneliness evolves? Is resolved?

As you work with children individually and in small groups, you will find that some of them tend to write about small stuff. These children's pages will be full of specific, concrete, detailed references, and they will not have grown many ideas. Other children will be just the opposite. They will tend to write expansive, abstract ideas without much detail or grounding. A rule of thumb is that if children start small, they profit

---

"Then usually you can write a strong thesis if you say, '*Some* people think this is a story about (and you summarize the external sequence of events), but *I* think this is a story about (and you summarize the internal sequence of events).' Just for practice, let's try that for 'Spaghetti.' I could write a thesis that goes like this":

> Some people think that Cynthia Rylant's short story "Spaghetti" is about a homeless boy who adopts a stray cat, but I think this is really a story about a lonely boy who learns to love again.

"Of course, writers change the words around a bit. So I could say it differently":

> When I first read Cynthia Rylant's story "Spaghetti," I thought it was a story about a boy who adopts a stray cat but now I realize it is really a story about a lonely boy who learns to love again.

"Or I might write":

> A first read of Cynthia Rylant's story "Spaghetti" suggests that it is a story about a boy who adopts a stray cat; a careful reread, however, shows that it is really a story about a boy who learns to love.

continued on next page

> In the short story "The Marble Champ" by Gary & Soto, Lupe learns to overcome her difeculties by working hard and believing in herself

Fig. VII-2 Judah's draft thesis statement

from instruction that helps them shift toward big, abstract, general ideas. That is, if a child starts by writing, "The character's Australian shepherd went for a walk and didn't return," he will profit from being nudged to shift toward writing, "Things are always leaving this character." On the other hand, if a child tends to start by writing big, abstract ideas, such as, "This story is about loss and dealing with loss," she will profit from being encouraged to write that the character's Australian shepherd went for a walk and didn't return.

You will also want to help children realize that most of their ideas have parts, and it helps to articulate the parts of an idea. Eventually, writers will probably develop one part fairly completely before progressing to the next part.

Often children's ideas seem obvious to them, and therefore they don't feel compelled to defend their ideas. Help those children to realize that others may see an idea differently, and they need to address that different view.

Another common pitfall is that when writing about their thesis statements, students do not state their ideas as clearly as possible. Children need to try writing their ideas in four or five ways, until they can read them to a partner and the partner understands them. Their statements need to be simple and clear, and should pop out to the reader.

For example, at first Max wrote his thesis statement this way: "Rachel is a girl who acts, wants to be, or feels different ages on her birthday." While at first glance that seems clear, Max is waffling. Then, too, when I talked with him and learned what really fired him up as a reader of this text, it was clear to me that his rough-draft thesis lacked the part of the statement that tells the reader his real thesis—the *why* of it. Finding the whole of the thesis takes time and thought. The final draft of a thesis is not apt to be in the notes the students have written already—instead, students need to explore, write, and talk more to push their thinking. In Max's case, he needed to figure out which of his three statements about Rachel he really wanted to advance. Then he needed to figure out *why* he thought she did that. Or, *what happens inside of her* because of this.

After some talking and writing and conferring, Max changed his thesis statement to "Rachel is a girl who wakes up on her eleventh birthday expecting to feel older on her birthday, but ends up feeling disappointed by the way the day goes." This thesis statement more clearly shows the reader what he is going to prove as he continues the essay.

continued from previous page

"Listen, for example, to Jill's lead. You'll see that her content is very different, but she follows the same template for a thesis statement":

> Many people read Sandra Cisneros's essay, "Eleven," and think it is a story of a girl was has to wear a sweater she doesn't want to wear. But I think it is about a girl who struggles to hold onto herself when she is challenged by people who have power over her.

"So if today or another day you find yourself struggling to write a strong thesis statement, you can usually move past this impasse if you think of your story's internal story mountain. Then write, 'Some people think this is a story about (and retell the external story mountain), but I think this is a story about (and retell the internal story mountain).'"

> Many people read Sandra Cisneros's essay "Eleven" and think its about a girl who has to wear a sweater she doesn't want to wear. But I think the story is about a girl who struggles to hold onto herself When she is challenged by people who have power over her.

Fig. VII-3 Jill's lead with thesis statement

SHARE

Interpreting Texts

Tell students that when writers decide what to write, they think about the story—the events and the places they happen—as well as its deeper meaning—what the story is really about.

"My favorite writer, Annie Dillard, wrote a memoir called *An American Childhood*. She said that when she was writing it, she thought, 'What shall I put in?' She decided what it was she really wanted to say. 'It's about the passion of childhood. It's about waking up.' That's the internal part. But Annie had to use something concrete to show that deep message. So she decided to use the landscape of her childhood as the external part, and then angle the text to show her waking up over and over again: noticing things, loving the rocks, the tiny creatures, the adventures she has. Every story has that same dynamic: the plot and the deeper meaning. As readers, we need to consider both of them as we think and write about texts."

"So, readers, as you work on framing your thesis statements and planning your boxes and bullets, remember to pause and think about the internal and external story mountains in the texts. Annie Dillard isn't really writing about the rocks and the butterflies she saw, she's really writing about how it felt to grow into an awareness of herself and the world. In the same way, Cynthia Rylant and Gary Soto and Sandra Cisneros are not really writing just about finding a kitten, learning to shoot marbles, or a red sweater that didn't belong to Rachel. They are writing about deeper, more powerful ideas."

Ask children to work with a partner to read their thesis statements and notice whether they have included both the external and internal story mountains for their stories.

"Right now, would you share your thesis statement with your partner? Look at what you have said to see if you have included the internal and external story mountains in your statements. When you look at what you have written, does it include what the story seems to be about (the plot or external story)? Does it also include what the story is *really about* (the internal story, the character's change, or the deeper meaning)? If not, don't worry. See if you can help each other revise the thesis statement. Ask each other that very important question: 'What is this story *really* about?' Another way to think about that is to ask, 'What is the significance the author wants to highlight?' Or, 'What does the character learn in this

This session guides students to consider the internal and external story lines in the texts under study. Some students will need to hear more about this before they can successfully incorporate the strategy into their writing. This session focuses on choosing and crafting a seed idea, but it also expects that children will be able to consider what the story is really about—the internal aspect of the story. If your children need help doing this, you'll need to either teach this in strategy lessons and one-to-one conferences or develop additional minilessons.

I could have reminded writers that they already learned about Annie Dillard's writing shed and the photograph she has there of a boy standing deep in rapids, a picture with a deeper message about feeling all of life intensely.

Notice that this lesson reminds students of what you have just taught as well as important things they have worked on as readers all year.

Listen in on students' conversations. Take note of the students who are still struggling to name and/or phrase the internal story. You might intervene now, as in the example following. Or you can convene them for a group conference later.

story?' Once you answer one of those questions out loud, think about whether the answer can in some way fit into your thesis statement. Let's add this new question to our chart":

Questions Essayists Ask of a Thesis Statement
- Does this relate to both the 1st and 2nd halves of the text?
- How would I support this?
  - At start of story, then at end of story
  - One character, then another
  - One reason, then another
- **Does the thesis address what the story is really about, the internal as well as the external story?**

"Janica, can I stop you? I heard you telling Peter that you are not sure what the story 'The Marble Champ' is really about, because you think it could be about lots of things. That's such a good point. But let me teach you something that good readers do: They realize there are lots of possibilities for what a story is really about—but they choose one, because it seems the most important or powerful to them. So out of all your possibilities for 'The Marble Champ,' which one do you think is most important?"

● HOMEWORK *Crafting Theses Quickly Using a Template* In class today, we spent lots of time crafting and revising our thesis statements and our plans for essays. In many situations, however, you'll want to write a thesis really quickly. So tonight, would you practice writing thesis statements quickly? Try this:

Think of a fairy tale you know well. For now, let's take "Little Red Riding Hood." Quickly think, "What's the external plot line of the story?" Remember that it helps to think of the main character, what he or she wants, what gets in the way, how this is resolved. Quickly plot the external story line. For example, for "Little Red Riding Hood," you might sketch this story mountain:

Story Mountain for Little Red Riding Hood

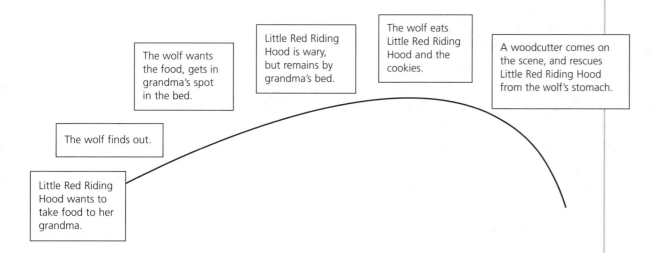

The wolf wants the food, gets in grandma's spot in the bed.

Little Red Riding Hood is wary, but remains by grandma's bed.

The wolf eats Little Red Riding Hood and the cookies.

A woodcutter comes on the scene, and rescues Little Red Riding Hood from the wolf's stomach.

The wolf finds out.

Little Red Riding Hood wants to take food to her grandma.

Now think, "What might this story really be about?" or "What life lessons does the character learn?" You are now thinking about the internal story. For "Little Red Riding Hood," you might write this:

> Little Red Riding Hood is naïve and trusting, unaware and unsuspicious. She therefore gets into trouble, and almost dies.

> The story is really a reminder that evil lurks along our pathways, and we need to be less naïve, more suspicious.

Now use the template I gave you earlier for one way a thesis statement could go—contrasting the external and internal story mountains—and draft one possible thesis. For "Little Red Riding Hood," for example, my thesis might be:

> Some people think "Little Red Riding Hood" is the story of a girl, dressed in a red hood, who wants to give cookies to her grandma but instead is eaten by a wolf. I think, however, this is also a story of a girl who goes into the woods of life utterly trusting and naïve, and learns that she needs to be more suspicious.

Tonight try using this template to produce an instant thesis about the story you have in mind: "Some people think (the fairy tale you've chosen) is a story about (the external story line), but I think it is also a story about (the internal story line)."

TAILORING YOUR TEACHING

If your students are voicing shallow, wooden responses to texts . . . you could teach them that when they form a thesis, the important question isn't "What is the author saying?" but "What idea does this text support?" In our own education, many of us were taught to write literary essays as though there was only one possible thesis to argue. We were taught to ask, "What is the author trying to say?" or "What is the author's message?" These kinds of questions erect barriers for us, limiting our thinking and making us doubt insights we glean from reading. Students need to believe that readers can come away from texts with different understandings, so long as sufficient evidence in the text exists to support them. Imagine how productive and provocative their writing will be if they have the chance to share and argue those understandings, rather than timidly putting forth guesses as to the author's one and only True Meaning.

If your students are having a hard time figuring out if a seed idea would make a good thesis . . . you could teach them to study the work of literary critics. Literary critics usually focus on a few key ideas in stories when they write their reviews: how a character's journey progresses, how a plot and setting mirror a real-world social issue, how a story compares or contrasts with previous works by the same author. Students who have a hard time figuring out if a seed idea would make a good thesis can lean on literary critics as mentors for writing about reading, and ask themselves questions like, "Does this seed idea deal with a character's journey? Does it deal with a social issue that's reflected throughout the text? Is this seed idea similar to (or different from) something the author has written about in another text?" As we teach these growing writers about literature, we need to give them lenses that help them recognize the kinds of seed idea that will carry them through an entire essay.

ASSESSMENT

When I wanted to put down new carpet in my living room, I wasn't sure whether I wanted pink, blue, or green. I didn't have carpet swatches, so I found a few shirts and sweaters that matched the optional colors. I first laid the grayish blue sweater onto the floor, then stepped back and squinted, trying to see only the sweater, and to imagine it stretching out between the wallpapered walls. "If this little patch of color were room-sized, how would it look?" I asked. Then I tried this with a spring-green T-shirt.

Today, you'll want to reread each of your student's efforts to frame out thesis statements and bullet points in a similar way, trying to imagine what the work will "look like" when it's expanded into an essay. It's usually more helpful to intercede now, setting the child up for success, rather than to let the writer go forward with a plan that is flawed from the start.

For students to be able to write a great essay, it is essential that they start with a strong, clear thesis statement. Students will feel easily discouraged and find it hard to proceed unless they have an idea that is central to the story and that matters to them.

Let me show you how I read and assess drafts of thesis statements.

When I first read Harrison's thesis, it sounded very professional. I know, however, that it's easy to be conned by a thesis statement that sounds overly polished, so I resisted the temptation to give his thesis only a cursory glance and a stamp of approval. Instead I deliberately and carefully looked it over, almost as if I were expecting to find problems. After all, the work is being written by nine-year-olds, writing their first thesis statements about a literary text—chances are great their efforts will require revision. This was Harrison's draft of a thesis statement:

> In the short story "The Marble Champ" by Gary Soto, a girl named Lupe, through practice, devotion, and persistence, has to overcome not being an athlete and not being a good athlete. This is all new for Lupe because she is very academic.

Right away, I reduced this to its simplest form, just so I could see the plan Harrison had laid out for himself. I may or may not teach him to do this in the end, but to think through the work entailed in supporting the thesis, it definitely helps me to consider whether a clarified version of the thesis could be easily defended.

> In the Short Story "The Marble Champ" by Gary ~~Soto~~ Soto, a girl named Lupe, through Practice, devotion + Persistance, has to overcome not being a good athlete. This is all new for Lupe because she is very academic.

Fig. VII-4 Harrison's draft thesis statement

> Through practice, devotion, and persistence, Lupe overcomes not being an athlete and not being a good one. This is hard because she is academic.

I thought to myself, "What will Harrison need to prove?" To support his claim, Harrison would need to support many claims.

Through practice, Lupe overcomes not being an athlete.

Through practice, Lupe also overcomes not being a good athlete.

This (practicing and overcoming not being an athlete/ a good athlete) is hard because Lupe is academic.

Through devotion Lupe overcomes not being an athlete.

Through devotion she overcomes not being a good athlete.

This, also, is hard because Lupe is academic.

Through persistence, Lupe overcomes not being an athlete.

Through persistence she overcomes not being a good athlete.

This, also, is hard because Lupe is academic.

Looking at this, I realized that this configuration of claims was so complicated that it would be very difficult to defend. Also, of course, it would be tricky to defend the idea that the difficulties Lupe faces over not being athletic derive from the fact that she is academic. Why would being academic make it especially hard for her to deal with the fact that she's not an athlete? Because these issues popped up, I encouraged Emily to consolidate and clarify her thesis. I also suggested that once she did this, she'd want to be really sure she could prove her points. In the end, she wrote this:

In Gary Soto's short story, "The Marble Champ," an academically talented girl named Lupe, through persistence and practice, becomes also an athletic success.

Now I weighed what Emily would need to prove, and the answer was much more reasonable.

Lupe is an academically talented girl.

Through persistence, Lupe becomes an athletic success.

Through practicing, Lupe becomes an athletic success.

I wondered, still, if the two main claims would be significantly different from each another, but at least the plan seemed workable.

I'm accustomed to eyeing categories, asking, "Are these significantly distinct, one from the next?" When I ask this, I'm trying to predict whether, when the writer goes to elaborate on each bullet point (each topic sentence), he or she will find that the same content belongs in several categories. I also am accustomed to asking, "Is this claim warranted in the text?" The two questions sometimes overlap. For example, although one could conceive of practice and persistence being distinctly different, in this text I suspect the lines between them will blur.

Often we must decide whether to tell children the issues that we see with a thesis or let them encounter these problems along the way. In this instance, I decided it was likely that Emily would see for herself that her two bullets overlap once she began gathering and sorting evidence. Even if she collapsed these two categories into one, she would still have a viable thesis, so I let the categories stand.

IN THIS SESSION, YOU'LL TEACH STUDENTS THAT WRITERS PLAN THEIR ESSAYS, MAKING SURE THEY CAN DELIVER THE EVIDENCE FROM THE TEXT THAT THEIR THESIS PROMISES. YOU'LL DEMONSTRATE SOME WAYS ESSAYISTS REVISE THESES AND SUPPORTING PARAGRAPHS.

GETTING READY

- Child's draft and revised thesis statements that illustrate the process of analysis and revision
- "Spaghetti," by Cynthia Rylant
- Class thesis statement for "Spaghetti," written on chart paper
- Questions Essayists Ask of a Thesis Statement, updated with latest bullet points
- List prepared as a handout: Tips and Tools for Writing a Thesis and Topic Sentences for a Literary Essay
- See CD-ROM for resources

FRAMING ESSAYS

Once I decide to write a nonfiction text to address a particular theme or topic, one of my earliest steps is drafting and revising a succession of outlines. My outlines aren't complete with Roman numerals and capital and lowercase letters, but they do divide the terrain into subordinate categories and then divide those subordinate categories into subsections. Just as I can look at a timeline of a narrative and mull over whether I want to eliminate some dots or clump other dots together, I can also look at a rough draft of an outline, imagine the text it represents, and weigh whether that is the text I want to write. I anticipate the problems that I will encounter writing the text I've outlined. I revise my outline countless times, and love doing so. It's much more efficient to revise an outline than to revise an entire book!

For children, it is equally important that they draft and revise outlines before they begin to write their essays. A child's energy for revision is far from endless, and the texts children write for this unit will be longer than most that they've written. It's not likely that they'll be game for writing a succession of entirely new drafts.

Today's session will hark back to Session VIII of Breathing Life into Essays. In this session, you'll help children draft, reflect on, and revise possible outlines for their now-literary essays. You'll coach the whole group through the sequence of work involved in imagining the boxes and bullets that can provide the framework for their essays. But most of your teaching will occur as you help individuals and small groups of children see and resolve difficulties that are inherent in the essays they've outlined. Eventually children will be able to draw on prior experiences writing essays (and especially literary essays) to anticipate problems, but for now they'll be fairly dependent on you to help them foresee difficulties.

To help children critique their rough-draft boxes and bullets, you'll need to hone your own abilities to read these very closely and critically. This is not a time to skim!

MINILESSON

Framing Essays

CONNECTION

Tell children that you stayed up late reading their boxes and bullets. Acknowledge that even though the texts are short, reading a pile of thesis statements is nevertheless demanding.

"Writers, I took your thesis statements home last night and stayed up very, very late reading them. I put them beside me while I ate dinner, and read them as I ate. I told my family they'd need to clean up from dinner—that I had a ton of reading to do. All evening I read your thesis statements, and I was still reading them as, one by one, the people in my family went to bed. Finally, when it was very, very late, my husband asked, 'What have you been reading anyhow?' I showed him the stack of pages—one for each of you—on which you'd written your thesis statements and bullets."

"'Okay,'" he said, eyeing the stack. "'And what else have you been reading?'"

"'Just this,'" I said.

"'And it's taken you *all these hours*?'" he asked. "'How is that possible?'"

"How could I explain the kind of reading that you and I have been doing? How could I tell him that we read our thesis statements and imagine the implications that each word has for our essays? How could I explain that a thesis isn't just regular writing—that it's almost a blueprint for a building, a contract for a business relationship? It lays out terms, makes promises. How could I convey to John how important it is for us to read our thesis statements and understand what we are setting ourselves up to do?"

Name your teaching point. In this case, tell children that it is far easier to revise a thesis statement and topic sentences than to revise whole essays.

"Today I want to teach you that writers need, at this juncture, not only to read with critical, cautious eyes. We also need to be tilted forward, expecting to revise. It's much more efficient to do the front-end work of revising a thesis rather than the rear-end work of repairing a problematic essay."

COACHING

This is not a usual Connection. I'm not naming the work the children have been doing or the lessons I've tried to teach.

William Zinsser, author of On Writing Well, *suggests that one of the most important qualities of good writing is surprise. If we can surprise our readers (and our listeners), we earn their attention. In this minilesson I deliberately go a little bit off track, telling an anecdote that I know will surprise children, and I do this because I want their attention.*

Notice these terms. A thesis is a blueprint for a building. A contract for a business relationship. Say these words so that children hear them. You are saying, "Writing matters."

Notice the parallel structure here. "It's easier to do the front-end work of revising a thesis rather than the rear-end work of . . . ." I'm trying to use rhetorical devices to make my teaching memorable.

TEACHING

Tell children about one child who scrutinized her thesis statement, imagining implications and potential problems.

"Oona drafted a thesis statement yesterday, then began the hard work of rereading what she'd written. She's got what some people refer to as 'lawyer's eyes.' When I wanted to buy a new house, I had a lawyer read the contract, the deal. Lawyers are trained to have eagle eyes. They can spot potential problems. My lawyer read my contract and pointed out all the risks I was undertaking, all the trouble I could get myself into. And yesterday I saw that Oona was able to do that for her own thesis! She read what she'd written": *[Figs. VIII-1 and VIII-2]*

> In "Boar Out There," by Cynthia Rylant, Jenny is a girl who believes that the wild boar in the woods is fearless and is hurt. She feels sorry for him and goes to look for him. When she finds him, she realizes that he has fears after all. The boar runs through the woods ignoring the sharp thorns and briars. The boar cries at the moon.

"And then she said, 'To support my thesis, I'm going to need to show that'":

Jenny believed that the wild boar was fearless.

Jenny believed the boar was hurt.

Jenny felt sorry for the boar.

Jenny wants to find the boar.

When she finds him, she realizes he isn't fearless.

"'That's a lot to show!' Oona realized. Then she looked at her planned bullet points and decided to revise her draft of the thesis statement. She cleaned it up, so now it read":

> Jenny is a girl who believes that the wild boar in the woods is fearless, but after finding the boar she comes to realize that he is not.

"Then she thought, 'What would my paragraphs be?' and tried planning her bullets. Then she used her lawyer's eyes to spot problems with that plan. She wisely questioned whether she could write a whole paragraph about Jenny finding the boar in the woods, so she tried a new outline":

- In the beginning Jenny believes the boar is fearless (runs through the thorns and briars).

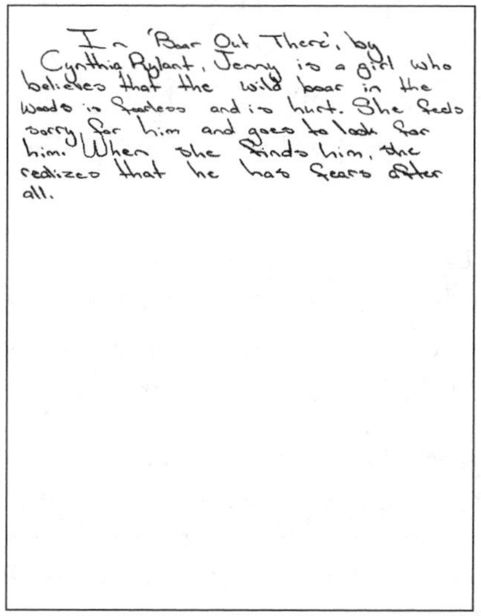
In 'Boar Out There,' by Cynthia Rylant, Jenny is a girl who believes that the wild boar in the woods is fearless and is hurt. She feels sorry for him and goes to look for him. When she finds him, she realizes that he has fears after all.

Fig. VIII-1 Oona's draft of a thesis statement

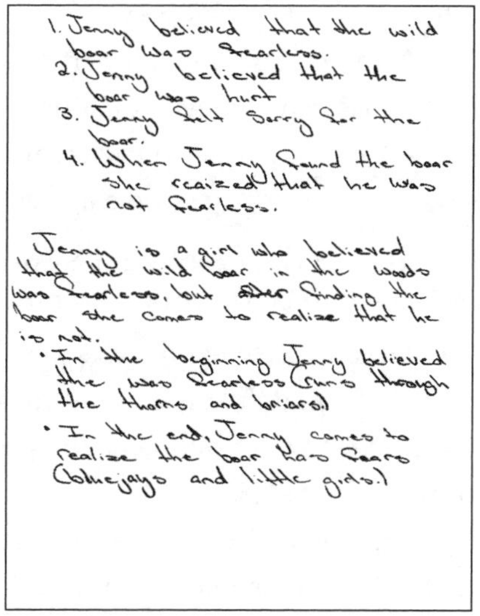
1. Jenny believed that the wild boar was fearless.
2. Jenny believed that the boar was hurt
3. Jenny felt sorry for the boar.
4. When Jenny found the boar she realized that he was not fearless.

Jenny is a girl who believed that the wild boar in the woods was fearless, but after finding the boar she comes to realize that he is not.
- In the beginning Jenny believed the boar was fearless (runs through the thorns and briars)
- In the end, Jenny comes to realize the boar has fears (bluejays and little girls.)

Fig. VIII-2 Oona realizes her first thesis is too complex and writes a simpler one

- In the end, Jenny comes to realize the boar has fears (bluejays and little girls).

"Do you see how Oona first read her essay plan with a lawyer's eyes, trying to understand what she'd set herself up for and to make sure she could do it? Then she wrote the plan for a literary essay, imagining what she might put in each paragraph, just to test out whether her thesis would work."

ACTIVE ENGAGEMENT
Using the latest thesis from the class story, set children up to read with a lawyer's eyes.

"Let's try this with the thesis statement we worked on yesterday for our 'Spaghetti' essay," I said, and flipped the chart paper to reveal this draft of a thesis statement:

> Some people think that Cynthia Rylant's short story "Spaghetti" is a story about a homeless boy who adopts a stray cat, but I think this is really a story about a lonely boy who lets a stray cat into his life and learns to love again.

- At the start of the story, Gabriel is lonely
- Then Gabriel lets a stray cat into his life and learns to love again.

"Would you and your partner read this over with a lawyer's eyes, searching for potential problems? Remember to ask questions such as these:"

"Remember to read each word very carefully, and to check whether this is precisely what we want to say." The children worked with each other for a few minutes.

Convene the class. Coach them to see potential problems with the planned boxes and bullets based on content that classmates propose.

Soon I convened the class, and gestured first to one partnership, then another.

"We couldn't figure out if the first paragraph has gotta support the first part of the thesis when we wrote that some people think this is a story of a homeless boy who adopts a stray cat," James said.

I nodded, "Good question, James. I don't think there is a right or wrong answer to that—this first sentence could be considered part of your thesis and therefore needs to be supported, but it could also be the lead-in to your thesis, a place for background facts, in which case you can assume your readers will trust you. Did you want to devote your first paragraph to that point, James?"

"Not really, 'cause it'd be dull."

Questions Essayists Ask of a Thesis Statement
- Does this relate to both the 1st and 2nd halves of the text?
- How would I support this?
  - At start of story, then at end of story
  - One character, then another
  - One reason, then another
- Does the thesis address what the story is really about, the internal as well as the external story?
- Can I deliver with my planned categories what I promise in my thesis?

"I think you're okay with not defending it, then," I said. "But that was really close and careful reading! What did others decide?"

"We figured how to show he's lonely at the beginning," Ali said. "We can tell that 'cause he's sitting on the stoop alone. Other people are talking but he doesn't join. Plus he daydreams that he's away by himself like living outside on the street."

I coached her to write in the air, dictating what she might claim in that paragraph and what her supporting information might be. She said aloud, with intonation that suggested she was dictating boxes and bullets:

1. At the start of the story, Gabriel is lonely.
   - Even though Gabriel was sitting on the stoop surrounded by other people who were talking to each other, he was not included or did not join in.
   - He daydreamed about being other places:
     - Living outside
     - Sleeping under the movie theater lights
2. At the end of the story, Gabriel learns to love again.

"What do the rest of you think of Ali and Emily's plan?" I asked. "Read their plan for the first support paragraph with a lawyer's eyes!" Soon the class agreed that the second point (that Gabriel daydreamed about other places) didn't necessarily relate to the claim that he was lonely, and the class reworded this (Gabriel had become so used to being alone that he imagined sleeping outside alone).

The class turned to the big idea and at first had no trouble with it. I then told them I could imagine arguing that the second topic sentence was not defensible. They read it again, this time realizing that the story doesn't *actually* show that Gabriel learned to love again. They revised this bullet point to read, "Gabriel isn't lonely anymore."

LINK
Remind writers that they'll soon make files for each of their bullet points, but caution them that it's efficient to first critique and revise their planned boxes and bullets.

"Writers, I know it's tempting to get started making files for each of your bullet points, and you'll no doubt do that today. But I hope that first you'll remember that it's much more efficient to do the front-end work of revising a thesis than the rear-end work of repairing a problematic thesis. So take the time right now to read your thesis and supporting statements with a lawyer's eyes, spotting potential problems. Have the courage to revise your plans many times before you go forward."

One of the many advantages of asking children to first talk with partners is that, before I call on a child, I already know what he will say. I can deliberately call on children who will bring up what I regard as the big, main questions.

It's possible to write one paragraph that relays the plot line of the story and then another that reveals the deeper story, but in "Spaghetti" the text is so simple that there is not a huge difference between the external and the internal story. For this reason, I don't especially recommend that children write one paragraph on the external and another on the internal story.

I deliberately jot Ali's proposed content, because I already know from hearing her share it in her partnership that it is somewhat problematic (as well as being impressive). I plan to seize this opportunity to give children practice reading with a lawyer's eyes.

This session relies upon you to teach youngsters how to read closely and critically. Notice these examples of careful reading. It would have been very easy to let the claim that Gabriel "learns to love again" slide right past us. Frankly, you'll need to decide how rigorous you want to be. If I am teaching third graders who are new to this work, I might not bat an eye at the notion that Gabriel learns to love again. But with more sophisticated students, I want to teach them to triple-check whether their claims are accountable to the text. But keep in mind: You'll be able to teach children to scrutinize their claims and imagine how they could be different only if you become accustomed to doing so yourself.

I like talking about the fact that revision requires courage. I actually believe that most qualities and strategies of effective writing rely on personal character: honesty, empathy, accountability, tenacity, high standards, optimism, confidence, a willingness to be vulnerable. Of course, I think qualities of good teaching are not very different!

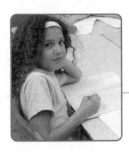

Writing and Conferring

Revising Essay Plans

I pulled my chair alongside Max and watched as he reread what he'd written: *[Figs. VIII-3 and VIII-4]*

> In the story "Eleven" by Sandra Cisneros, Rachel is a girl who wakes up on her eleventh birthday expecting a lot, but ends up getting disappointed by the way the day went.

> She expects to feel eleven.

- "When you wake up on your 11th birthday you expect to feel 11 but you don't."
- "You don't feel eleven, not right away. It takes days, weeks even, sometimes even months till you say 11 when they ask."

> She expected the other kids not to understand all the ages she has.

- "I feel sick inside like the part of me that's 3, but I shut my eyes down tight . . . and remember I'm eleven."
- "Rachel you put that sweater on and no more nonsense!"

> She expected everything to go perfect because it's her birthday.

- "Mama is making a cake for tonight and Dad will come home and everyone will sing happy birthday, happy birthday to you"
- She does not think she will get in trouble while fooling around with the sweater because it's her birthday.

Max set to work, looking first at "Eleven" and then at his outline, adding yet more references to the text under each of his topic sentences.

"Can I stop you?" I said to Max. "What are you working on?"

"I'm making my boxes and bullets, like you said," Max responded. "I'm on my second page."

"Max," I answered, "I love the way you are not just reading *your plans* closely, you are also reading the

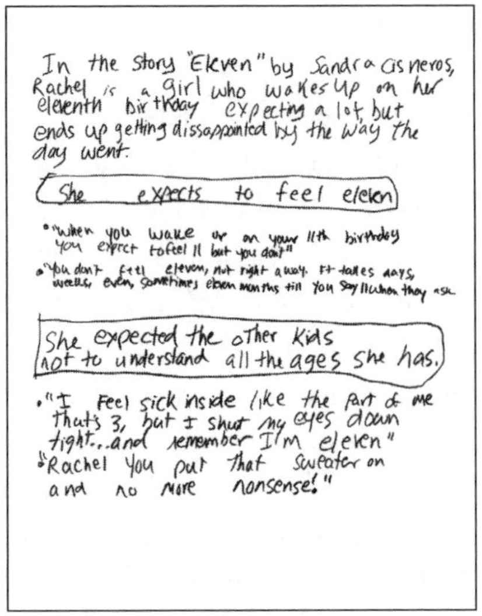

In the story "Eleven" by Sandra cisneros, Rachel is a girl who wakes up on her eleventh birtHday expecting a lot but ends up getting dissappointed by the way the day went.

She expects to feel eleven

• "when you wake up on your 11th birthday you expect to feel 11 but you don't"

• "You don't feel eleven, not right away. It takes days, weeks, even, sometimes eleven months till you say 11 when they ask.

She expected the other kids not to understand all the ages she has.

• "I feel sick inside like the part of me that's 3, but I shut my eyes down tight...and remember I'm eleven"

"Rachel you put that sweater on and no more nonsense!"

Fig. VIII-3 Max page 1

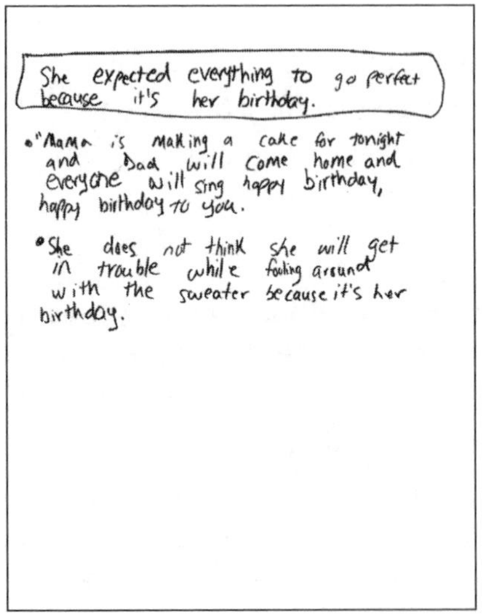

She expected everything to go perfect because it's her birthday.

• "Mama is making a cake for tonight and Dad will come home and everyone will sing happy birthday, happy birthday to you.

• She does not think she will get in trouble while fooling around with the sweater because it's her birthday.

Fig. VIII-4 Max's work page 2

short text closely. I love seeing you look back and forth between the text, your outline, the text, your outline. And I think it is really smart that you are looking for the textual evidence for each point."

Then I shifted my voice, saying, "But can I teach you one thing?" I waited for Max to nod, then said, "Writers really profit from being able to give ourselves self-assignments. And especially early on in our writing process, instead of doing one thing on and on and on, it helps to do one job for a bit, then to pull back and think, 'How's this working?' Instead of continuing on and on, you'd be wise to reread this with a lawyer's eyes, like I suggested today, thinking, 'What will I need to prove if this is my thesis?' and imagining possible problems."

Max looked stunned, "But I have the evidence," he said.

"Actually, I think a lawyer would tell you that your boxes (your topic sentences) don't match your thesis," I said. I did not point out that certainly his second box—"She expected the other kids not to understand all the ages she has"— didn't fit with his thesis. Instead I said, "You are smart enough and hard-working enough to see this if you give

> **MID-WORKSHOP TEACHING POINT** *Using Partners to Help Scrutinize Essay Plans* "Writers, can I have your eyes and your attention? I want to remind you that when I wanted to buy a house, I hired a lawyer and asked that lawyer to read my contract with eagle eyes, helping me imagine potential problems. You may need to recruit another pair of eyes to help you scrutinize your plans. I've set up extra conference areas around the edges of the room. If you think your boxes and bullets are okay, would you recruit someone other than your partner to read your planned thesis and supporting statements, to hear your intentions, and to help you see potential problems? And those of you who are recruited as lawyers, be sure you cosign the writer's plans. Your signature acts as a promise. Your signature says, 'You can go forward with this and not encounter problems.'"

yourself the job of really scrutinizing what you promise in your thesis, and really looking at the match between your thesis and your topic sentences," I said. "You also need to make sure the evidence you are gathering *really*, truly matches the point you are making."

Then I said, "Max, you've got a talent for getting a ton of work done, and for keeping on and on and on in a job. Those are very special talents. But you need to be not just the worker who grinds out a lot of sheer work. You also need to be the lawyer who is critical, thoughtful, and makes cautious decisions. To become the lawyer as well as the worker, you need to be willing to believe that a plan that feels great to you—one you want to get started with—could conceivably have problems. So right now, switch from being a builder to being a lawyer, from writing to reading, from going forward to looking backwards."

The next day, I returned to find that Max had made a few important revisions. He had altered his plan. This time, I congratulated Max and suggested he simplify, imagining that his essay might have only two or perhaps three body paragraphs.

> In the story "Eleven" by Sandra Cisneros, Rachel is a girl who wakes up on her eleventh birthday expecting a lot, but ends up getting disappointed by the way the day went.

> She expects to feel eleven.

- "When you wake up on your 11th birthday you expect to feel 11 but you don't."

- "You don't feel eleven, not right away. It takes days, weeks even, sometimes even months till you say 11 when they ask. And you don't feel smart eleven, not until you're almost 12, that's the way it is."

> She expected everything to go perfect because it's her birthday.

- "Mama is making a cake for tonight and Dad will come home and everyone will sing happy birthday, happy birthday to you."

- She does not think she will get in trouble while fooling around with the sweater because it's her birthday.

- She expects someone to come and take the sweater so she does not have to keep it.

> She learns that Eleventh Birthdays can be disappointing and not bringing what you expect.

- You wake up expecting to feel eleven but you don't.

- You don't feel eleven. Not right away. It takes days . . . weeks . . . even months to say eleven when they ask you.

- You don't feel smart eleven. Not until you're almost twelve.

- And maybe one day when your all grown up you will need to cry like you're 3. And that is fine. That's what I tell mama when she's sad and needs to cry. Maybe she is feeling three.

> She understands that you can still feel a different age, even if you're older.

- Someday you may say something stupid and that's one part of you that's still ten. And that's okay.

- Or maybe sometimes you are scared and need to sit on your mama's lap, and that is the part of you that still is five.

SHARE

Writing Thesis Statements on Demand

Compliment children on crafting and scrutinizing their essay plans.

"Writers, lawyers, can I have your attention? You've done some powerful work today. Most of you will end today with a viable thesis and with a plan for your topic sentences, and that will mark an enormously important step forward. We have been working for more than a week, and as a result of all this work we'll each have a plan—one we can write in three or four lines—that is solid and trustworthy."

Ask children to join you in charting the tips and tools for planning an essay.

"It's pretty amazing, isn't it, to think that we've been writing and reading and revising and thinking and planning for more than a week—and we end up with about fifty words! But of course, the truth is that we've not only written a strong thesis, we've also each developed a whole backpack full of tips and tools for writing a thesis statement and for planning our supporting paragraphs. Before we go forward, let's gather some of the tips and tools we've learned. This time, would you talk not just with your partner but with another set of partners as well, and see how many helpful tips and tools you can recall."

Soon I solicited their input and compiled this chart:

Tips and Tools for Writing a Thesis and Topic Sentences for a Literary Essay

- First gather lots of ideas about the text you've read. Be sure you read closely, <u>really</u> noticing stuff, and then write, "The idea I have about this is . . . ." Use thought prompts to write long. Reread, looking for ideas that are true and interesting. Box them and write more about them. Then reread again, looking for ideas that are true and interesting.

- Pay attention to characters and their traits, wants, struggles, changes, and lessons. Think about the whole story as a story of a character who wants something, struggles, and then changes or learns a lesson.

- Think about the issues in your life and ask, "How does this story go with my issue?" This can help you find something to say that really matters to you.

The chart you make in your class will be slightly different from this one. You can certainly use this one as the handout for children to keep in their notebooks or folders, but it is still important to allow children the process of creating this list together.

Tips and Tools for Writing a Thesis and Topic Sentences for a Literary Essay (continued)

- Ask, "What's this story <u>really</u> about?" Look how the author wrote it, and think, "Why did the author do this?" Expect the author to make craft decisions that highlight the meaning the author hopes to convey.

- Reread all your ideas and find things that seem interesting and true and important. Compile these.

- Draft a possible thesis statement, then test it out. Ask, "Does this go with the whole story?" and "Can I support this?"

- Maybe write, "Some people think this is a story about . . . but I think it is <u>really</u> about . . . ." Consider whether your thesis addresses the internal as well as the external story line of the text under study.

- Write your thesis and plan your paragraphs. Your paragraphs might be organized to show how your thesis is true at the beginning and the end of the story, or in one way and another way, for one reason or another reason.

- Reread your thesis with a lawyer's eyes. Look at what you have promised to prove and make sure you can do that. Check every word. Be sure your subordinate claims match your thesis. Rewrite over and over.

This list might be too wordy or too lengthy to be helpful, depending on your children's developmental stage. Alter it as you see fit!

"We've spent many days writing a thesis and planning an essay, but I'm pretty sure that you've also learned that you can do this really quickly if you need to do so. Let's try it."

Ask children to go through the whole process again in a condensed, faster version, using a text they all know well.

"Pretend you are writing a thesis about Gary Paulsen's book *The Monument*, which we read earlier this year. Let's imagine you want your thesis to address a deep message in the book. Work with a partner, and see if you can come up with a thesis in exactly five minutes. Remember, if you are stuck you might think about the external and internal story lines and use the template, 'Some people think such and such is the story of . . . but I think it is really the story of . . . .' Remember, too, you might think about what two or

This quick drill is something you can ask children to try throughout these units at nearly any stage of the writing process. Not only is it a way for children to consolidate and review what they know about the writing process of a given genre, it also helps prepare them for the writing on demand that they will invariably be asked to do.

three things the main character learns or ways the main character changes. Are you ready? Go!"

Soon I'd written some of the children's best ideas on chart paper:

> Some people think this is a story about a girl who is adopted and goes to live in a dull Kansas town, but I think this is a story about a girl who learns to be an artist.

> In The Monument, a girl named Rocky learns to see the world as an artist and to not be so tough.

> In Paulsen's story, The Monument, an artist teaches with examples and with advice.

"So remember, it may be that you'll be asked to write literary essays quickly on tests—look how well you are set up to do that, already! The process you'll use when you write essays on demand is the same as the one you already know."

[HOMEWORK]   ***Providing Thinking About Texts by Making Connections***   Writers, this morning I asked many of you to tell me all about the new ideas you came up with at home about "Spaghetti," and many of you looked at me like I'd just asked the stupidest question. You said, "I didn't even take the story home!" But you did. I know I gave it to every one of you. I read it to you! Once we've read (or heard a text read to us), that text is ours. We carry it with us. And we not only carry the text with us, we continue reading it—even if it's not there! We continue reading it because reading is mulling, thinking, questioning, and envisioning. I have a quote over my bed, the words of a great poet, and it says, "The poet is working," meaning that poets work on poems even in their sleep! But I *could* also have a quote over my bed that says, "The reader is reading." Readers, you need to carry texts with you all day long, all night long, mulling over them, finding new significance in them. To help you do that, notice intriguing bits of stories and life around you—collect anything fresh you can get your hands on, and use it to help you think about the text you are working on! The material you collect might not exactly make sense with the text you are reading at first, but if you work at it, you can often make extraordinary connections that will eventually help make your points in fresh and intriguing ways! Tonight collect some interesting tidbits, some great quotations, and try to make them apply to the reading you are doing now. See what you can come up with!

If your students are writing theses that are complex and confusing . . . you might highlight the importance of simplicity and elegance in thinking. In order to write a strong thesis statement, one that is both thoughtful and clear, a writer needs to take a complex idea and make it simple. You may, therefore, want to teach a minilesson on the importance of simplifying. It may help to tell a story about the genius, Albert Einstein. He insisted always on using hand soap for shaving, despite the discomfort. When asked why, Einstein replied, "Two soaps? That is too complicated!" This from a man who created theories of relativity and so forth! Many people believe that Einstein's genius came from a willingness to be dissatisfied with anything which wasn't simple, elegant, and clear.

If students need help in planning the categories that support their theses . . . we can remind them to draw on the strategies they learned while writing personal essays. Some theses are more easily supported by discussing them in terms of *parts* or *kinds*. Here we can show how this essay will explore the kinds of risks the main character faces in the story:

> Despite the risks and dangers that challenge her on the long, perilous journey to the duchess' palace, Irene continues on and shows her love and devotion to her mother in *Brave Irene*, by William Steig.

> - Despite the strong, biting wind, Irene continues on to the palace.

> - Despite twisting her ankle in a hole, Irene continues on to the palace.

> - Even despite the approaching darkness, Irene continues on to the palace.

Students need to understand that we are not teaching a set of disconnected lessons for writing, but that we are arming them with a cache of strategies to fuel their writing throughout life.

COLLABORATING WITH COLLEAGUES

You and your colleagues will probably want to spend some time together looking over your children's thesis statements and supporting claims. Help each other to sort the children's work into two piles: *on track* and *in need of help*. In this way, you can triage your problems and guard against children doing a great deal more work if their entire plan is totally flawed.

As you reread children's plans, consider whether there are ways to help children simplify and consolidate what they have written. For example, this is Judah's plan for her essay: [Fig. VIII-5]

> In the short story "The Marble Champ" by Gary Soto, a girl named Lupe does good in everything she tries. But, she is not good at sports. To overcome this problem, she practices every day and believes in herself to become good at marbles.

> In the beginning Lupe wins a lot of academic awards, but she is not good at sports.

- Ex. of what she won
- Explanation about Lupe not good at sports

> Lupe decides to play marbles. She practices and believes in herself to become good.

- Lupe likes the idea of marbles
- She starts practicing right away.
- She really believes in herself and she practiced three good hours.

> In the end Lupe has overcome not being good at marbles. She won the championship.

- She won! Practicing paid off.
- Self belief—kept going, never gave up.
- Her awards—she worked at goal, finally overcame it.

Fig. VIII-5 Judah's plan for her essay

With a bit of help, Judah consolidated her thesis statement. She first rewrote it this way:

> In Gary Soto's short story, "The Marble Champ," Lupe changes from being good only at academics to being good also at sports. By practicing everyday and believing in herself she becomes a marble champ.

Her final draft of her thesis statement and supportive claims is as follows: *[Fig. VIII-6]*

In literature, characters face challenges and learn to survive. In the short story, "The Marble Champ" by Gary Soto, Lupe learns to overcome her difficulties by working hard and believing in herself.

- Lupe overcomes her difficulties through hard work.
- Lupe overcame her difficulties, not only by hard work, but also because she believed in herself.

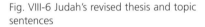

Fig. VIII-6 Judah's revised thesis and topic sentences

Paulina's draft looked like this: *[Fig. VIII-7]*

This essay shows how Rachel—the girl in Cisnero's "Eleven"—feels about growing up and being eleven. Sometimes growing up feels slow—like when the teacher makes Rachel wear the sweater, or right after your birthday—and sometimes it feels fast—like when Rachel stops being excited about her birthday cake or like when you act younger than you are.

- Sometimes growing up can feel really slow. When you want to be older than you are, growing up feels slow.
- However, growing up can also feel fast.

Growing up is hardly ever right on schedule . . . or maybe it is—just not a schedule you agree with. Sometimes growing up is behind schedule and sometimes it's ahead.

Fig. VIII-7 Paulina's boxes and bullets

IN THIS SESSION, YOU'LL
DEMONSTRATE WAYS THAT
ESSAYISTS COLLECT AND ANGLE
MINISTRIES AS EVIDENCE TO
SUPPORT THEIR CLAIMS.

GETTING READY

- First portion of "Spaghetti," by
  Cynthia Rylant, on transparency,
  chart paper, or as handouts
- Timeline of "Spaghetti" that
  you can quickly summarize
- Specific ministry from
  "Spaghetti" you can retell
  to support a thesis
- ⦿ See CD-ROM for resources

USING STORIES AS EVIDENCE

Throughout the year, your children will have written about tiny moments in ways that convey the biggest meanings of their lives. My stories about searching for a place to sit at the basketball game, and about hoping that by receiving a part in the school play I'd also receive a place in the popular group, both conveyed my yearning to find my place in the world. Stories can be powerful vehicles for conveying Big Truths.

Earlier in the year, your children collected stories to support the main ideas in their personal essays. Now you'll invite them to collect stories that support the ideas they've chosen to advance in their literary essays.

You may need to reteach lessons from the personal essay and narrative units, reminding children to bring what they know about writing effective stories to this unit. Above all, children will need reminders about the differences between summarizing and storytelling. Although there are appropriate times to summarize a bit of the short text to make a particular point, today you will emphasize the value of storytelling bits of the text, and of angling their rendition of the text to illustrate an idea. Today, then, you'll help children recall how to write short chronological stories, and you'll teach them to angle these stories to convey big ideas. This may sound easy, but it's actually very complex and challenging work.

Interestingly enough, in our minilessons, we as teachers are constantly required to do just what we're teaching children to do. That is, we are frequently called upon to retell a story, angling it to make one point or another. We therefore have a repertoire of strategies to bring out our angle (or our interpretation) of an event. For example, we may highlight the point we want to make by mentioning counterexamples, saying something like, "Donald Crews didn't write about his whole summer down south; instead he wrote about just one episode on the train tracks." This is a technique children can learn as well. We also angle our stories by starting with an overarching statement that orients listeners: "Listen to what I do," we say, "and notice especially . . . ." Children, too, can learn to preface their stories with comments that establish their angles.

MINILESSON

Using Stories as Evidence

CONNECTION

Remind children that in the personal essay unit, they collected and filed evidence that supported each of their topic sentences. Ask children to do the same when writing literary essays.

"Writers, you'll remember that after you wrote your thesis statements and planned your supporting statements during the personal essay unit, you each became a researcher, collecting the evidence that would allow you to make your case."

"So it won't surprise you when I suggest that you need to do similar work now. In fact, you can look back on our charts from the personal essay unit, and remind yourself of materials you can collect to support your thesis. Many of you, I'm sure, will decide to collect Small Moment stories that support your claim, your thesis."

Name your teaching point. Specifically, tell children that when writers want to tell stories in the service of an idea, they tell these stories with an angle.

"Today I want to remind you that when you are telling a story in the service of an idea, you need to angle that story to highlight the idea you want to convey."

TEACHING

Demonstrate that before a literary essayist can tell a story to illustrate a topic sentence, the writer must reread the text and identify bits that could make the point.

"I first need to reread 'Spaghetti,' looking for small moments that could illustrate my first point—that at the start of the story Gabriel is lonely." I used an overhead projector to enlarge the text, and skimmed the first half of it, writing stars in the margins whenever I found a potential story.

"I could tell a tiny story about Gabriel sitting alone on the stoop," I said. "Or, alternatively, I could tell a tiny story about how he didn't hear the meow at first, then did, and wondered if someone was calling for him."

Ask children to watch as you tell one portion of the text as a story. Highlight the steps you take.

Then I said to the children, "Watch how I write the first story, and then you'll have a chance to use similar techniques to write the second story."

"First I'm going to reread the text and just get the timeline of what happened straight. But I need to remember that I won't be simply telling the story of what happened; I'll be telling the story of what happened that shows Gabriel was lonely."

"I'm going to retell what happened in order. Some of these things might have happened all at once, but I'll put them on a timeline. I'm going to fill in some of the details that the author didn't exactly say but did suggest." Then, touching one finger after the next, I listed these events:

First Gabriel was sitting on the stoop alone.

Other people around him were chatting with each other, but he didn't hear them.

He remembered his sandwich and wished he still had it.

He remembered being alone in school too when he was the only one who knew the answer and the kids were mad at him.

Then he imagined that he'd like to sleep outside alone.

Then he heard something.

"Now I'll tell it as a story, remembering to start at the beginning and remembering, every line or two, to say something about how this story shows Gabriel being lonely."

One evening Gabriel sat on the stoop outside—

"No," I said, "I should tuck in something about him being lonely so people know from the start that this story shows his loneliness."

One evening Gabriel, a homeless boy, sat alone on the stoop outside the shelter where he lived. Other people sat on far corners of the stoop, but they were all talking with each other.

"I better mention the alone parts again."

Gabriel sat alone. He remembered his lunch sandwich and wished he still had it.

"I want to make the sandwich relate to the fact that he is lonely. Umm . . . ."

He felt extra lonely because he was hungry.

When children retell portions of a novel to make a point, the text itself is long enough that it's not challenging to cull a sequence of events. When writing about a very short text such as "Eleven," however, the entire text is so abbreviated that writers must really zoom in on microevents to extract a sequenced story. But a sequence is necessary to create a story.

We always make decisions over whether something is worth recording. In this instance, I do not plan to revisit this timeline or ask children to work with it, so I don't think it needs to be written on chart paper. If you decide otherwise, I'd record only a word to signify each new dot on the timeline.

When retelling a sequence of events to make a particular point, children are apt to abbreviate the start of the event instead starting the story at the climax, because it is usually the section that most pertains to the idea the child wants to advance. I try to remind children that even ministories must have a beginning, a middle, and an end.

"Writers, do you see that I first extracted the timeline of activities, retelling the sequence of events across my fingers and making sure to tell the events that illustrate that Gabriel is lonely? Then I storytold, but after every line or two I thought, 'How do I highlight the "Gabriel is lonely" theme?'"

I advise you and your children to literally return to the key words—in this case, to the word lonely—*after every sentence or two. Many of us are taught to avoid repeating a word— don't take that instruction too seriously. Repetition can be an important source of cohesion.*

ACTIVE ENGAGEMENT

Describe the way you've created a file system in anticipation of data collection. Tell children you plan to collect a few tiny stories to support each topic sentence.

"Like most of you, I've already made files, so I'll have a place for the material that I will gather to support each of my bullets. I have one file that says, 'At the start of the story, Gabriel is lonely,' and another file labeled, 'Then Gabriel lets a stray cat into his life and isn't lonely anymore.' Today, I'll want to collect at least one or two tiny stories for each of my files."

Although my real point will be to show children ways writers angle stories to illustrate a particular idea, I have minor points that I'm also hoping to make. One concerns productivity. I find some children call it a day's work after they've retold one tiny snippet of a short text, and I'm modeling a very different expectation for productivity.

Reiterate the steps you hope students take: finding an episode, extracting a sequence of events, recalling the main idea, telling the story. Help one partner start doing this.

"So remember that after finding a little bit of the text that could illustrate my point, my topic sentence, I reread it and extracted a timeline. I retold the sequence of events across my fingers. Remember how I kept threading my big idea in and out of the story."

"Would you try that with the second small moment we've marked? We've already located the episode. Remember, this is the episode when Gabriel is sitting on the stoop and there is a meow, but Gabriel almost misses hearing it because he is lost in his own thoughts. When he does hear the small cry, at first he wonders if someone is calling him, and goes looking, looking."

To get them started, I said, "Partner 1, extract the sequence of events, telling them across your fingers. Start at the beginning—'Gabriel sat alone on the stoop, imagining sleeping outside all alone . . . .'" I paused, then added, "Keep going," and gave them a moment to do this.

If you feel your children would profit from extra support during Active Engagement, you could retell two-thirds of a story only and then ask them first to retell the story you've just told, and then to continue, adding on the rest of the story. This, of course, would provide them with much more scaffolding than the request to proceed in a similar way, retelling an entirely new small story.

Notice that when referencing the small moment, I provide children with subtle help seeing this as a sequence of microevents all pertaining to the main idea.

Record the sequence of events that many are articulating on chart paper. Remind children that the goal is to storytell, angling the events to make a point. Launch partners into doing this.

As partners talked, I recorded the sequence of events they mentioned on chart paper. "Writers, most of you retold a sequence that goes like this," I said, and showed this timeline:

You'll notice that I helped children get started retelling the sequence of events. By telling the first dot on the timeline, I made it considerably easier for them to be successful with this activity. My role is often to function as training wheels so that children get a felt sense for what the strategy I've taught feels like.

Gabriel sat alone on the stoop, imagining sleeping outside alone.

There was a meow.

Gabriel almost didn't hear it because he was lost in his thoughts.

Meow again

"Is someone calling me?"

Looked

Heard again

Excited, looked more

"Now, partner 2, would you storytell this to partner 1? Remember, after every dot or two, you'll want to highlight ways this story shows that Gabriel was lonely and longing for company."

Demonstrate, recruiting children to help you angle the story toward the point.

Children did this, and I coached those that I overheard to bring out the loneliness theme. "Writers, can I stop you?" I said after a bit. "I'm going to storytell, and I'll pause after every dot or two. Will you help me highlight the theme of loneliness?"

> One day Gabriel sat on the stoop outside his building, imagining sleeping outside.

I gestured to Emily. "Emily, I'm going to repeat my story. Then will you write in the air what you might add next to bring out the message about Gabriel being lonely?" I said, and repeated my lead.

> One day Gabriel sat on the stoop outside his building, imagining sleeping outside.

Emily added:

> He sat all alone. He imagined sleeping alone with just coyotes and on the grate outside the movie theater, all alone too.

I continued:

> There was a meow.

Again, notice that I find a way to intercede with additional support. Of course, not all the children will have arrived at this timeline of events. By recording this on a chart, I offer children a leg up as they approach the second portion of this work.

Because I know that children will need help fully understanding what it means to angle a story to make a point, I add this extension.

I deliberately call on Emily to work with me here because I know she's fairly adept at this, and I want her to provide yet another demonstration.

I gestured for Emily to add her part, and she said:

> Gabriel didn't hear it. He was off in his dreams.

I gestured for her to say even more.

> He wasn't expecting anyone to call or anything. He was just used to being alone.

I added:

> There was another meow.

Emily added:

> Gabriel thought someone was calling him.

I gestured for her to say more, and to stay with the lonely theme.

> He was glad someone was calling. He was so lonely that he couldn't believe someone was calling him.

You'll notice that I don't complete this; earlier, too, we began but didn't finish a demonstration. After a bit, I think the point has been made and that children won't benefit from prolonging the demonstration.

LINK
Remind writers that essayists collect ministories to advance their point. Remind students that literary essayists can collect several stories for each topic sentence within a single day.

"So, writers, you already know that when you are writing an essay you need to collect material to support each of your topic sentences, and you already know that essayists often collect stories to make a point. Today you've seen how writers of literary essays reread, finding portions of the text that can be told as stories, and then how we angle those tiny stories to make the point we want to make."

"Today, I know each of you will collect several stories. You may collect a story for each file, or several stories in one file. The challenge will be to angle those stories to highlight the idea you are advancing, as Emily just helped me to do."

Just before sending them off to work, I remind children of the productivity goals for today.

WRITING AND CONFERRING

Collecting and Angling Stories to Support Ideas

You'll probably want to conduct table conferences today. That is, you will probably not need to invest lots of time in research. You can count on the fact that children will profit from help, and you can anticipate the sort of help they'll need.

For starters, children will need help seeing the microstories they can extract from these short texts. For example, if a child wants to make the point that Rachel is silenced by Mrs. Price, she is apt to see only one possible story that might illustrate this, and that story encompasses the whole text of "Eleven." (Mrs. Price says she's seen Rachel wearing the sweater, Mrs. Price doesn't listen to Rachel's protests and moves on to math, Mrs. Price makes Rachel put on the sweater, Mrs. Price acts as if it is no big deal when the sweater turns out not to be Rachel's.)

You'll need to show children that they can also regard "Eleven" as containing several different episodes, each of which shows Mrs. Price's disregard for Rachel. For example, one of these episodes happens early:

- Mrs. Price asks whose sweater it is, and Rachel thinks, "Not mine."

- Mrs. Price listens to Sylvia and not Rachel, believing Sylvia when she says that the sweater is Rachel's.

- When Rachel sputters "Not mine," Mrs. Price ignores her and acts as if she knows better than Rachel.

- When Rachel tries to protest, Mrs. Price turns to math as if the sweater question is now resolved.

- Rachel is about to cry, but Mrs. Price doesn't notice.

Then, too, children will need help retelling a sequence of actions as a story. Many will be apt to cut to the chase, summarizing rather than storytelling the event. For example, a child might write:

> When Rachel tried to tell Mrs. Price the sweater wasn't hers, Mrs. Price ignored Rachel.

MID-WORKSHOP TEACHING POINT **Finding Ministories to Illustrate Topic Sentences** "Writers, can I have your eyes and your attention? Writers, you all are doing a superb job at finding tiny ministories inside your short texts and then telling these to advance the ideas you've chosen. Ali, for example, wanted to tell a story to show that Lupe had never been good at sports. She reread the start of 'The Marble Champ'—listen to it and think about whether you could find a ministory here":

> Lupe Medrano, a shy girl who spoke in whispers, was the school's spelling bee champion, winner of the reading contest at the public library three summers in a row, blue ribbon awardee in the science fair, the top student at her piano recital, and the playground grand champion in chess. She was a straight-A student and—not counting kindergarten, when she had been stung by a wasp—never missed one day of elementary school. She had received a small trophy for this honor and had been congratulated by the mayor.
>
> But, though Lupe had a razor-sharp mind, she could not make her body, no matter how much she tried, run as fast as the other girls'. She begged her body to move faster, but could never beat anyone in the fifty-yard dash.

continued on next page

You will want to let this writer know that he has just summarized rather than storytold. Although essayists *do* sometimes summarize pertinent bits of a text to defend a point, a wise writer recognizes the difference between a summary and a story, and can produce either one.

Above all, children will need help angling their storytelling so that every line or two references the point they want to make. You could teach children these tips:

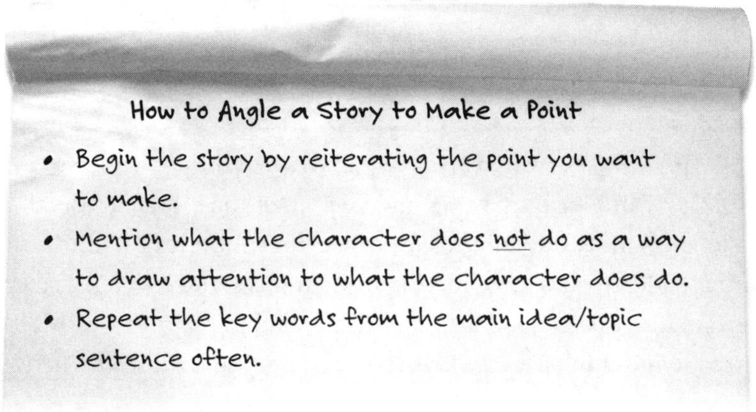

How to Angle a Story to Make a Point

- Begin the story by reiterating the point you want to make.
- Mention what the character does **not** do as a way to draw attention to what the character does do.
- Repeat the key words from the main idea/topic sentence often.

As you conduct table conferences, don't hesitate to ask every child to stop what he or she is doing and watch you work with one child. For example, I asked children to watch while I worked with Harrison, who had decided to retell the story of Lupe's dinner conversation to support the idea that Lupe overcame her difficulties through the support of her family. The excerpt from "The Marble Champ" that Harrison wanted to storytell goes like this:

That night, over dinner, Mrs. Medrano said, "Honey, you should see Lupe's thumb."

"Huh?" Mr. Medrano said, wiping his mouth and looking at his daughter.

"Show your father."

"Do I have to?" an embarrassed Lupe asked.

"Go on, show your father."

Reluctantly, Lupe raised her hand and flexed her thumb. You could see the muscle.

The father put down his fork and asked, "What happened?"

"Dad, I've been working out. I've been squeezing an eraser."

"Why?"

continued from previous page

"Listen to the story Ali wrote": [*Fig. IX-1*]

At the start of "The Marble Champ," Lupe had never been good at sports. She lay on her bed wishing she could play a sport. There was never a sport she could play. She stared up at her awards shelf. She looked at awards—for spelling, reading, science, piano, chess, and for going to school every day of the year. Not one of her awards was for a sport. "I wish I could win at a sport," she thought.

At the start of "The Marble Champ," Lupe had never been good at sports. She lay on her bed wishing she could play a sport. There was never a sport she could play. She stared up at the her awards shelf. She looked at awards— for spelling, reading, science, piano, chess, and for going to school every day of the year. Not one of her awards was for a sport. "I wish I could win at a sport," she thought.

continued on next page

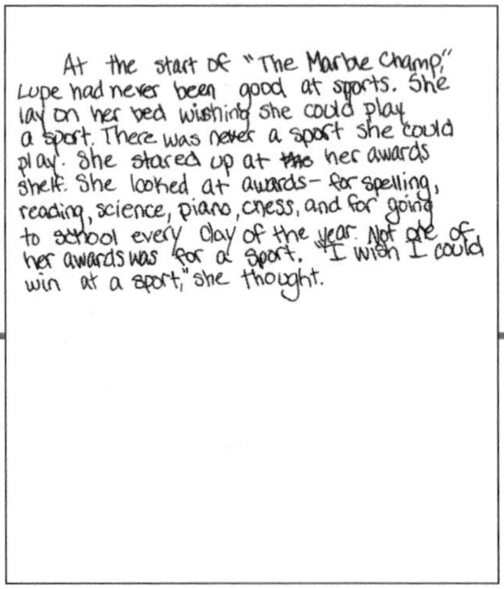

Fig. IX-1 Ali's ministory

"I'm going to enter the marbles championship."

Her father looked at her mother and then back at his daughter. "When is it, honey?"

"This Saturday. Can you come?"

The father had been planning to play racquetball with a friend Saturday, but he said he would be there. He knew his daughter thought she was no good at sports and he wanted to encourage her. He even rigged some lights in the backyard so she could practice after dark. (Soto, p.116)

Harrison had initially written:

> For example, one dinner Lupe asks her father to come to the marble competition. "When is it?" her father asks. She said, "This Saturday." The date wasn't good for him but he decided to come anyway.

I said, "Harrison, when I reread my stories to check whether I've angled them to support my claim, I do this: I underline the parts of my rough-draft story that directly show my main idea. Right now, could you underline the parts of your microstory that show that Lupe overcame her difficulties through the support of her family?"

Harrison began doing this. Partway through, he paused and said, "I get it. I stretched out the wrong point 'cause my details about Saturday are ones that don't really show the big idea. I need to add on to the part about the dad switching his plans to support her." In the end, this is what Harrison wrote: [Fig. IX-1]

> Lupe overcomes her difficulties through the support of her family. For example, one dinner, Lupe asks her father to come to the marble competition. Her father drops his fork and drops into deep thought. He had finally planned to spend that very day playing racquet ball, his favorite activity. But he looked into Lupe's eyes, thought about how important it was that she was risking entering a sports competition, and announced he would be there. Lupe grinned.

I debriefed for the observing children. "Do you see that Harrison reread his draft and realized he'd stretched out and provided details for an aspect of the story that didn't make his point? So he redid it. Notice in the next version, he ends by talking about how this episode shows his claim, his idea."

"Harrison added into his version of these events the notion that Lupe's father thought about the racquetball game he'd planned, and then thought about the risks his daughter was taking before he made his decision."

continued from previous page

"Ali has done just what essayists often do, finding a ministory that illustrates the idea she wants to advance. And I want to point out something special Ali has done that can help the rest of us. As you did, she paraphrased sections of the text that go with her big idea. But she did something else—she added her own insights and her own envisionment. Listen again to the excerpt from 'The Marble Champ' and then to Ali's ministory, and you'll see that Ali inferred, she added bits to her story that *aren't in the text itself*." Then I read both aloud.

"Ali's reading between the lines in this instance, seeing what's not quite written in the actual words and showing how that supports her ideas too. Today, if you find yourself copying or paraphrasing bits of the actual text that go with your idea, that's fine. But try to do as Ali has also done and sometimes collect evidence that is suggested but not explicitly stated in the texts."

SHARE

Celebrating the Use of Ministories and Other Bits of Wonderful Writing

Remind writers of the teaching point. Celebrate an aspect of their writing that is going particularly well, and ask them to reread their writing with their partner, talking about both ministories.

"Writers, earlier today I taught you that literary essayists search for sections of a text that can make our point, and then we storytell those sections, starting at the beginning of the story and angling the story. But today, *you've* shown me other things writers do that are so, so important. Your stories are incredibly powerful because they act like the smells of salt air and sea roses, which for me always conjure up the presence of the ocean. You include tiny, emblematic details in your ministories that evoke the entire story in your literary essay. I'm not sure what makes some details have such magical power—but there is no mistaking these details when I see them in your folders."

"Would you and your partner each reread one of the stories you wrote today and notice ways it is angled to highlight the point you want to make. And would you notice, also, specific details you've used that have magical powers?"

⚫ HOMEWORK *Studying a Literary Essay* During the next two weeks, you'll be working toward writing a literary essay. It helps, I think, to be able to imagine the sort of text you're hoping to make. For homework, then, I'd like you to study Jill's essay on "Eleven." I've made a copy for each of you. *[Figs. IX-2, IX-3, and IX-4]*

Literary Essay on "Eleven" by Sandra Cisneros written by Jill

In my life, not everything ends up like a fairytale. I like to read books where characters are like me. They don't live fairytale lives. We have the same kinds of problems. Many people read Sandra Cisneros's essay "Eleven" and think it's about a girl who has to wear a sweater she doesn't want to wear. But I think the story is about a girl who struggles to hold onto herself when she is challenged by people who have power over her.

Literary Essay On "Eleven" by Sandra Cisneros
written By Jill

In my life, not everything ends up
like a fairytale. I like to read books
where characters are like me. They don't
live fairytale lives. We have the same
kinds of problems. Many people read Sandra
Cisneros's essay "Eleven" and think its
about a girl who has to wear a
sweater she doesn't want to wear. But
I think the story is about a girl who
struggles to hold onto herself when
she is challenged by people who have
power over her.

When Rachel's teacher, Mrs. Price, challenges
Rachel, Rachel loses herself. One day Mrs.
Price puts a stretched out, itchy, red sweater
on Rachel's desk saying "I know this is your
I saw you wearing it once" Rachel knows
that the sweater isn't hers and tries
to tell Mrs. Price, but Mrs. Price doesn't
believe her. Rachel reacts to Mrs. Price's
actions by losing herself "In my head
I'm thinking...how long till lunch time,
how long till I can take the red sweater
and throw it over the school

Fig. IX-2 Jill's literary essay page 1

When Rachel's teacher, Mrs. Price, challenges Rachel, Rachel loses herself. One day Mrs. Price puts a stretched-out, itchy, red sweater on Rachel's desk saying, "I know this is yours. I saw you wearing it once!!" Rachel knows that the sweater isn't hers and tries to tell Mrs. Price, but Mrs. Price doesn't believe her. Rachel reacts to Mrs. Price's actions by losing herself. "In my head, I'm thinking ... how long till lunch time, how long till I can take the red sweater and throw it over the school yard fence, or leave it hanging on a parking meter, or bunch it up into a little ball and toss it over the alley?" This shows that Rachel loses herself because she's not listening to her teacher, she's dreaming about a whole other place. It is also important to see that Rachel has all this good thinking about the sweater but when she wants to say the sweater isn't hers, she squeaks and stammers, unable to speak. "But it's not," Rachel says. "Now," Mrs. Price replies. Rachel loses herself by not finding complete words to say when Mrs. Price challenges her.

When Rachel's classmates challenge Rachel, Rachel loses herself. Sylvia Saldivar puts Rachel on the spot light when she says to Mrs. Price, "I think the sweater is Rachel's." Sylvia is challenging Rachel, she is being mean and she makes Rachel feel lost. Rachel cries to let her emotions out. Rachel feels sick from Sylvia. Rachel tries to cover herself up by putting her head in her sleeve. Tears stream down her face. She doesn't feel special like it's her birthday. Instead she feels lost in Sylvia's challenge.

In "Eleven" Rachel is overpowered by both Mrs. Price and Sylvia Saldivar and this causes her to lose herself. I used to think that when people turn eleven they feel strong and have confidence but I have learned that when your eleven you're also 10, 9, 8, 7, 6, 5, 4, 3, 2, and 1.

Would you circle Jill's thesis statement and her topic sentences? Notice where they are in her essay, and notice the way in which they channel everything she writes.

Would you also notice (and star) her use of a story to illustrate one of her topic sentences? Notice and star ways Jill angles her story so that it develops her topic sentence. Finally, notice that after Jill tells a story from the text, she writes a sentence discussing how the story addresses her topic sentence. This sentence begins, "This shows that . . . ."

Finally, would you look again at the ministories you wrote today and revise them, using what you learn from Jill's essay to help you? Be sure that, like Jill, you include a sentence that discusses how your ministory addresses your topic sentence. Your sentence, like Jill's, can begin, "This shows that . . . " and it needs to refer back to the topic sentence.

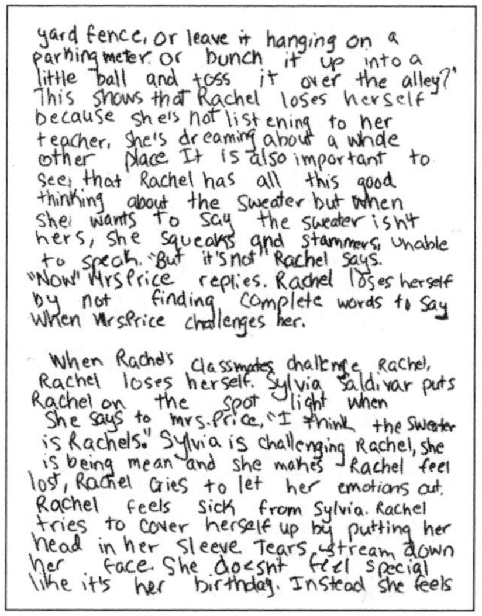

yard fence, or leave it hanging on a parking meter, or bunch it up into a little ball and toss it over the alley? This shows that Rachel loses herself because she's not listening to her teacher, she's dreaming about a whole other place. It is also important to see that Rachel has all this good thinking about the sweater but when she wants to say the sweater isn't hers, she squeaks and stammers, unable to speak. "But it's not" Rachel says. "Now!" Mrs Price replies. Rachel loses herself by not finding complete words to say when Mrs Price challenges her.

When Rachel's classmates challenge Rachel, Rachel loses herself. Sylvia Saldivar puts Rachel on the spot light when she says to Mrs. Price, "I think the sweater is Rachel's." Sylvia is challenging Rachel, she is being mean and she makes Rachel feel lost, Rachel cries to let her emotions out. Rachel feels sick from Sylvia. Rachel tries to cover herself up by putting her head in her sleeve. Tears stream down her face. She doesn't feel special like it's her birthday. Instead she feels

Fig. IX-3 Jill's literary essay page 2

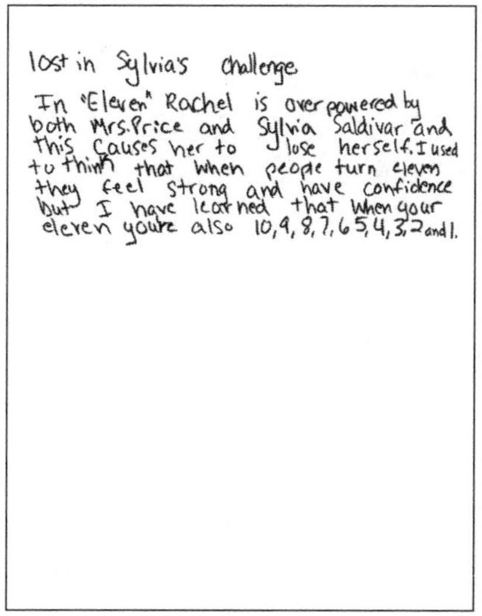

lost in Sylvia's challenge.

In "Eleven" Rachel is overpowered by both Mrs. Price and Sylvia Saldivar and this causes her to lose herself. I used to think that when people turn eleven they feel strong and have confidence but I have learned that when your eleven you're also 10, 9, 8, 7, 6, 5, 4, 3, 2 and 1.

Fig. IX-4 Jill's literary essay page 3

If your class of children studied this unit during a previous year and you want to add complexity . . . you might teach a variation of this lesson to more clearly illustrate that the way we angle our story—the point we want to make—alters the story. You could, for example, point out that if you wanted to say that Jenny, the protagonist in "Boar Out There," was curious towards the boar, you'd retell the story one way. If, alternatively, you wanted to suggest she's sympathetic towards the boar, you'd tell it differently. In such a lesson, you could first timeline a section of the story:

- The people of Glen Morgan knew about the boar.
- Jenny whispered to the boar sometimes.
- Jenny imagined the boar as fierce.
- Jenny went looking for the boar.
- Jenny heard the boar.
- Jenny saw the boar.
- The boar left.
- Jenny felt a new understanding for the boar.

Then you could demonstrate a retelling that shows Jenny is curious about the boar:

- Jenny whispered to the boar sometimes. Leaning over the fence that separated its world from hers, she imagined that it could talk back and wondered what it would say.
- Jenny imagined the boar as fierce. She could see his large angry eyes as he charged through the woods, spearing everything in his path with the golden horn on his head.
- Jenny went looking for the boar. As she walked quietly through the woods, Jenny felt afraid. She thought of how the boar could come charging at any moment, and wondered if it would even spear a little girl.
- Jenny heard the boar. She heard loud, stomping feet that could have been the feet of a giant. Jenny was terrified as the sound grew louder and louder, and the branches on the trees starting swaying back and forth. She was scared but didn't move. She wanted to see what the boar looked like.

Finally, you could demonstrate how the retelling would be different (and the same) if Jenny instead felt sympathetic towards the boar. You could, for example, simply retell the rest of the story to show this:

- Jenny saw the boar. He was large and ugly, but also sad looking. His ears were bloody and torn and he shivered, silent. Jenny felt sorry for him right away. He seemed so fragile, even in his large frame, that she started crying.

- The boar left. It went charging past Jenny as quickly as it had arrived. The boar looked scared. Its eyes were very large and gleaming. Jenny wished she could put her arms around the boar and convince it she didn't mean it any harm.

- Jenny felt a new understanding for the boar. Now whenever Jenny leaned on the fence, she felt both sad and happy when she thought about the boar. She was glad he wasn't the mean beast she'd imagined, but felt sad that she could never be his friend. He was still wild and didn't understand that she would never hurt him.

Collaborating with Colleagues

You'll probably find that before you can help your children with this minilesson, you need to spend some time with your colleagues developing your own skills at this work. I suggest you reread minilessons from earlier in this series, searching for instances when I have angled a story to make a particular point. Notice exactly what I do to accomplish this goal. For example, in the personal narrative unit, in Session VI, I model how I can tell the same story about the classroom window getting stuck to show two different things. First, I show children how to angle this story so that it's about how broken items in the classroom make it impossible to get through a single lesson. This is how I begin that version:

> Yesterday, our teacher read aloud. It was so hot that sweat
> was rolling down our faces, so our teacher stopped and went
> over to open the window. She pushed. Nothing happened.
> Flakes of paint rained down.

Notice that I include details to show how the window is stuck shut: the teacher pushing and nothing happening, flakes of paint raining down. The emphasis in this story is on the window being beyond repair. Next I tell the same story, but this time I angle it to be about how the class works together, as a community, to overcome problems:

> Yesterday our teacher read aloud. She looked out and saw that
> we had sweat rolling down our cheeks. So she knew she had
> to help us. She went over and tried to open the window. It
> was stuck. Soon Ori had jumped up.

Here, the emphasis is on how members of the class—the teacher, Ori, and, presumably, as the story continues, others—help each other solve problems. Many of the details from the earlier version have been dropped from this new story.

Once you've studied how we have angled stories in minilessons, you'll develop your own list of tips for doing this. My list is given here, but use your own. Next, tell an angled story by working together (orally if it is easier) on a joint text. For example, if you and your colleagues have been pulling your hair out over the pressures wrought by standardized testing, then you could retell a shared moment showing how this is true. You could retell the story of a recent faculty meeting that prioritized standardized tests, using these tips:

- Name what did not happen, but could have happened, in a way that highlights the aspect of this event that you want to highlight.
- Mention the specific actions that further your point and bypass others that don't do this.
- Bring out the internal story—your thoughts, observations, remarks, worries—in a way that allows you to elaborate on the aspect of the story you want told.
- Frame the story with explicit comments that make your point.

Your story might begin like this:

> Last Monday we gathered as usual for our after-
> school faculty meeting. But this time when we
> gathered, no one was smiling and jovial. Ms. X (the
> principal) especially didn't smile. She looked as if she
> were gritting her teeth in anxiety. We sat in our usual
> places, but this time, instead of a gorgeous children's
> book as a place setter, we each had a stack of
> bubble paper and copies of printout tests. "Let's skip
> the usual amenities," Mrs. X said, bypassing all the
> rituals that made us a community. I glanced at my
> grade level colleague and we rolled our eyes. This
> faculty meeting would contain no small-group
> collaboration, no collegiality, no problem solving—it
> would contain none of what sustains us. School systems
> need to realize that tests only wreak havoc on
> morale, dissipate energy, and jettison all that works
> well in schools.

USING SUMMARIES AS EVIDENCE

The Inuit are rumored to have dozens of different words for snow—one for falling snow, one for the last grey patches that remain long after most of winter has melted away, and words for all the kinds of snow in between. Because many Inuit work closely with snow, it makes sense that they have specialized terms for it. Children will need specialized terms for their essay writing as well. When children first learn to write about literature, they will probably talk often about the need to cite evidence (or examples) from the text. The goal will be to "give evidence." Most third, fourth, and fifth graders will not know that, just as the Inuit might call on a specific set of words and phrases to refer to snow, literary essayists draw on a set of terms to help state claims and make cases. Literary essayists have a vocabulary to help us incorporate evidence from a text into an essay. Starting in this session, we'll introduce children to some of this specialized vocabulary.

The majority of this session, however, will be devoted to helping children learn how to summarize bits of a text as evidence to support their theses and claims. In the preceding session, children learned that they can find bits of a text that illustrate the idea they are advancing and then retell those bits as microstories. Today you'll help children learn that as literary essayists they have a palette of optional ways to refer to the text under study. They will sometimes choose to tell a story to make a point, but other times they'll summarize (paraphrase) or quote a section of the text to provide evidence.

IN THIS SESSION, YOU'LL EXPLAIN SUMMARIES AND OFFER AN EXAMPLE, THEN DEMONSTRATE HOW ESSAYISTS USE SUMMARIES TO HELP THEM SUPPORT THEIR POINTS. YOU'LL OUTLINE THE STEPS CHILDREN CAN TAKE TO CREATE SUMMARIES FOR THEIR ESSAYS.

GETTING READY

- Example of a paragraph that summarizes a book, transcribed onto chart paper
- Passages from "Spaghetti," by Cynthia Rylant, transcribed onto chart paper and as a handout
- Example of a paragraph that summarizes an episode from "Spaghetti" as supporting evidence for an idea
- Transitional Phrases to Link Evidence in Essays chart
- See CD-ROM for resources

MINILESSON

Using Summaries as Evidence

CONNECTION

Point out to children a place in their lives where they encounter summaries. Tell them that essayists use summaries just as they use stories to support their claims.

"Have you ever asked a little kid—say a five- or six- or seven-year-old kid—'What was the television show about?' and then had the kid take this huge breath of air and start off, telling one thing and then the next, the next, on and on and on? After a bit, you interject and say, 'So how did it end?' because you're trying to nudge the child to finish the retelling. Well, today I want to tell you that what you wanted the kid to give you—what you expected when you asked the question, 'What was the show about?'—was a summary. You hoped for a brief, encapsulated synthesis of the plot. You hoped for something resembling the blurb on the back cover of a book."

"I want to talk to you about summaries today, because all year long I've nudged you to storytell, not to summarize. Today, I want to take that all back and teach you that essayists sometimes decide to storytell and sometimes decide to summarize—and we need to be skilled at doing both."

"Essayists make choices. When we want to cite evidence (or give an example), we can decide to *storytell* the detailed, step-by-step timeline of what happened first, next, next—or we can quickly *summarize* just the main highlights. These are closely related but distinctly different ways to bring bits of a text into our literary essays."

Name the teaching point. Specifically, tell children that writers use summaries to support their claims.

"Today I will teach you that literary essayists often summarize bits of a text. When we summarize a story, we convey a miniature version of a text. We mostly use our own words, but we also often borrow a few specific words from the story—words that capture the feel of the story's language."

TEACHING

Explain the elements of a summary and offer an example.

"A few years ago, hundreds of New York City teachers created a list of books that we hoped our city's mayor would put in every classroom across the city. The mayor did put

COACHING

You'll recall that earlier in this series I stressed that writers show, not tell, and then later I recapitulated, pointing out that although that is an adage of good writing, it is nevertheless true that writers actually show and tell. Now I'm going to—in a similar fashion—retrieve summarizing from the "reject" pile, and teach the craft and purpose of a summary.

those books in classrooms, and the teachers produced the series *Field Guides to the Classroom Library* that gave teachers and children just a glimpse of each book's contents. What these teachers and I wrote were summaries, and I want to share one with you. It's a summary of a book you know well: Karen Hesse's *Come On, Rain*."

"I want you to notice that this summary, like most summaries, tells the main features of the story. Usually that will mean that a summary captures the main character, conveying his or her traits and motivations. The summary will capture the story's setting, too, and the main sequence of events, especially those that involve a struggle and a resolution. I also want you to notice that often a story summary will use a few words from the text in a way that captures the tone and color of the text. Listen, then, for the elements of story, the story language. In a minute, I'm going to ask you to try to create an even more miniature version of this summary."

Turning the pad of chart paper, I read this summary:

> This jewel of a book uses poetic language to tell the story of a little girl, Tessie, who lives in the sweltering hot city. From her apartment balcony, Tessie stares past chimneys and roof tops to see, way off in the distance, a bunch of grey clouds bulging under a purple sky. Tessie whispers, "Come on, Rain!" Soon Tessie and her friends are in bathing suits, waiting for the rain, which finally comes after great longing. "The first drops plop down big, making dust dance all around us," Tessie says, and soon the Mamas have thrown off their shoes and stockings and joined the girls in a glorious dance through puddles. After the joyful rain celebration, Tessie and her mom head home "fresh as dew."

"Do you see how just that short little bit of text about *Come On, Rain* captures the important parts of the whole story? That's what a summary needs to do."

Demonstrate summarizing a short episode from a known text.

"Let's pretend we have claimed that Gabriel, in 'Spaghetti,' is determined, and let's pretend we decide that instead of storytelling the moment when he searches for and finally finds the cat as an example of him being determined, we will *summarize* that episode."

"Okay, we have to summarize that bit of the story that proves that Gabriel is determined. The first thing we need to do is reread the story, marking off the section that describes Gabriel finding the cat—with determination. The sections don't always come right next to each other in the story." With my pen, I highlighted the section of "Spaghetti" in which Gabriel almost missed hearing the cry. I also marked the sections of the text

There are lots of sources you can turn to in order to illustrate the components of book summaries. The American Library Association Web site, http://www.ala.org, contains lots of book lists, many with summaries.

In this minilesson, I demonstrate how I go about summarizing bits of a text. I'm scooting right past a potential lesson, showing children how I go from wanting to show that Gabriel is determined to locating the sections of the text that demonstrate that quality. I'm aware, however, that many children, when looking for evidence of a character trait, would skim through the text looking for explicit mention of that trait (here, determination). When that word isn't mentioned, these children would decide the text doesn't show the trait! This instruction, in this instance, will need to be reserved for small groups.

where Gabriel picked himself up and walked down the street. As I did this, I pointed out that there were sections of the story I wasn't marking.

"What I do next is I think back over what I have read and try to restate it in just a sentence or two, in a way that covers the highlights of it. I want to remember to mention the character, what he wants and does. I might repeat just a very few specific words or phrases from the story that help me summarize it and make my point. For example, the story said that the cry was so small it *could have been the wind,* but Gabriel still picked himself up. I think it is important that a cry as quiet as the wind got him to get up from that stoop! It also says that he didn't just look in the alleys, he *peered* into them. *He peered!* Here's my summary":

> In one section of the story, Gabriel heard a cry as weak as the wind. He was determined, so he picked himself up and started walking in the direction of the cry. He didn't just glance around to find the source of the cry, instead, he peered, determined to see what was making the noise. He didn't see anything but he knew something was there.

Debrief. Point out the steps of summarizing that you took and you expect they will take as they try this strategy for creating evidence for their essays.

"To recap, here's what I do when I want to summarize an episode to use it as evidence to prove an idea":

- I read and find the exact section of a story that supports my point (that Gabriel was determined).
- I reread the section and think about how I could tell it in my own words, more briefly, conveying the main elements of the story.
- I notice and underline the key words in the text.
- I retell the section, trying both to get my point across (that Gabriel's determined) and to recap a bit of the story for people who haven't read it. Although I mostly use my own words, I also incorporate a few key terms and weave in the main idea I want to advance.

ACTIVE ENGAGEMENT
Get children started summarizing another section of the touchstone text. Set them up to do this by recalling the components of a story summary.

"So let's pretend we are writing that Gabriel is a soft-hearted person, and we want to summarize (not storytell) what happened when Gabriel saw the cat and decided to take him in. On your copies of the text, would you and your partner mark the sections of 'Spaghetti' that show he is soft-hearted? These will be the sections that, for now, you want to summarize."

It is important to stress that a literary essayist often lifts key words from a text, bringing those words into the essay itself. Children may worry about plagiarism, and it is true that a writer doesn't borrow more than four or five consecutive words without using quotation marks, but this doesn't mean there's a problem with lifting a sprinkling of key words.

In this instance, I am teaching a few complex ideas at once. For example, it is complex enough to simply teach children to summarize—and I am teaching them to summarize in an angled fashion to make a specific point. You may decide to teach summary at another time—perhaps during reading—so that this minilesson isn't too ambitious. If you are teaching children to summarize a story, it can help to teach them that a summary usually answers the who, where, when, why, and how questions. Alternatively, it can help to teach them that a summary is generally structured like a tiny story, containing a character who has traits and motivations, and who goes through a struggle and changes in the process.

You may decide that during this Active Engagement, you'd like to switch to another text altogether. You could ask children to think of a part of the story that they could cite as evidence for a claim you state, and to summarize that part of the story. Alternatively, you could ask them to try this with a fairy tale.

"Reread the section and think how it conveys elements of story—a character who wants something, does this and then this, and perhaps changes. Now will you circle any exact words that either help your case or that capture the flavor of the excerpt?" I waited a few minutes while the children worked in pairs. Then I said, "Thumbs up if you've done this." Most of the children indicated they were done. "Okay, writers, now would you write in the air a summary of this section, weaving in the idea that he was soft-hearted. Start by saying: 'Gabriel is soft-hearted. In one section of the story, Gabriel . . . .'"

Present the thinking of the group for comment. Demonstrate that after we write a summary, we have the opportunity to revise it.

As I listened, children summarized. I then convened the class, and retold (and improved upon) one child's summary. "I heard many of you summarize like this," I said:

> Gabriel is a soft-hearted boy. In one section of the story, Gabriel saw a scrawny kitten. Gabriel held the kitten next to his cheek. It smelled of pasta so he named it that, and it purred.

"After we write a summary, we often reread it to see what we could delete. You could, of course, do this," and I deleted some phrases before their eyes, resulting in this summary:

> Gabriel, a soft-hearted boy, picked up a scrawny kitten that smelled of pasta and held it against his cheek.

LINK
Remind children of the repertoire of options before them.

"Writers, artists make masterpieces by drawing on a palette of colors, and today when you collect more evidence for your files, you'll draw on a palette of choices. You may write ministories to illustrate your topic sentences, filing each one in your folder for all the writing that goes with that topic sentence. On the other hand, you may take some time to reread one of the stories you have already written and decide to angle that story to bring out the idea you want to advance. Or you may decide that instead of storytelling to make your point, you'll summarize bits of the text. Whenever you write literary essays, you'll want to remember that as a writer you have options. You need to provide evidence from the text to support your claims, but you can do so by telling stories or by summarizing portions of the text, among other options."

You could say, "Let's try this with 'The Three Little Pigs' . Let's say your claim is that the three pigs work hard to be safe from the wolf. Can you summarize the part of the story that illustrates this claim? I've got copies of the fairy tale if you need it."

The work you are asking children to do is very complex. Expect rough approximations. It would help if you find summaries elsewhere and point them out to the class.

Your children may not know the term "palette." When this is the case, tuck a synonym into your sentence and use gestures and drama to help convey your meaning. But don't detour around unfamiliar words!

WRITING AND CONFERRING

Summarizing to Support a Claim

To help Tyler, Rebecca, and John understand how to summarize in ways that develop a claim, I convened them into a small group. "Let's practice together first by differentiating between how a writer storytells and summarizes. Let's take something—anything—you guys did together. Say . . . what you did in art class this morning. (For now, we'll pretend you aren't making a special point about art.)"

"If you want to storytell the events of this morning's art class, first recall what you did. (I gave them a few seconds to do this.) Now go back to the start of art class when Mrs. Pressley walked into our room. Can you recall her entering, dragging that cart behind her? Make a movie in your mind of it." I gave them a moment to do this. "Okay, Rebecca, storytell art class, starting with, 'I heard a bump on our door and looked up to see Mrs. Pressley pushing through the door, dragging the art cart.' What did she say or do?"

Rebecca continued, "She said we were going to make God's eyes today, and asked if we ever made them. Then she showed us some God's eyes. She said, 'Aren't they beautiful?' Then she passed out two sticks to each of us."

Taking over because I wanted the story to be especially drawn-out and step-by-step, I added, "Then she passed out a pattern, didn't she? Then she passed out the yarn. Then she showed us how to attach the yarn to the stick. Then she showed us how to turn the yarn to get our God's eyes started. Then she showed us how to change yarns. She called it magic."

As Rebecca and I storytold, I scrawled the main events that we repeated onto the pages. Turning to the group, I said, "Now let's try to summarize this," and I gestured toward the list. "Before we do, would you think about where there are places in this version that Rebecca and I detailed in a step-by-step, drawn-out way that could instead be described in a phrase. Like instead of saying, 'I went on the swings, the seesaw, the slide,' I could say, 'I played on the playground equipment.'"

Children agreed that the summary could say that the teacher passed out the supplies (not listing each item) and gave directions (instead of listing each instruction). Then the youngsters worked with partners to jot down a summary. Most went something like this:

MID-WORKSHOP TEACHING POINT   *Linking a Sequence of Summaries*   "Writers, can I have your eyes and your attention? Earlier today I taught you *how* writers summarize episodes from a story, but I didn't teach you *why* we do this. Usually we decide to summarize episodes because no single example is powerful enough to make our point, and therefore we gather a few examples, chaining them together. So, for example, if I wanted to convey that Gabriel is lonely, I might decide that it would be hard to write really well about Gabriel sitting alone on the stoop; I might instead decide to summarize a few different examples that showed his loneliness."

"Max, for example, has a folder titled, 'Rachel realizes when you are 11, you are also 10, 9, 8 . . .' He decided to summarize a time when Rachel feels younger than she is. So he wrote this":

> In the story, Rachel sits at her desk staring at the nasty red sweater Mrs. Price made her keep. She was disgusted with it and wanted to cry like she was three.

continued on next page

Today in art, Mrs. Pressley told us we'd make God's eyes and showed us examples. Then she passed out the supplies and gave us directions.

"Now let's try something trickier," I said. "You just summarized *everything* that happened in art. You could, instead, summarize those things that support a claim that you have about art class. Then you would need to pick and choose what to say. Let's imagine you wanted to say, 'It is hard for Mrs. Pressley to teach art from a cart,' and you wanted to explain that lots of time is taken up just giving out stuff. How might you summarize that part of art class in a sentence or two that makes your point?"

The children looked back on the storytold version. I called on John, reminding him to start by saying his claim. He said:

It is hard for Mrs. Pressley to have art on the cart. Today in art she had to pass out about five things so we could make God's eyes.

"Let's say we want to make the point that having art supplies on a cart is hard by writing a couple of summaries in a row," I said. "What *else* happened in art that shows it is hard to have it on a cart?"

Then children recalled the way art class had ended, and soon had written a chain of two summaries to make their point:

It is hard for Mrs. Pressley to have art on the cart. Today in art she had to pass out about five things so we could make God's eyes. At the end of art, we weren't done and we couldn't leave them in the room, so we had to mark which God's eye was ours, and that is hard because you can't write on yarn. She couldn't fit them all on the cart so some of us carried them to her closet.

"So now," I said, "could you turn to your writing, think about what you'll do next, and get started while I watch."

"My hunch is that if you've collected one summary, you'll probably find that there is another episode in the story you could also summarize to help you make the same point. If so, you'll want to use a transitional phrase such as Max used when he said, 'There are other sections of the story where Rachel . . .' and 'For example . . .' and 'Another example is when . . . .' Or like Diana did when she said, 'At the beginning of the story, Jenny . . .' and 'Later . . . .' I've written several transitions on chart paper—you can use these to help you now and whenever you write essays! Essayists have special words they use to help them, and little by little we'll learn lots of those words in this unit."

continued from previous page

"Then Max wrote":

There are other sections of the story where Rachel understands that when you are eleven, you are also all the ages inside. For example, she says "When you are scared and need to sit on your Mama's lap, that is the part of you that is still five." And another example is, "When you say something stupid, that is the part of you that is still three."

"So Max has strung together three examples, one of which is a summary, all of which prove his point."

"Diana has a folder on 'Boar Out There' titled 'Jenny imagines that the boar is ferocious and special.' Diana compiled a list of instances in the story when Jenny thinks about the boar in ways that support this claim. Then she summarized each of those two parts. She wrote this":

At the beginning of the story, Jenny imagines the boar as a wild and ferocious beast. For example, early on, she leans against the fence and whispers to the boar, and pictures that he is fierce. Jenny also imagines the boar as magical, with a golden horn.

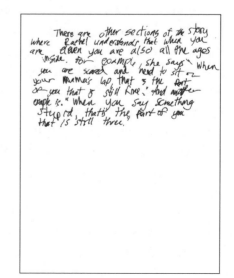

Fig. X-1 Max's examples

SHARE

Studying Collections of Entries

Ask children to study and talk over their work with their partners, paying careful attention to the parts of the essays they've worked on to date.

"Writers, last night for homework you studied Jill's essay, and looked especially closely at the way in which she used stories to support her topic sentences. It seems to me that we need to also study *your* work, because so many of you have found wise ways to use both stories and summaries to support your claims. Would you share your stories and summaries with your partner? Just as you noticed Jill's thesis statement and her topic sentences, would you notice each other's thesis statements and topic sentences? Notice your stories, too, and your summaries. Talk in detail about the ways in which you've angled these to support your topic sentences. If you've neglected to write a sentence after your story or summary that refers back to the topic sentence, help each other to do so." The children shared, and I listened in.

⊙ [HOMEWORK] *Using Quotations as Evidence* Jill did something in the exemplar piece we have been studying that some, but not all, of you have done. She included a quoted section from her story in her essay. Read Jill's essay again and notice that she has used a quotation that is a complete sentence—it doesn't rely on Jill's words to prop it up. It stands alone, even though it has ellipses showing that a section of the sentence has been left out.

Jill could have *instead* written with a partial quote, lifting just a phrase from "Eleven" as I do here: "Rachel was unhappy putting on a sweater that wasn't hers. She thought it was disgusting to put on a sweater that was 'full of germs' that weren't even hers." That phrase, *full of germs*, isn't a full sentence, it is just a few words that support your claim. Essayists use both kinds of quotations.

Find a few different sections from the text you have been studying that you could quote to support your claim. Copy those sections onto separate pages to file in the folders you've made for each supporting section. Bring them to school tomorrow and file them in your folders.

If your students are not seeing a difference between storytelling and summarizing . . .
you might design a minilesson to help them see the difference. It might go something like
this: "Writers, I am blown away by the stories and summaries that you are telling to support
your ideas. And most of you are telling these in ways that highlight the meaning you are
trying to show!"

"One thing I've learned about writing about reading is that our readers don't always
notice what we want them to notice. Yesterday when I was reading an essay in the *New York
Times* about Lance Armstrong, I read quickly and when my friend and I were talking about
it, I realized I'd completely missed the part where the writer said Lance Armstrong is a hero
of our country!"

"When you write your literary essays, you need to keep in mind that your readers might
be in a hurry and do the same thing. They might fly right past whatever you have said. The
way you can help prevent that is to unpack your stories or your summaries and stretch them
out a bit."

"For example, earlier we summarized part of 'Spaghetti' like this:"

> In one section of the story, Gabriel heard a cry as weak as the wind. Still, he got himself
> up and started walking in the direction of the cry. He didn't just glance around, he
> peered, and when he saw the cat waiting, he was amazed. (That's the summary.)

"Now, watch what I add on to the end of that story as I unpack it so that my readers
really get my point:"

> This episode is important because Gabriel might have just looked up and then
> returned to his daydreaming. But instead he went forward, into the gray street.
> Most people wouldn't have done that—they'd have chickened out or ignored the cry.
> Gabriel did not. This proves he was determined to find out what the cry was.

Teaching writers to summarize has implications across the curriculum, and it will be
important for you to show children how they can summarize in math, social studies, and
science as well as in literary essays. Although all year long you will have taught children to
write with details, summaries are a place where generalizations can be helpful. Show
children that they can describe the step-by-step sequence that occurred in a specific battle at
the start of the Revolutionary War—say, at the Battle of Bunker Hill or the Battle of
Lexington—or they can, alternatively, say something general that acts like the overview on
the back of the DVD box, conveying the main idea of those early battles.

COLLABORATING WITH COLLEAGUES

In today's minilesson, you taught children that when they want to support an idea by citing evidence from the text, they can summarize or storytell to make a point. In a study group with colleagues, you will probably want to consider ways to use the reading workshop and read-aloud time to help children develop the requisite skills.

For example, it's not necessarily easy to read a text and find specific instances that support a specific idea. In today's minilesson, I suggested that I could show that Gabriel is determined by showing that he persisted in tracking down the source of the sound he heard. It's important to bear in mind that it's no easy matter for a child to recognize that Gabriel's tenacious search for the source of the noise shows determination. Many children would survey the details of this vignette, see that Gabriel is not described as determined, and decide this episode can't be used to support the claim that Gabriel is determined.

Some children, then, will find it very challenging to locate sections of the text that support a claim they've made. You and your colleagues can consider

Examples of Increasingly Advanced Textual References

1. Gabriel is determined. An example is when he finds the cat.

2. Gabriel is determined. We see this when he looks and looks for the cat.

3. Gabriel is determined. When he hears a cry, he gets up to look for what is making the sound. He peers into the alley. He finds the cat.

4. Gabriel is determined. When he hears a cry, he doesn't just glance around for the source of it. He actually gets up and walks down the street, looking for the source. He doesn't just glance in the alleys—he peers into them. When he hears the noise a second time, he walks faster and searches more. Other people might just glance around, looking for the source of the noise, but Gabriel's determination makes him look until he spots the tiny kitten.

ways to teach the requisite skills during your read-aloud. For instance, you might pause in the midst of reading and ask yourself, aloud, "So what kind of person does this character seem to be?" You could proceed to demonstrate developing a theory, generating a variety of words that could possibly suffice, and then read on, saying, "Let's see if the upcoming text supports or challenges that theory."

Of course, as you read on, chances are good that nothing in the text will exactly match the words you've used to characterize the character, so you can show children the process of weighing whether or not an event in the story can function as evidence for the theory the class is advancing.

Similarly, you may want to suggest that children record on sticky notes the ideas they form as they read their independent books. When children are midway into a book, they can reread all their notes, thinking, "So what is one big idea that feels important to this whole story?" Again you could suggest that children read on, expecting the upcoming text to either support or challenge their theories. They may, in fact, want to create "theory charts," accumulating page numbers that support, extend, revise, or dispute their theories.

In these ways, then, you and your colleagues can invent ways to be sure that the work you are doing in the writing workshop pertains also to the reading workshop. If you want to go a step farther and use summarizing in the context of a reading workshop, you could show children how to transform a theory chart into a summary.

You and your colleagues will want to work together to develop wise responses to the summaries your children produce. It can help to spend time talking about what it might look like for children to progress from beginning-level summaries to more intermediate-level summaries, and from intermediate to advanced summaries. Then you'll need to imagine specific ways in which a child's efforts could become more skilled.

You can create such a ladder of difficulty by collecting examples from your children's work and thinking, "Is this a more mature version? How so?" In this way, you can slot children's work into a ladder of development . . . and design teaching that helps children progress along a pathway you've imagined.

USING LISTS AS EVIDENCE

When this nation was young, *rhetoric was part of each school's core curriculum. Children grew up with as firm a foundation in oration as in multiplication. In school, they learned to articulate their ideas loudly and clearly, using their voices to gather and command attention and to rally listeners to action.*

Essay writing was inexorably linked to public speaking. Children delivered their essays at speaking contests, and learned to write in ways that would appeal to the ear. Perhaps for this reason, parallelism is a crucial part of many essays—and many speeches. Think of the greatest, most memorable speeches you can, and you'll probably find yourself remembering lines that were repeated: "Ask not what your country can do for you, ask what you can do for your country" and "I have a dream."

Today's work with lists invites children to use the parallelism of the list structure to bring rhetorical power to their writing. This session also invites children to write with attentiveness to sound as well as to meaning.

IN THIS SESSION, YOU'LL REMIND CHILDREN OF WORK THEY DID DURING THE PERSONAL ESSAY UNIT IN USING LISTS TO SUPPORT THEIR CLAIMS. YOU'LL AGAIN ENCOURAGE THEM TO WRITE "TIGHT LISTS" IN WHICH THEY WRITE WITH PARALLELISM.

GETTING READY

- Examples of well-known repeating phrases from familiar children's texts
- "Spaghetti," by Cynthia Rylant, and "The Marble Champ," by Gary Soto
- Example of a thesis used as the repeating chorus for a list
- Example of one student's thesis and supporting ideas, written on chart paper, from which the whole class can develop a list using parallel structure to support a claim
- Types of Evidence to Support Claims, listed on chart paper
- See CD-ROM for resources

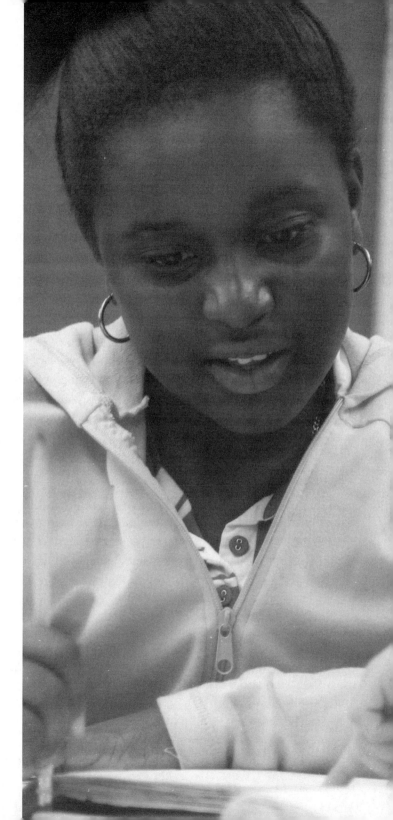

Minilesson

Using Lists as Evidence

Connection

Celebrate children's powerful read-aloud voices. Point out that the repetitive phrases in the books children are reading act as signals for how to read in powerful ways.

"The other day I listened while you read aloud books to your first-grade reading buddies. Every one of you read aloud really well. Your voices were rhythmic and flowing, and you used your voices to hold parts of the books together. I've been thinking about the read-aloud voices you use when you work with first graders, and it occurs to me that you don't use equally powerful voices when you read your own writing aloud. Part of the secret may be that many of the books you read to your reading buddies contain lists, held together with repetitive phrases, and those repetitive phrases help you read aloud in powerful ways."

"'When I'm five . . .' one book says, listing over and over what the young narrator will do when she is five years old. 'When I was young in the mountains . . .' is the refrain in Cynthia Rylant's list of memories from when she was young, growing up in the mountains of Appalachia. We all know the famous words of 'The Little Engine That Could': 'I think I can, I think I can.' When texts contain lists held together by phrases or repeating lines, it's almost as if the texts become a song containing a chorus."

Name your teaching point. Specifically, remind children that their writing should appeal not only to the eye but also to the ear. Lists, held together by repeating phrases or lines, can hold an essay together.

"I'm telling you this because as writers you need to remember that you are writing not only for readers' eyes but also for their *ears*. And readers' ears welcome lists and repetition. Lists, held together by repeating lines, can hold an essay together, just as repeating verses can hold a song together."

Teaching

Demonstrate that literary essayists often use a claim, a thesis, as the repeating chorus for a list. Then show students that any important simple sentence can be used to create and extend a list.

"Often when writing literary essays you'll find yourself making a claim. That claim might be your thesis or one of your bullet points (these become topic sentences), or it could just be a claim that you make in the middle of a paragraph. Either way, once you've made a

COACHING

Initially, I'd also written an example from my family, but I try to delete any example that doesn't contribute something new. This is the deleted example:

"In my family, my brothers and sisters seem to know all the verses to every Christmas carol. Meanwhile, I often stumble along through those verses. But when the chorus comes, I'm always happy. The repetition of those lines allows me to join in heartily to sing 'Oh! Jingle bells, jingle bells, jingle all the way . . .' or 'Oh-oh, Star of wonder, Star of night, Star with royal beauty bright. Westward leading, still proceeding, Guide us to thy Perfect Light.'"

This session introduces a skill which has turned out to be more challenging for youngsters than I ever anticipated. You'll invent your own adaptations.

claim, stated an idea, you can often use that claim as the basis for a list. For example, let's take the claim, 'Gabriel is lonely.' Once I have a claim, I think to myself, 'How could I extend this claim by adding some detail?' I'd probably think, 'I could list *times* when he's lonely, *places* where he's lonely, or *reasons* why he's lonely!' Then I could take one of these and try it. I'll think about times when Gabriel is lonely. As I write my list, I lift specific terms and details from the text itself. The list, then, is less original than it might seem."

"You should notice that I develop a claim into a list in the same ways that I develop a thesis. Earlier we learned that after we have made a claim (My father's been an important teacher), we can think of reasons (because he taught me to write, to fail, and to be my own person). Alternatively, we can think of times—instances—or of parts; the work I do here is reminiscent of that."

"For example, we could instead have said, 'Gabriel is lonely because he lives alone, Gabriel is lonely because he's isolated by his classmates, Gabriel is lonely because he distances himself even from the people who are around him.'"

> Gabriel is lonely when he eats his butter sandwich at school.
>
> Gabriel is lonely when he sits on the stoop outside his building.
>
> Gabriel is lonely when he walks the dark street, peering into alleys.

"I can create a list by starting with almost any claim, any sentence that conveys one of my ideas and feels important. I just need to think, 'Can I repeat part of this sentence in a way that creates echo lines?' For example, I could write":

> Gabriel doesn't mind that the kitten smells like pasta.

"Then I could try extending this. When I go to do this, I have no idea what I will say, but I just repeat the phrase I've chosen and squeeze my brain to see if I can come up with something":

> Gabriel doesn't mind that the kitten smells like pasta.
>
> Gabriel doesn't mind that kitten's legs are wobbly.
>
> Gabriel doesn't mind that the kitten meows pitifully.

Much of education includes learning to apply what one already knows to new situations. When children learned to plan an essay by considering whether they could support their claim with reasons, times, or places, they can apply this to lots of different situations.

ACTIVE ENGAGEMENT
Enlist children to work in pairs, helping a classmate write a list, with support from you.

"Let's help Harrison write a list. His thesis is this":

> Lupe overcomes her athletic difficulties through hard
> work and family support.

"Remember yesterday, we heard Harrison's story of the father at dinner time, agreeing to come to Lupe's game? Well, today Harrison wants to list other ways in which Lupe's family supports her. Harrison has already reread the story and looked for and starred sentences that show what Lupe's family did to support her." I read aloud from chart paper:

> So Lupe ... listened to her brother, who gave her tips on
> how to shoot: get low, aim with one eye, and place one
> knuckle on the ground.
>
> (The father) even hung some lights in the backyard so
> she could practice after dark.
>
> (The mother) asked why her thumb was swollen.

"So writers, can you help Harrison turn these into a list? Your items won't necessarily progress in this order, and you needn't include all of this data, or use these exact words. Work with a partner to decide first on the repeating stem, then plug in the details. Turn and talk."

The children immediately began talking. Many of them simply lined up these excerpts, using the exact words of the text.

Intervene to lift the level of the children's work. In this instance, remind them that for the most part, their lists will contain their words, not the words of the text they are referencing.

"Writers, can I stop you? The author, Gary Soto, may have used beautiful words, but your essay can't just repeat his story. You will need to *replace* many of his words with your words! That's hard to do, I know, because it feels almost arrogant. It's easy to think, 'His words work so well; why get rid of them?' But remember, *you* have an angle on this that you want to bring out—you are trying to highlight how helpful Lupe's family has been—so that's one reason to use your own words. Go back and work some more."

Notice that during an Active Engagement, we do everything possible to set children up for success with the strategy we've taught. Typically, we do half the task, leaving the children with only the part of the task that is most pertinent to that lesson. In this instance, Harrison and I fed the children the data to draw upon in making their lists, and got them started with an initial claim that they could build upon with success. The examples we've provided could be channeled into a list of people who support Lupe, of times when the family supports her, or of places or ways in which the family supports her.

You will want to watch for times when children's work during the Active Engagement is not exactly what you want. You can intervene, coaching the class as a whole with more specific pointers, and let them have a second go at whatever you are hoping they practice.

After children had worked for a bit longer, I said, "Let's listen to the lists a couple of you suggest for Harrison." Soon we'd heard (and I'd charted) these lists:

- Lupe's brother gave her tips on shooting well, Lupe's father gave her lights for practicing in the dark, Lupe's mother gave her attention.

- Lupe's family gave her tips, materials, and interest.

- Her family did all they could. Her brother told her tips, her father rigged some night lights, her mother tried not to doubt her too much.

- Lupe's family supported her with tips on shooting low and with one eye, with lights for practicing late at night, and with observations of her thumb.

LINK
Remind children of the options they have when collecting material to support their topic sentences.

"Writers, today, and whenever you write literary essays, you'll draw on lots of different options as you collect material to gather in your files. Some of you may draft and revise *stories* to support your topic sentences, rewriting those stories so they are angled to make your point. Some of you will *summarize* a bunch of small sections that illustrate your point. And some of you will try your hand at writing *lists* using parallel structure. You'll want to write several items for each folder today."

Types of Evidence to Support Claims
- Stories
- Summaries
- Lists

Try creating a list yourself before you read the children's ideas, because you want to be able to say to a child in a conference, "Might you want your list to go something like this?" and then get them started with the first two items in a list.

When you cite options, those choices should be on a chart, and you'll want to gesture toward the chart as you speak. Make it likely that children will rely on it as a resource.

WRITING AND CONFERRING

Arguing on the Page

As you confer, be sure that you are helping children draw from their entire repertoire of ways to collect evidence. You'll want to begin every conference by asking the writer what he is working on. Richard looked up from Cynthia Rylant's story "Slower Than the Rest" to say, "I am proving that Charlie matches the turtle 'cause they are both slow. I'm not sure if it is a summary or a story because it is a little of both." He showed me what he had written:

> Leo said that "It wasn't fair for the slow ones." This shows that Leo hates being slow. He thinks that it isn't fair for the slow ones. Leo talked about how there are great things about Charlie. He was really saying that even slow kids have things that they are good at. Charlie represented Leo and all of the other slow kids in Leo's class.

I asked Richard what he thought of what he'd written, and he said it was good but he had more stuff to say and hadn't figured out how to put it—whether it was a list or a summary or whatever.

"Richard," I responded, "you have just taught me something that I need to tell the kids. Because when I tell you about the different kinds of things you can collect in your files, I definitely do *not* want you to be so worried about whether you are writing this kind of thing or that kind of thing that you focus on the rules for how to write rather than on what you really want to say! I am so glad that your mind is fired up about this story. That is like you: You always are someone who pushes yourself to have smart ideas on any and every topic. That is a great gift of yours. Different people have different talents, and your talent is that you have so, so much to say. Never forget that."

Then, shifting from the compliment section of the conference to the teaching part, I said, "And I need you to know that another way to fill up your files is to talk on the page, saying whatever it is you'd say if you were arguing your point and wanted to be sure people understood your claim." To get him started and to test whether my advice would work, I said, "Can you and I just talk together a bit about this story— writers sometimes do that; we find a friend who is interested and we talk over what we are going to write. So tell me more about Charlie the turtle, representing Leo the boy, and them both feeling trapped. Is this story saying it is really awful to be slow?"

"Yes and no. 'Cause when Leo said that Charlie (that's the turtle) was sluggish, he said, 'It wasn't fair for

---

MID-WORKSHOP TEACHING POINT · *Arguing and Collecting Like Essayists* "Writers, can I have your eyes and your attention please? I want to remind you of something that the writer Philip Lopate said in his preface to a book entitled *Best Essays of 1999*. Lopate read thousands of essays in order to select the very best for his anthology, and from all that reading he learned that very few things can be said about all essays. Essays are different, one from another. Some contain long narratives; some take inventory (like a shopkeeper takes inventory of merchandise). But Lopate does say that *all* essays are both arguments and collections."

"I want to suggest that all of you in this class are natural at doing both things. You argued very convincingly for an extra-long recess yesterday, in fact. And you are born

continued on next page

> Leo said that "It wasn't fair for the slow ones." This shows that Leo hates being slow He thinks that it isn't fair for the slow ones. Leo talked about how there are great things about Charlie. He was really saying that even slow kids have things that they are good at. Charlie represented Leo and all of the other slow kids in Leo's class.

Fig. XI-1 Richard's notebook entries

the slow ones,' but he also talked about the good things for Charlie. 'Cause Charlie was a phenomenal turtle and he helped Leo win an award."

"So why do you think Rylant put a turtle in here," I asked, "and not a frog?"

"Because turtles are slow like Leo and she wanted Charlie to be like the slow kids."

"You mean, she wanted to use Charlie as a metaphor for the slow kids, so as to teach a lesson about slow kids not being only slow?" I replied, tucking some literary language into my retelling of what Richard had just said. Then I added, "You definitely need to write this." I pushed paper in front of Richard. Before he resumed work, I said, "You could start one entry, on one of these pieces of paper, by saying, 'You might ask, "Why did Rylant decide to make Leo a turtle?"' because essayists do that; we take other people's questions and put them right into our essays." This is what Richard gathered: *[Fig. XI-2]*

> Leo said that "It wasn't fair for the slow ones." This shows that Leo hates being slow. He thinks it isn't fair for the slow ones. Leo talked about how there are great things about Charlie. He was really saying that even slow kids have things they are good at. Charlie represented Leo and all of the other slow kids in Leo's class.
>
> You might ask, "Why did Cynthia Rylant decide to make Leo find a turtle and not a frog?" The reason is because turtles are slow animals just like Leo. Cynthia Rylant wanted to use Charlie as a metaphor for slow kids.

Later, when I saw Richard's work, I turned what he'd done into a brief Mid-Workshop Teaching Point, reminding Richard and all the other kids of a few things. First, sometimes they will simply have ideas pertaining to one of their claims, and it is a great thing to fill their folders with those ideas, not worrying whether those ideas are written as a list, a summary, a story, or whatever. And if a child wants to realize that he or she has lots of ideas, it can help to talk to someone about the story. Then, too, if people in those discussions ask us questions about our ideas, we can record the questions and our answers to them. Often these make very strong additions to an essay.

continued from previous page

collectors—as is clear from the pins and badges on your backpacks, the songs on your iPods. Because you are already good collectors, could you look over your files and think, 'What else could I collect that might help me make my case?' Because as essayists, we especially collect evidence and ideas that will help us make our cases, win our arguments."

"In the end, an essayist is like a trial lawyer. You will go before a jury (yours will be a jury of readers) and you will argue for your claim. Adam will argue that Mrs. Price took her fury out on Rachel who, in turn, passed it on to others. Jill will argue that 'Eleven' is about a girl who struggles to hold on to herself. Many of you will make claims about other stories. Either way, each of you will each make an argument and will hope to be convincing. Like Perry Mason, you will present evidence to support your claim—and to do that, you need to collect! You need to decide what to collect, too; I have given you some ideas, but in the end you need to collect whatever ideas, facts, information, or observations can allow you to make your case. Right now, would you talk with your partner about the collecting you plan to do, and make yourself a planning box?"

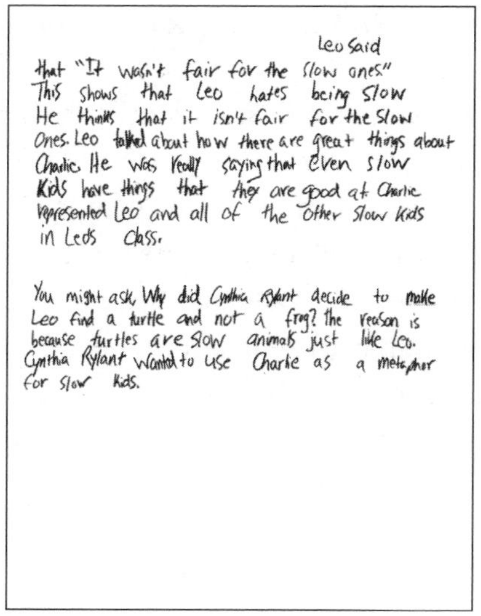
Leo Said that "It wasn't fair for the slow ones." This shows that Leo hates being slow He thinks that it isn't fair for the Slow Ones. Leo talked about how there are great things about Charlie. He was really saying that even slow Kids have things that they are good at Charlie represented Leo and all of the other Slow kids in Leos class.

You might ask, Why did Cynthia Rylant decide to make Leo find a turtle and not a frog? The reason is because turtles are slow animals just like Leo. Cynthia Rylant wanted to use Charlie as a metaphor for slow kids.

Fig. XI-2 Richard's notebook entries

SHARE

Reading Lists Aloud

Gather children on the rug with their list work from today. Ask them to take a list they've written and practice reading it really well to themselves and to a partner.

"Writers often read their work aloud, so we can hear the words we've written, to hear how they sound—and lists especially are meant to be read aloud. So let's do this Share like a symphony. Each of you, and your lists, will be a part of the music we create. So take a second and find, in your files, a list you wrote today that you really like."

"First, you need to practice reading your list aloud *really* well. You won't want to read it like this." I read the first part of my list very quickly, running the words together as if they were one word: "'Gabriel is lonely when he sits on the stoop outside his building. Gabriel is lonely when he eats his butter sandwich at school.' Instead I will want to read my list as if the words are worth a million dollars." (This time I read my list slowly and rhythmically—giving each word weight.)

"Practice reading one of your lists to yourself in your head before we begin," I said, and gave them a minute to do so. "Now would you work with your partner? Give each other help and advice, so each person's words sound as wonderful as they can be."

After a few minutes, remind children how the symphony works, and elicit their contributions.

"I'll be the conductor. When I gesture to you with my baton, read your list aloud in your best voice. Do this even if it is practically the same as a list we heard previously. Remember, in a musical symphony, the composer uses a repetition of phrases to make the symphony sound beautiful and resonate for the listener!"

I gestured to one child, then another, not in a round-robin fashion and not including every child. For example, I gestured to Judah and she read, "Lupe believes in herself to try and win those academic awards. Lupe believes in herself to work and try to become good. Lupe believes in herself to go to the game and win." Finally, I closed the reading by saying, "The music of words, Room 203."

Not only is this Share lovely and exciting for students, it also helps them develop a felt sense for parallelism in structuring language. Developing this felt sense makes teaching parallelism later much easier. Often, powerful language and powerful structures are easier to feel than to explain.

You may find that one child's lists resemble another's. This is not surprising, considering they are working with the same short texts.

HOMEWORK *Saying Essays Aloud* You've all heard the expression "Practice makes perfect." It's no secret that when you want to get good at something—anything—you need to practice. In the story "The Marble Champ," Lupe, a girl who's never been good at *any* kind of sport, proves that hours of practice can help her overcome the odds. She outshines even the expert marble players at the marbles championship. Lupe doesn't just *decide* to enter the competition and win, though. She spends hours each day for weeks and weeks exercising the precise muscle—her thumb muscle—to perfect the skill of shooting marbles.

It's impossible to master something all at once. Mastery takes time and practice, and practice involves steps. Singers sometimes warm up by singing some scales. Basketball players warm up by shooting some hoops. And writers sometimes warm up by talking in the voice, the persona, we want to assume. Sometimes before I write a minilesson or a letter to your parents, I practice by saying the words aloud to myself. When you wrote personal narratives, you practiced by storytelling to each other, trying to give each other goose bumps, but now that you will be writing a literary essay, you need to practice by using your professor voice.

Tonight, put a fresh sheet of paper in front of you, write your thesis, and write your first topic sentence. Then use your professor voice to fast-write a little lecture on that topic. Do the same for your second topic sentence. As you do this, pretend you are actually giving a little course on your topics. Bring your papers to school. They will be first drafts of your essays!

TAILORING YOUR TEACHING

If you find your children are stuck on old ideas or that the content of their writing isn't as complex as it could be . . . you might suggest that these children spend some time writing simply to think harder about their topics. Sometimes children are so caught up with the structure of essay writing that they don't spend enough time developing their thinking. Freewriting is a great way to get new ideas flowing, to ask questions and entertain answers, and to push thoughts forward. Specifically, children might ask themselves, "Do I believe what I've written?" "What have I not considered in all that I've said?" "Is the opposite of what I'm saying also true?"

If children are quoting whole paragraphs of text from the stories to support their claims . . . you may decide to teach them ways to use only exact, meaningful quotes to support their arguments. When children are first learning to quote, they may be tempted to replace their own writing with large portions of the texts they're writing about. Explain that using quotes often involves going back to the text and taking just bits of it to support, not replace, your argument. For example, a child arguing that Lupe's father in "The Marble Champ" is a supportive, proud father wouldn't cite Soto's entire paragraph on this, but would instead pick parts of it that highlight the thesis. Often this involves a bit of summarizing, interspersed with portions of quotes. Here is an example:

> Lupe's father is incredibly supportive and proud of his daughter. He sacrifices his Saturday racquetball game because "he knew his daughter thought she was no good at sports and he wanted to encourage her." He even goes out of his way to help Lupe practice at night, rigging lights in her backyard. It's clear that Lupe's father is not only supportive but also proud of his daughter, because Gary Soto writes that Lupe's father is "entranced by the sight of his daughter easily beating her brother."

For an Active Engagement, children could take paragraphs such as the above and, in partners, talk about the use of quotation marks and summary to support a claim or topic sentence.

MECHANICS

If you collect your children's folders and pore through them, you'll see that this unit has posed new challenges to your children's command of conventions. You may decide to design minilessons and strategy lessons to address these challenges.

This is probably one of the first times your children will have been asked to craft literary essays. Just as kindergartners and first graders write with incomplete, approximate spellings when writing is new for them, your children will in a similar fashion write with an incomplete and approximate command of the conventions that accompany this form of academic writing. If you decide to address the most common problems that crop up in this unit, the following are some you'll want to highlight.

Past versus Present Tenses   Your children will not know whether to write about a short story in present tense (because Gabriel, in the story, is still there on the page, holding his cat) or in past tense (because it was yesterday that the child read about Gabriel, and the child's life has moved on, and because the author wrote this book long ago). Some children may write in whichever tense the text is written.

When your children are in secondary school, they'll be taught that when retelling what they found in the pages of a story, they should generally use present tense. This is not usually the tense in which the story is written (stories are more often told in past tense). For this reason and others, your children will quite frequently shift between present and past tense, as Max does in this summary:

> In the story, Rachel sits at her desk, staring at the red sweater Mrs. Price made her keep. She was disgusted with it, and wanted to cry like she is three . . . she then realizes that she was not just eleven . . .

Max will need to correct his summary to put it in the present tense:

> Rachel sits at her desk, staring at the red sweater Mrs. Price made her keep. She is disgusted with it, and wants to cry like she is three . . . she then realizes that she is not just eleven . . .

Transitions   Transitions can be tricky, but they are essential to the flow of writing, so make it a priority to help children understand them. Transitions are connections between two thoughts on a page. A transition can be a word, a sentence, or several sentences.

> <u>One example of this</u> is her saying Mrs. Price is older.

> <u>And one more place is</u> when she blabbed and stuttered to Mrs. Price when she wanted to say something.

> <u>It is interesting how she says</u> "because she's older and the teacher, she's right . . . "

> <u>Other parts of the text where I see</u> that Rachel thinks being eleven can be a letdown are "You don't feel eleven . . . "

Pronoun-Verb Agreement Pronoun-verb agreement becomes more complicated when the pronouns are indefinite. You may want to teach your most advanced students that words such as *anybody, anyone, nobody, no one,* and *neither* are all singular. It is correct to say, "Neither of his friends *is* going." When subjects are separated by *or* (as in Paul *or* Jerry) the verb must be singular (is going).

> Gabriel *is* a lonely boy who *wants* company.

> Gabriel and his cat *want* a home, but Gabriel *sits* on the stoop.

USING DESCRIPTIONS OF AUTHOR'S CRAFTSMANSHIP AS EVIDENCE

IN THIS SESSION, YOU WILL TEACH CHILDREN THAT WRITERS STUDY THE CHOICES AUTHORS MAKE IN THEIR TEXTS IN ORDER TO FIND EVIDENCE TO SUPPORT THEIR CLAIMS. YOU WILL SUPPORT CHILDREN IN LEARNING TO DO THIS.

GETTING READY

- "Things," by Eloise Greenfield
- Your own thesis and supporting folders related to "Things"
- Recording of a talk or lecture, demonstrating a "professor's voice"
- See CD-ROM for resources

Literary essays, historical essays, and personal essays all resemble each other. In each one, the writer articulates a claim and several subordinate ideas. To support their ideas, writers draw on anecdotes, quotations, lists of examples, and so forth.

One of the few features that set literary essays apart from other essays is this: Literary essayists pay attention to the author's craftsmanship and to the literary devices an author has used. That is, the writer of a literary essay notices not only what a text says, but also how the text creates emphasis and meaning.

In this session, you'll teach young essayists that they are wise to notice not only the content but also the craftsmanship of the text under study. The session could introduce a whole series of minilessons (teachers of middle-school students may decide to stretch this one session into several). For most elementary-school classrooms, however, it's enough to expose children to the notion that they will want to notice how an author uses literary devices to convey the deeper meanings in a text.

MINILESSON

Using Descriptions of Author's Craftsmanship as Evidence

CONNECTION

Celebrate that students have collected a variety of evidence in a variety of ways and have learned ways to connect it to their claims.

"Yesterday we talked about essays being collections. You all are natural-born collectors, so it is no great surprise to me that you have collected dozens of entries in your files. And the great thing is that just as you all collect a variety of songs on your iPods, and just as Harrison collects a variety of hats and Diana collects a variety of horse statues, most of you have collected a variety of evidence to support your ideas. Give me a thumbs up if you've collected ministories. If you've collected summaries? Quotes? Lists? I am glad you've collected such a rich variety of materials, because your essays, like quilts, will be more interesting if they are constructed from variety. But I am glad not only that you have learned to gather a variety of evidence to support your ideas, but also that you know strategies for collecting evidence in general. For example, you know to restate your ideas often, threading them in and out through your information. You know to angle your information so as to highlight the point you want to make. I'm starting to worry about whether I'll ever win another argument in this class, because you are definitely learning to be convincing!"

"In another day or two, we're going to piece together the evidence and construct our essays."

Name your teaching point. In this case, tell children that writers of literary essays pay attention to an author's craftsmanship techniques, trusting that authors use these techniques on purpose, hoping to highlight deeper meanings.

"Before we do this, I want to teach you that good readers pay attention not only to character development, to the author's message, and to ways in which texts speak to the issues of our own lives. Good readers also pay attention to literary devices. Good readers know that an author deliberately crafts a story—or any text—in ways that highlight the deeper meanings of that text."

COACHING

During the lead of a minilesson, we have a chance to help children recall what we've taught them. The way in which we recall previous instruction matters, because we can make students feel as if prior lessons contained armloads of hard-to-remember, discombobulated instructions and directions—or we can make them feel as if our teaching had turned the light on in a new space, illuminating the way. By suggesting that children already love to make collections and that this is what an essayist does, I hope to help children feel at home with these strategies.

TEACHING

Show children that authors use literary devices to highlight what they want to say. Share your own thesis and folders related to a short and familiar text. Demonstrate rereading to study craftsmanship.

"I want to show you how I pay attention to what people refer to as literary devices, looking to see ways in which these literary devices support the message conveyed in a text. To show you this, I'm going to work with a poem you know well, 'Things,' by Eloise Greenfield ." (1978)

"I've already written and thought about this poem, and I've come up with a tentative idea, a tentative thesis: '"Things," by Eloise Greenfield, is a celebration of poetry.'"

"Things" celebrates poetry by showing that it is joyful, it reaches everyone, and it lasts forever.

"I've already made folders for each of my bullet points, and collected some evidence in my folders. Now I want to specifically look to see if the writerly devices Eloise Greenfield has used, the craft moves she's made, match the idea I have about her text."

"In my mind, I have a list of literary devices that authors sometimes use: language decisions (these include sound effects, dialect, incorporating words from another language, alliteration, and repetition) and comparisons (known as metaphors and similes)."

"Watch while I think about the language decisions Greenfield has made."

"Things"

Went to the corner

Walked in the store

Bought me some candy

Ain't got it no more

Ain't got it no more

"I notice that the narrator says things like 'ain't' and speaks in half-sentences, as when she writes 'went to the corner.' Before I read on, I'm going to think whether this language decision goes with one of my topic sentences," I said, as I scanned my folders and then the poem. Taking hold of one of my folders, I said, "The language decision to use casual talk *does* support the idea that poetry is for everyone. So I'll write an entry about this. Watch."

Of course, the way in which I went about forming my thesis involved reading the poem carefully and letting its literary devices work their magic on me. So it is not surprising that when I look back to see why the poem created the effect it did, I find that Greenfield used particular techniques. Perhaps in an ideal world this minilesson might have come before the lesson on developing a thesis statement, so that the sequence of instruction conveyed the idea that readers first attend closely to the choices authors make, and only then grow ideas about the text from this close, analytic reading.

There is nothing subtle or complex about my ideas. I think that when I'm demonstrating, it's helpful to choose examples that are extraordinarily clear.

Picking up a marker pen, I wrote on chart paper:

> The way that Eloise Greenfield wrote "Things" shows
> that she wants to convey that poetry is for everyone.
> She doesn't use fancy, elitist language. For example, she
> says "Ain't got it no more" instead of "I'm not still in
> possession of the candy."

To the children, I said in an aside, "Notice that to describe the craft decisions Eloise did make, I mention other choices she did not make."

"So let me think about another literary device: simile or metaphor. Hmm ... I better read on":

> Went to the beach
>
> Played on the shore
>
> Built me a sandhouse
>
> Ain't got it no more
>
> Ain't got it no more
>
>
> Went to the kitchen
>
> Lay down on the floor
>
> Made me a poem
>
> Still got it.
>
> Still got it.

"She doesn't *exactly* compare things, but ... hmm ... she *does* line up three things—building a sand castle, buying candy, and writing a poem! So it's sort of like she compares them. In a way, she's saying writing a poem is like eating candy or making sand castles. And that's comparison! That's metaphor! And it goes with my idea that she makes poetry seem joyful. So now I could write an entry on that."

"I've still got to think whether there is craftsmanship that supports the idea that this poem is a celebration of poetry—and I bet the evidence is here!"

I use a very brief and familiar poem because the concept I am teaching is a complex one, and I think couching it in this well-known poem makes the lesson itself more accessible.

ACTIVE ENGAGEMENT

Set children up to work with partners, looking for other literary devices the author you have been examining used. Help children see how the author's use of a literary device supports one of your ideas about the text.

"Why don't you try it? Take repetition, for example. See if you find instances of it, and then ask, 'Did Eloise Greenfield use this literary device in a way that supports the idea that poems are lasting, joyful, and for everyone?' If you find evidence that Greenfield's use of repetition supports this view of the poem's message, then tell your partner what you'd write about this." The children did this.

"I heard many of you say that it's probably important that she repeats 'Ain't got it no more, ain't got it no more' and the contrasting line 'still got it.' And you felt this *does* go with the idea that 'Things' is a celebration of poetry. Smart work."

LINK

Send children off, reminding them that they now have yet another way to collect evidence supporting their idea.

"Usually I'd tell you that you have lots of optional ways to collect evidence to support your ideas, but tomorrow we're going to move on to actually write our essays, so it's important that you spend today doing one of two things. First, if you have a folder that is somewhat empty, try to gather some material for that folder, or check whether the idea is really arguable. You may want to eliminate it. And second, you will definitely want to pay attention to literary devices."

There is absolutely no question that Eloise Greenfield's use of repetition helps to convey her messages, so I definitely have set children up for success in this Active Engagement. As usual, I use the trickier examples in my demonstration, leaving for students the work that is bound to work for them.

The work you teach today is important enough to the genre of literary essays that you'll probably want to insist children look at ways in which an author's craft supplies the text's meaning. This work definitely merits more than a day—extend the work if you can!

WRITING AND CONFERRING

Supporting the Study of Craftsmanship

You won't be able to spin among your children fast enough to reach them all today, and most of them would profit from some scaffolding and encouragement. Therefore, I suggest you convene small groups of children who are studying the same text. Each child will have his or her own unique angle, of course, but they can help each other apply the new lens to their text.

Once you convene a group, you may want to teach them that instead of scanning the text, hoping a craft move or literary device will pop out, saying "Here I am! Look at me," it can help to almost arbitrarily take a passage and think, "I'm *sure* there are literary devices and craft decisions within this paragraph. Let me read very, very closely to find them, and see whether they support my claim."

"Let's pretend that your claim for an essay on 'Eleven' is that Cisneros is actually writing about how and why she became a writer. Your claim is that Cisneros has written an essay that celebrates the importance of writing."

"Zoom in on any paragraph. Let's take the top of page two":

> Not mine, not mine, not mine, but Mrs. Price is already turning to page thirty-two, and math problem number four.

Show children that you squeeze your mind and try to come up with something to say about the way Cisneros has crafted this sentence. Let the children see that you at first feel speechless. "Umm . . . well . . . it's long!" Let the children see that you are tempted to brush your first thought aside, but resist. "The sentence is not just long; it also has lots of parts. 'Not mine, not mine, not mine' is what Rachel is thinking. But there isn't a period at the end of it. Instead the sentence keeps going, almost as if it is a run-on sentence, and at the end of it Mrs. Price is ignoring Rachel, turning to page thirty-two."

MID-WORKSHOP TEACHING POINT   *Using Descriptions of Authors' Craftsmanship as Evidence* "Writers, can I have your eyes and your attention? Writers, I'm seeing amazing insights. It's as if your minds are on fire. Listen to what you've discovered!"

"Max says that because Cisneros wants to emphasize that when you are one age, you are also all the ages you've ever been, she stretched all those other ages out into a long repeating list, saying, 'When you are eleven, you're also ten, and nine, and eight, and seven, and six, and five, and four, and three, and two, and one.' She could have just said, 'You are all the other ages,' but instead she stretched out what she means by being other ages."

"The way Max thought about what Cisneros *did do*—by considering choices she *rejected*, alternatives she opted against—is really smart. I suspect others of you will borrow that strategy."

"Ali wrote that Gary Soto uses lists in the beginning of the story to convey the point that Lupe has been a winner. For example, she's 'the school's spelling bee champion, winner of the reading contest three summers in a row, blue-ribbon awardee in the science fair, the top student at a piano recital, and the playground

continued on next page

"I'm realizing that Cisneros sometimes uses long, run-on sentences, and in this instance, she does so in a way that shows that Rachel's voice gets lost in her teacher's actions."

You'll want to show children that you shift between very close reading of the text and consideration of your claim. "Now how might this connect to the idea that this is an essay about writing? Hmm . . . Maybe Cisneros' sentence structure reinforces the idea that Rachel feels voiceless? Rachel's thoughts get lost in this long sentence that ends up being all about the teacher's actions and decisions. Perhaps 'Eleven' is not just the story of Rachel but also of Sandra Cisneros and how she struggles to find and claim her own voice. Perhaps the story culminates in the fact that Cisneros gets the last word in. She—that's Cisneros but also Rachel—perhaps *does* find her voice because look—she's writing this essay! She's gotten the last word in, even if at the time Mrs. Price rolled right over her."

You'll need to demonstrate this in an efficient manner so that the conference is not a soliloquy. Shift soon to a second passage, and suggest that children assume there's a craft move in that paragraph that relates to each child's different thesis. (Of course, this may prove incorrect, but that is unlikely.) Then support children in identifying that move.

continued from previous page

grand chess champion.' Soto wants readers to notice that although Lupe has excelled in many areas in her life, she has not been good in sports."

"Judah wrote: 'I notice the way that Gary Soto uses lists in the beginning of the story really carries through the point that Lupe was no good in sports. For example, "she could not catch a pop-up or figure out in which direction to kick the soccer ball." This is a place where Gary Soto uses a list to show some things that Lupe tried but never succeeded in.'"

"Both Ali and Judah noticed that Soto uses lists to emphasize his point that Lupe was good at many things but not at sports. I know that many of you will be noticing when authors use lists to prove a point."

"Harrison noticed that Soto also uses repetition, like 'Tried again and again' and 'Practice, practice, practice, squeeze, squeeze, squeeze,' to show the character's determination."

"So, writers, if at first you don't notice literary devices that support your idea, look again, more closely. Look at what the author did and didn't do, as Max demonstrated. Pay attention even to something as clear as repetition, as Harrison did. And notice more craft moves that merit attention so we can add them to our list, just as we added Ali and Judah's observations about using lists for emphasis."

SHARE

Taking a Teaching Tone

Tell children that essayists sometimes write in the voice of a teacher, a professor. Set children up to talk in groups about how a teaching voice differs from a storytelling voice.

"Tomorrow you'll begin drafting your literary essays. You'll recall that before we wrote stories, I told you that the author Robert Munsch tells his stories at least a hundred times aloud before he writes them. We all did a bit of storytelling in our narrative units, and I think that helped us write in the voice of a storyteller."

"When we write essays, we need to write in the voice of a teacher, a professor. I know you tried this last night. Before we try it again, I want to teach you a bit about how to write and talk in a professor's voice. I tape-recorded a professor who was on television last night, giving a little lecture on bird migration. I want you to listen for just a second to her teaching voice, the explaining voice she uses. Jot down phrases you notice, phrases that go with the role. For example, she says, 'Notice . . . .' Imagine how she stands, too, and imagine her relationship with her readers, her audience. Jot notes on what you notice. After I play a bit of the tape, I'm going to ask you to talk in groups of four—two partnerships can clump together—about ways in which this woman's teaching voice seems different from a storytelling voice."

Share some of the children's observations with the class, and then have children teach each other their ideas.

We did this, and I listened to what children said. Convening the class, I said, "Many of you pointed out that the teacher seems to be trying to be clear. You said that even though you couldn't see the written version of her words, you still sensed that she was speaking in paragraphs because she talked on one clear topic, then the next. You said that you could almost imagine her holding up fingers to say, 'My first point is . . . ,' 'My next point is . . . .' You said that she came right out and spoke to her listeners, saying, 'It is important to notice . . .' and 'You may ask why . . . the reason is . . . .'"

"Now I'd like you to take a few minutes of silent time to get ready, and then I'm going to set you up to act as professors, teaching each other your ideas."

"Follow your essay plan. You can lay materials out in front of you to help you remember what you want to say, but don't read your entries. Instead, say aloud what you might write—and then say more. Add on. Elaborate."

Obviously, as these units of study unroll and you come to know your particular class of children better and better, you'll use your own experience with previous units to inform your work in this unit. If it has been incredibly helpful to set children up to say what they'll eventually write, you may have brought this Share activity into an earlier session. If your class was chaotic last time you tried this, you'll anticipate the potential problems and tweak my words so they channel your children in productive ways.

Notice that in this Share, I ask children to engage in table conversations involving two partnerships. You may decide to invite these larger conversations often.

HOMEWORK *Considering Purpose in Crafting* In today's session, you learned that it is important to notice not only what an author has written about, but also how that author has written, noting ways that the author's craft supports his or her message. This minilesson could launch another whole bend in the road of our unit. But time is short. Let's extend today's lesson at least for tonight, however. One way to do this is to reread the text under study and to notice what the author *did* do by noticing what he or she did *not* do!

When you and I write our own stories, we make choices about what to expand and what to skip past. We look over our own writing and think, "What is the heart of the story?" and then we stretch out that part. The authors of these texts that you are reading have made similar choices. They write with a lot of detail about some things, and bypass others altogether. So one way to learn what matters to an author is to think, "What has this author written about with extensive detail? What has the author skimmed past? And how might this support the author's real message?"

For example, we can look at Rylant's story, "Spaghetti," and we can ask, "What's missing here? What has she seemed to pass right by?"

I notice, for example, that Rylant doesn't say why Gabriel is lonely, or why he is sitting by himself. I think we are supposed to get the idea that he is homeless, and to infer that this means he doesn't have any friends. So I think Rylant is trying to sort of push poverty and loneliness together, blurring the line between them, making them into one overlapping category.

Once I have developed and written this thought, I need to decide which folder can best hold this thought, and then I'll file it just as I have filed other bits I have collected. If I want to hold on to the thought and it doesn't fit under any category, I will make myself a file titled "Other."

Tonight, will you reread the story you have been studying, and notice what your author has developed and what the author has skimmed past? Notice the details that are missing. Does one character not have a name? Is there a feeling in the story that is never really explained? Once you have noticed what's missing in the story, ask yourself, "How does the author's decision reflect the message of this story?" Write your thoughts, one on a page, and file those thoughts.

If you decide that your children are ready for a challenge . . . you might extend this session. As part of this, you could help them know that specialists in an area usually know and use specialized vocabulary. A chemist refers to valence and isotopes. A person who studies literature, too, has a toolchest of terminology, and many of these terms are words we can use to describe authors' ways with words. You might begin by reviewing terms that children know but may not always incorporate in their essays. They should identify the text's genre by name, refer to the speaker as the *narrator,* and describe parts of a text using terms such as *stanza* for poetry, *climax* or *resolution* for story.

Children probably know terms such as metaphor, but may not know and use terms such as alliteration, image, assonance, or hyperbole. In a single minilesson, you wouldn't want to dump fifteen terms on top of your kids, but you could definitely stress that they can convey that they are experts by using the specialized terminology of this field.

If you decide to extend this minilesson another day . . . you could teach children that when trying to surmise why an author made a decision to write in a particular way, they'll be conjecturing. That is, many children will notice that an author has done something, and not feel confident that they can discern *why* the author wrote as he or she did.

Children need to be encouraged to guess. Teach them that no one *knows* the answer. The difference between a person who is a very skilled literary essayist and a person who just sits there saying, "I don't know *why* Soto did that," is not that the first has more facts, more knowledge. The difference is that the skilled literary essayist is willing to surmise, to speculate, to conjecture, to hypothesize. That is, this is a person who is willing to think, 'Could it be that he does this because . . . ?"

Of course, once we make a tentative guess as to why an author could have decided to write in a particular way, we think this through. One way to do this is to ask ourselves, "How *might* he have written this? What different effect would he have created had he written it in that manner?" Then, too, we can say, "Is there any other evidence to suggest this might be why the author did this?"

Teach children that reading and thinking about literature is not altogether different than being a crime solver. We see what looks as if it could, possibly, be a clue, and we speculate . . ."Could it be?" Then we look for more clues, hoping to see a pattern.

COLLABORATING WITH COLLEAGUES

It's essential that you and your colleagues take time to study the ways in which craftsmanship can convey meaning in a text. You might, for example, look at "Spaghetti" and notice how Cynthia Rylant uses soulful, plaintive sounds—"the slow lifting of a stubborn window ... the creak of an old man's legs ... the wind"—to describe how Gabriel envisions the kitten's cry. Some people feel that implicit in these imagined sounds is the loneliness and longing that Gabriel hears in the kitten and feels himself. Rylant also uses repetition here: "It could have been ... it could have been ... it could have been ... But it was not." Does this not show how vivid an imagination Gabriel has, how he spends so much time in his own mind that he can imagine not one, not two, but three sounds he might be hearing?

You could next study "Eleven" by Sandra Cisneros. You might study the author's use of comparisons. About growing older and turning eleven, Rachel says, "Because the way you grow old is kind of like an onion or like the rings inside a tree trunk or like my little wooden dolls that fit one inside the other, each year inside the next one. That's how being eleven years old is." What do you make of the fact that the comparisons Cisneros has Rachel make are to physical things in her world that she can touch and see? They are also all layered things—circles and shapes that fit together—so why might Cisneros have chosen those things? In another simile, Cisneros has Rachel compare the sweater to something from her world of childhood, calling the sleeves "all stretched out like you could use it for a jump rope." Why that image? What specific purposes do you suppose it serves?

There are many more literary devices you might notice in these or other stories: metaphor, alliteration, consonance, hyperbole, and analogy, to name just a few. Why might the author have chosen to use these devices right where she does? What purpose does it serve? Bring the thoughts you and your colleagues come up with about these texts back to your students, and share the thinking that led you to them.

Sometimes studying literary devices can lead essayists to further evidence to support their claims. If the reasons we think authors have chosen specific comparisons and images don't fit with our claims about the story as essayists, what then? On the other hand, sometimes close reading of the story, of the crafting an author has done, may lead essayists to revise their thesis statements. If this happens to you or your colleagues as you study a text in depth, be sure to bring that story to your young essayists!

PUTTING IT ALL TOGETHER:
CONSTRUCTING LITERARY ESSAYS

When I was younger, a singing group named the Byrds sang a song—"Turn! Turn! Turn! (To Everything There Is a Season)"—and the refrain went like this:

> To everything—turn, turn, turn
>
> There is a season—turn, turn, turn
>
> And a time for every purpose under heaven.

Those words mean a lot to those of us who are writers—because in writing, as in farming, there is a rhythm to our work. The farmer plants, waters, weeds, and harvests, and the writer plans, gathers, outlines, drafts, revises, and edits. This ancient rhythm is in our bones; we remember it like a river remembers its seasonal rise and fall.

I hope the rhythm of writing is in your students' bones now as well. I hope that your students remember it, and can sense that the time has come to turn, turn, turn.

Today you'll help your children perform that miracle of miracles. They'll begin with a pile of folders and that will turn, turn, first into a writer's version of solitaire. Throughout the room, your children will sort through their material, deciding what to keep and what to discard. Then they'll turn, turn again. With scissors and tape, they'll place one entry next to another, constructing an essay. They have a feel for how to do this by now—it's in their bones.

Also today, you will remind writers about that special kind of reading that writers do. You will teach them first to read the work of another author, one who has written something similar to the essay they'll be writing. You will teach them to look over this other writer's work, thinking, "How has she constructed this text? What has she done with her text that I, too, can do with mine?"

Finally, you will teach your students to critically reread the notes and entries they've accumulated, scrutinizing their own drafts of stories, lists, and reflections in order to say "yes" and "no" to each bit of their material. You will teach them to read with imagination, too—with the imagination that allows them to envision ways in which one piece of thinking can be linked to another, and another, creating a path of thought. There is a tall agenda for today!

IN THIS SESSION, YOU WILL TEACH CHILDREN SOME OF THE WAYS THAT WRITERS CREATE DRAFTS OUT OF COLLECTIONS OF EVIDENCE. YOU'LL ALSO TEACH CHILDREN WAYS TO STUDY PUBLISHED LITERARY ESSAYS IN ORDER TO FIND STRUCTURES FOR THEIR OWN LITERARY ESSAYS.

GETTING READY

- Enlarged copy of first two paragraphs of Jill's essay from in Session IX
- Copies of Jill's essay for each child
- See CD-ROM for resources

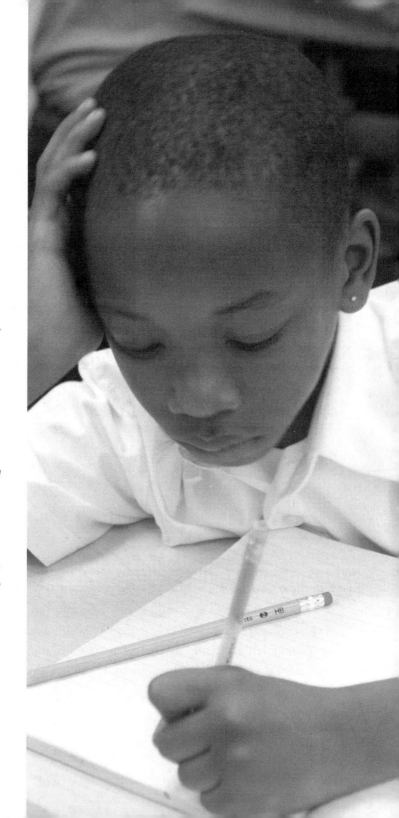

MINILESSON

Putting It All Together: Constructing Literary Essays

CONNECTION

Celebrate that children are ready to construct their literary essays.

"Writers, yesterday you and your partner spent time talking about the material you have collected. You pretended you were literature professors, teaching each other about your theories. You took on the voice of teachers, of professors; you gave little talks to each other about your theories. That was your dress rehearsal: Today's the day!"

"You no doubt can already feel that this will be the day to draft your literary essay. And you no doubt can recall a day like this from our earlier unit of study on the personal essay. I bet you recall how, in the space of a day, you went from having scraps of paper to having a draft of an essay. It was like magic. Presto! That same magic will happen today."

"I do not need to teach you that you will open up the file you want to write first, lay out the contents, and sift through all of the stuff you have collected, thinking, 'What should I throw out?' and 'What should I keep?' I do not need to teach you that you'll tape one bit of data alongside another."

Name your teaching point. Specifically, tell children that before constructing their raw material into essays, it's useful to read other writers' work, examining what works well.

"Today I want to teach you that writers take raw materials and piece them together to form a coherent essay, and that writers especially need to be strong, smart readers. One kind of reading that writers do just before we make a draft is this: We read the work of other writers, asking, 'What has she done that I, too, could do?'"

COACHING

It is a bit harder to rally children to step into the role of being literary essayists. They know fiction writers or poets, and aspire to create texts like they create. Still, it's important to try to help children know that they are not just producing a text, they are also becoming the kind of person who makes this sort of text.

I am hoping that by listing all that I do not need to teach children, referencing appropriate visuals for each stage that I mention, I manage to remind children of those very things! That is, while saying, 'I do not need to teach you this,' and 'I do not need to teach you that,' I allow myself to quickly review both. In art—and teaching must be an art—selection is crucial. Although I mention in passing what I hope children already know, I highlight the one new goal for today—and it is contained in my teaching point.

You could look back across the series and locate half a dozen other similar teaching points. One challenge in teaching writing is that the strategies we talk about are more easily said than done, and therefore our teaching will often revisit what we taught earlier. If we simply repeated the same minilessons six times, students might well tune us out, so we're always working to find ways to make old ideas feel new enough to be noteworthy.

TEACHING

Demonstrate that before writing a draft of an essay, it helps to look at an example and box the parts, noticing how it is put together. Use one child's draft to model this.

"When I was your age, my sister and I loved jigsaw puzzles—the more pieces the better. Every Christmas we would ask for a harder, more intricate puzzle than the year before. After unwrapping our newest challenge, we would clear off the round table in the corner of the living room and start to discuss our plan. First, we'd dump out all the pieces and turn them right side up. Second, we'd separate out all the edge pieces. Third, we'd each pick a side that would be our responsibility. Fourth, we'd study the picture on the cover of the box and build the frame."

"Once we had accomplished those steps, we would still spend hours sorting the remaining pieces into piles. We often consulted the picture on the cover of the box to see where the pieces might go best, and then we would slowly piece together the puzzle. Sometimes we were determined that certain pieces went together, and we would push and push until they lay flat and looked liked they belonged. Each night after dinner, my father would come and survey our progress. He would compliment each of us on the work we had accomplished, but he also always seemed to notice the one or two spots where my sister and I had forced pieces together that didn't fit smoothly. He'd ask, 'How do these two pieces fit together?'"

"When your audience reads your work, they will be piecing together your essay and asking themselves, 'How does this part fit with the part I just read?' They will be thinking about your thesis statement and combining it with one bit of evidence, like two puzzle pieces, and then with another bit of evidence, like more pieces of a puzzle. So you need to be smart about how you piece your bits together."

"Specifically, before you begin to piece together your essay, it is helpful to look at another author's essay and to examine how it is constructed. Let me show you how I go about doing this. I'm going to study the first section of Jill's essay—remember, you worked with this essay earlier in this unit. I want to study Jill's first body paragraph, because today you'll each write a body paragraph or two. So let's study the ways Jill pieced together that paragraph." I used an overhead projector to enlarge Jill's opening paragraph and her first body paragraph, and read it aloud. *[Figs. XIII-1 and XIII-2]*

> In my life, not everything ends up like a fairy tale. I like
> to read books where characters are like me. They
> don't live fairy tale lives. We have the same kinds of
> problems. Many people read Sandra Cisneros's essay
> "Eleven" and think it's about a girl who has to wear a

Over the sequence of units, I've used a variety of metaphors to depict this process. I've likened the writer's work to the work of a builder, a quilt maker, and now a person who constructs jigsaw puzzles.

sweater she doesn't want to wear. But I think the story is about a girl who struggles to hold onto herself when she is challenged by people who have power over her.

When Rachel's teacher, Mrs. Price, challenges Rachel, Rachel loses herself. One day, Mrs. Price puts a stretched out, itchy, red sweater on Rachel's desk saying, "I know this is yours. I saw you wearing it once!! Rachel knows that the sweater isn't hers and tries to tell Mrs. Price, but Mrs. Price doesn't believe her. Rachel reacts to Mrs. Price's actions by losing herself. "In my head, I'm thinking ... how long till lunch time, how long till I can take the red sweater and throw it over the school yard fence, or leave it hanging on a parking meter, or bunch it up into a little ball and toss it over the alley?" This shows that Rachel loses herself because she's not listening to her teacher, she's dreaming about a whole other place. It is also important to see that Rachel has all this good thinking about the sweater but when she wants to say the sweater isn't hers, she squeaks and stammers, unable to speak. "But it's not," Rachel says. "Now," Mrs. Price replies. Rachel loses herself by not finding complete words to say when Mrs. Price challenges her.

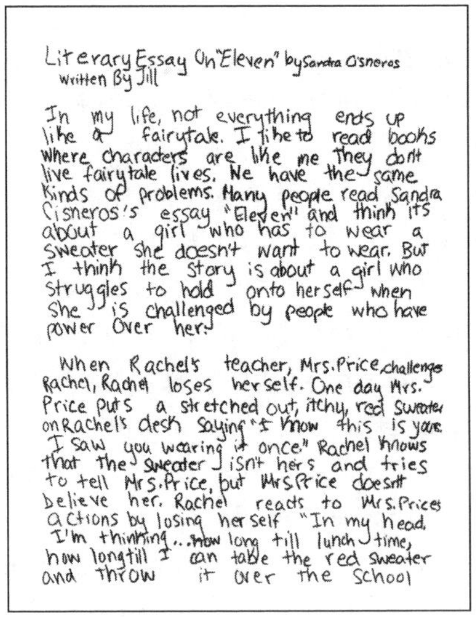

"Okay, I'll first box Jill's thesis:"

> I think "Eleven" is about a girl who struggles to hold onto herself when she is challenged by people who have power over her.

"I'm noticing that Jill begins her first body paragraph with her topic sentence, the one she had probably written on the outside of her folder, her first bullet point." I said, circling that section of the essay as I read it aloud again,

- When Rachel's teacher, Mrs. Price, challenges Rachel, Rachel loses herself.

"Then Jill tells the story of how Rachel loses herself (how she struggles to hold onto herself) by not being able to speak up and tell her teacher that the sweater isn't hers. Jill thinks that when Rachel tunes out of class, sitting in the room dreaming of ways she might get rid of the sweater, this shows that Rachel is losing touch with herself." I circled those several sentences where Jill summarized that part of the text. "Let me see how Jill connected

Fig. XIII-1 Jill's final literary essay page 1

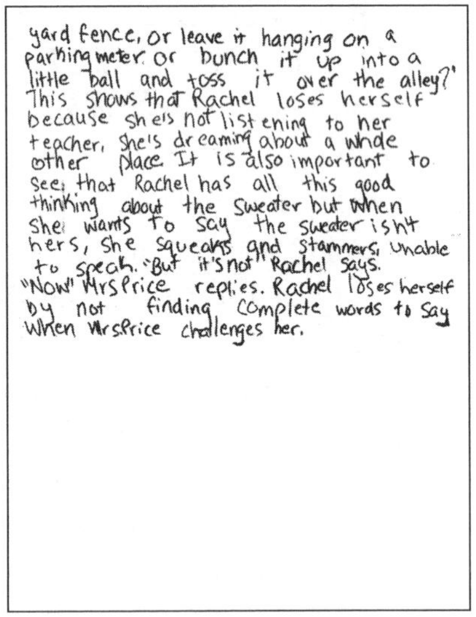

Fig. XIII-2 Jill's final literary essay page 2

Of course, literary essayists often structure essays differently than this one. For example, essayists often entertain points of view other than their own, writing, "Some might argue differently . . . " and then providing a counter-argument. Then, too, essayists often compare and contrast the one text to other texts, or to life. The actual components you teach aren't especially crucial, and I encourage you to make your own decisions, taking into account the standards in your region.

her topic sentence to this example, this story that illustrates her point—oh! After her topic sentence, Jill just jumped right into this story with only the connector words 'One day' to signal she is telling a story." I underlined the words 'One day.'

I continued to reread:

> This shows that Rachel loses herself because she's not listening to her teacher, she's dreaming about a whole other place.

"I'm noticing that Jill has 'unpacked' how this example refers back to her topic sentence. Do you see how she does that? She explains how the little story about Rachel dreaming of ways to get rid of the sweater relates to her topic sentence, doesn't she?"

Then I reread the next bit of text:

> It is also important to see that Rachel has all this good thinking about the sweater but when she wants to say the sweater isn't hers, she squeaks and stammers, unable to speak. "But it's not," Rachel says. "'Now,' Mrs. Price replies.'

I pointed to the chunk of text, rereading it several times to myself. "What point is Jill making here, I wonder? What kind of evidence is this? Oh! Now I see! Jill is pointing out that Rachel's actions highlight the fact that Rachel loses herself. Rachel had lots of thoughts, but when she went to talk, Cisneros made it so Rachel couldn't get words out, she only stammered. How does Jill connect that bit of evidence to her paragraph? Ah-ha, she uses the transition 'It is also important.' I'll underline that so we remember she used a connector for that bit of evidence too."

"Does Jill explain that bit of evidence too?" I read on:

> Rachel loses herself by not finding complete words to say when Mrs. Price challenges her.

"That's Jill explaining her evidence again, isn't it? Yes, she is saying exactly why that part of the story supports her point, just like she did the first time she had evidence."

ACTIVE ENGAGEMENT
Ask children to work in partners to study and label what the author has done to construct her second paragraph.

"Now it is your turn. Would you sit with your partner and study Jill's second paragraph? Do as I did, noticing each sentence and thinking, 'What is this? Is it a story? A list? A discussion of the writer's craft moves?' Would you pay special attention, as I did, to

This may be more detailed than your children can handle. If so, select the items you want to showcase. Alternatively, you can analyze just the start of this paragraph before sending children off to do the same for the start of the next paragraph, continuing with both paragraphs in the Mid-Workshop Teaching Point.

You always have the option of using this brief interval as a time for children to help each other get started doing whatever you've just taught them to do. So you could say, "Let's get started on our own essays right away," and then ask children to lay out the materials from one of partner 1's files, and begin to think about which material needs to be eliminated because it doesn't align with the claim, is repetitive, and so forth.

how Jill makes her transitions from one bit of data to another, and to the times when she unpacks the data she has just shared? Mark up the text of Jill's essay that I have given you and label what it is that Jill has done. Notice what Jill has done that you could also do when you build your body paragraphs." [Fig. XIII-3]

> When Rachel's classmates challenge Rachel, Rachel loses herself. Sylvia Saldivar puts Rachel on the spot like when she says to Mrs. Price, "I think the sweater is Rachel's." Sylvia is challenging Rachel, she is being mean and she makes Rachel feel lost. Rachel cries to let her emotions out. Rachel feels sick from Sylvia. Rachel tries to cover herself up by putting her head in her sleeve. Tears stream down her face. She doesn't feel special like it's her birthday. Instead, she feels lost in Sylvia's challenge.

I gave children a couple of minutes to do this. "You've done some really good thinking and decision making."

LINK
Set students up to review the contents of their folders, deciding what to include and how to sequence the information within each of their paragraphs. Ask them to decide which bits need to be revised.

"So writers, today you will want to reread Jill's essay, thinking again about what she has done that you could also try. I have given you a copy of it. And from this day forward, always remember that when you go to write something, it helps to study—to analyze— similar texts that other authors have written."

"After you study Jill's essay, you will be doing the work that you know how to do. You'll take one of your folders, and you'll spread the contents out before you. Then you'll reread each bit that you have collected, deciding, 'It this really powerful evidence? Is this something to include?' Keep in mind the overall shape you intend to follow in your essay. You'll need to decide how to sequence the information within your paragraph. Finally, you'll need to decide whether all that is required is some tape—or whether bits of information need to be revised before they can be put into your essay. Off you go!"

Children may notice that in the sentence, "Sylvia is challenging Rachel, she is being mean . . . " Jill has listed all the bad things Sylvia does to Rachel. The reader feels as if there is a giant pile of evidence because Jill writes this as a list. Then again, Jill writes another list, this time cumulating all the ways in which Rachel acts distressed in response to what Sylvia has done. The paragraph ends with a sentence which returns to the thesis.

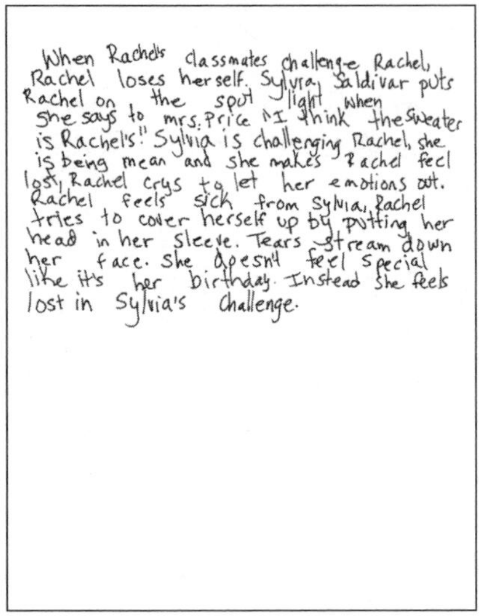

> When Rachel's classmates challenge Rachel, Rachel loses herself. Sylvia Saldivar puts Rachel on the spot "light when she says to mrs. Price "I think the sweater is Rachel's." Sylvia is challenging Rachel, she is being mean and she makes Rachel feel lost, Rachel crys to let her emotions out. Rachel feels sick from Sylvia, Rachel tries to cover herself up by putting her head in her sleeve. Tears stream down her face. She doesn't feel special like it's her birthday. Instead she feels lost in Sylvia's challenge.

Fig. XIII-3 Jill's body paragraph

WRITING AND CONFERRING

Making Parts into a Cohesive Whole

As you confer with young writers today, you can predict that you'll need to show them how to write sentences that link their bits together into a cohesive whole. For example, when I pulled my chair alongside Harrison, he had spread before him the contents of a folder titled, "Lupe overcame difficulties through hard work." He had two microstories in his pile. One read:

> Lupe lay in front of her shelf full of academic trophies and medals. She wished there was at least one trophy that showed that she could do sports – but there were none. She decided that she would work hard, day and night, to win a marble tournament.

Another story began:

> Lupe came home from school and immediately tossed down her backpack and got out her marbles...

Harrison's first job was to decide on the sequence of his stories, and he decided these would follow the order I just described. His next job, then, was to link his topic sentence with the start of his first story. If he simply stapled these alongside each other, they'd read:

> Lupe overcame difficulties through hard work.
> Lupe lay in front of her shelf full of trophies.

I told Harrison, "You need to set readers up for the story by coming right out and explicitly telling us that this story pertains to Lupe overcoming difficulties through hard work." Then I said, "I could imagine it might go like this," and I wrote-in-the-air to give Harrison a sense for sure of his options. "Lupe decided to work hard and become a marble champ one day when she lay ..." or "Lupe didn't just become a marble champ by luck or talent. She worked hard to become a marble champ. This hard work began one day when ..."

Harrison needed less help building a bridge between the one story and the next. I simply reminded him that generally writers use transition words such as these:

MID-WORKSHOP TEACHING POINT   *Piecing Together Evidence*   "Writers, once you've selected a few pieces of evidence that you believe should be brought together in one of your body paragraphs, you'll want to use a stapler or transparent tape to literally piece together a rough draft of your essay. Use a sheet of notebook paper as your foundation, and leave space between the assembled bits so that you can write transitional sentences that link your various pieces together. We'll learn more about how to write those transitions tomorrow, but have a go at them if you can, and in any case, leave space for them."

"As you construct your essay, keep in mind that you are arguing for your claim. You may be claiming that Cisneros believes that growing up is hard. If that's your belief, then you need to think, 'How can I really drive my point home?' Sometimes you'll realize that the material you've collected doesn't really speak as forcefully as you'd like, and so sometimes you'll decide to put one of your notes on the corner of your desk, and you'll pick up your pen and say exactly what you meant to say all along. Don't hesitate to do this. None of the early reading and thinking and writing and collecting will be wasted, because all of that good work has brought you to the place where you are now."

- Another example
- Not only did she . . . but she also . . .
- Later
- Furthermore

I told him, "I just take one, try it out to see how it sounds and fits, then take another."

I also find that children need lots of encouragement letting go of materials. If they've collected four stories, three quotes, and a few lists, they want to stick all of those together to make a gigantic paragraph. Over and over I find myself reminding children that they can't revisit the same material three times in a single paragraph, first, and, furthermore, that in general less is more. "Choose the most compelling, best-written material," I say. "Decide which evidence will be especially convincing."

Then, too, when conferring with children today it's important to think about the help they'll need editing their essays so that the instruction we give in the ensuing days can be as targeted as possible.

SHARE

Rereading as a Means to Revise

Advise writers to stop and to revise as they construct their essays.

"Writers, it's been exciting to see you sort through your materials and begin constructing your essays. Look at what a change Adam made today!"

Adam's thesis began like this: [Fig. XIII-4]

> Some people might think "Eleven" is about a
> girl whose teacher yells at her to put on an
> ugly red sweater. Really it is about how
> Rachel has to cope with her teacher who
> won't listen to her.

He then revised it in this way: [Fig. XIII-5]

> In literature, authors write a lot about one
> character being upset and taking it out on
> another person. Sandra Cisneros' essay,
> "Eleven," is about a girl named Rachel who is
> mistreated by her teacher and in return
> mistreats her classmates.

- Rachel is mistreated by her teacher.
- In return for Mrs. Price mistreating Rachel,
  Rachel then goes on to mistreat her classmates.

"He realized his evidence was supporting a different thesis from the one he'd written. You could either continue sorting, selecting, and assembling until you've constructed all your body paragraphs, or you can pause midway to look over your work and revise it. I tend to suggest pausing earlier rather than later, because I think if we not only construct but also revise one paragraph before proceeding on, we can avoid making the same mistakes twice. Today, let's use our Share session as a time to read what we've assembled with critical eyes, so that we leave school with a plan for revision work we need to do at home tonight."

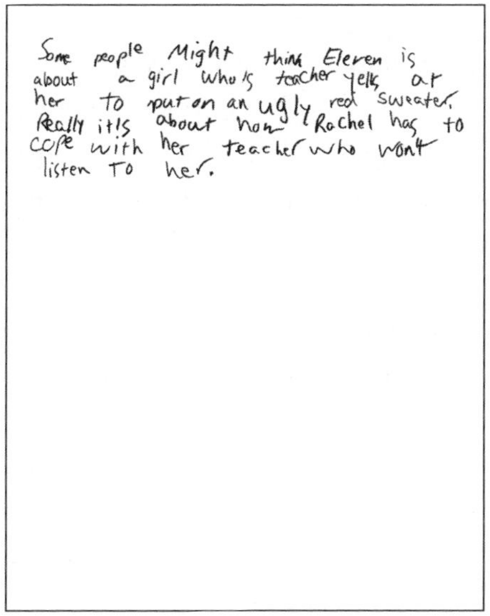

Fig. XIII-4 Adam's first thesis

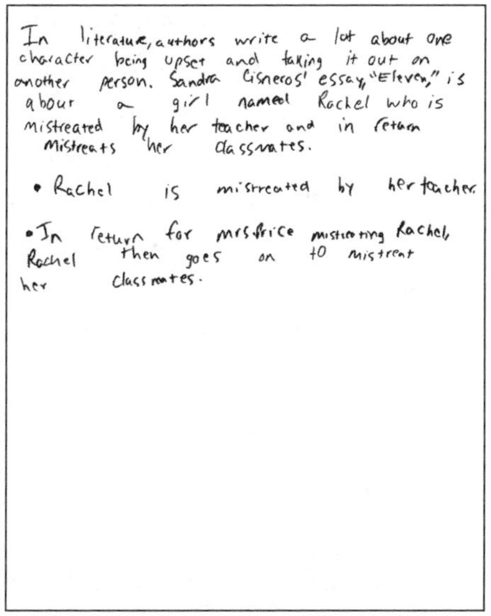

> Some people Might think Eleven is
> about a girl who is teacher yells at
> her to put on an ugly red sweater.
> Really it's about how Rachel has to
> cope with her teacher who won't
> listen to her.

Fig. XIII-5 Adam's revised thesis

> In literature, authors write a lot about one
> character being upset and taking it out on
> another person. Sandra Cisneros' essay, "Eleven," is
> about a girl named Rachel who is
> mistreated by her teacher and in return
> mistreats her classmates.
>
> • Rachel is mistreated by her teacher.
>
> • In return for mrs. Price mistreating Rachel,
> Rachel then goes on to mistreat
> her classmates.

Advise children of some predictable problems writers encounter when constructing essays. Ask children to help each other reread and revise.

"Would you and your partner look at first one person's writing and then the next person's writing? Reread the section that you assembled today and, as you read, would you check for a couple of the predictable difficulties that essayists often get ourselves into, and see if you've encountered any of this trouble."

"First of all, sometimes we find that we have collected so much evidence that each paragraph in our essay could be three pages long! Harrison, for example, has at least two pages of evidence showing that Lupe overcame her difficulties through hard work. If you're in Harrison's predicament, you can be very selective, choosing only the most compelling evidence."

"Meanwhile, however, keep in mind that you can write several paragraphs to support one of your ideas. So Harrison's thesis is that Lupe overcomes her difficulties through hard work and support from her family. If we wanted to do so, Harrison could show that Lupe received support from her family early on, and then again later—and these could be divided into two paragraphs. Or Harrison could tell in one paragraph about the support she received from her father, and in another paragraph about the support she received from her brother. So in the end, you may have two or three paragraphs supporting each of your topic sentences."

"Then, too, it is important to reread a rough-draft essay checking for clarity. A stranger should be able to read the essay and understand it. Sometimes, for example, a reader will be unclear over the pronouns. 'Who is he?' the reader might wonder. Every writer needs to be able to shift from writing to reading, to reread our work looking for places which will be confusing, and then to revise those places for clarity."

"So, writers, take some time to reread your own and each other's work, checking to be sure you've selected the most compelling and pertinent evidence, written in shapely paragraphs, and that you've been clear."

⊙ HOMEWORK *Revising for Strength and Clarity* Writers, tonight you have an opportunity to revise the draft that you assembled in school today. Revise it first for power. You are writing an essay that aims to be persuasive. You'll be most convincing if every portion of your argument is fresh, new, and compelling. So read over the bits of evidence you've collected, and decide whether some sections of it seem redundant or unnecessary. Do what any skilled writer would do—and cross those out. Then look at the evidence which is compelling and convincing enough to remain in your essay, and think, "How can I make this even stronger? Even more convincing?" Finally, double-check your draft for clarity. If you can rope someone from home in to listening, read your draft aloud. Notice where you stumble as you read, or when your words no longer feel like they are reaching your listener. Revise these places, aiming to be precise, clear, and convincing!

TAILORING YOUR TEACHING

If your children need more time to construct and revise their body paragraphs . . .
which is very likely, you might teach them that they, as writers, need to do their very best work before passing the draft on to you for final corrections.

Don Murray, author of *A Writer Teaches Writing*, once told me the story of a senior editor at a publishing company who sent his people out to do some writing. "Bring your articles in on Friday," he barked.

Friday came, and the writers brought drafts to the great editor. He collected them in a folder, then tucked them in his briefcase, saying, "Come in on Monday morning and we'll discuss these."

Monday came, and the writers assembled. Pulling the folder of drafts from his briefcase, the editor waved them in front of his team, asking, "Was this your best?"

The writers shifted uneasily from one foot to another, looked at their feet, shrugged. One said, "I tried, but . . . " Another said, "Mine started strong, but . . . "

Brushing aside their excuses, the editor said: "Take your drafts. Make them your best. Bring them back tomorrow at 3:00 p.m."

The next day came and again the great man collected them. Hours later, he again convened the team and again asked sharply: "Was this your best?" And again, their excuses were met with a wave of dismissal. "Take these, then, and this time do your best."

That Friday, he again collected the papers, and this time, after he collected them, he turned to his team. Holding the stash of drafts, he said, "Now, for the third time, I ask you—'Is this your best?'"

The people looked him in the eye and said, "Yes."

"Good," the editor said. "Now I'll read them."

In the same way, your children need to do their very best before they bring their drafts to you for help. Use this story to remind them that it is the writer's job, not the editor's job, to make the text the very best that the writer can possibly make it. Then the editor can make the best even better.

If your children need help constructing a coherent text out of the bits and pieces they've collected . . . then you'll probably want to spend another day helping them to grasp the big picture of how literary essays go. You might decide to do this by teaching children how writers go about writing "instant essays," a lesson your children will probably need to learn as part of test prep.

You might alter the normal schedule of the day, keeping children with you in the meeting area for a collaborative work session. Give them each a copy of a text—and teach them that after reading a text, a literary essayist thinks, "What interesting idea do I have about this text? Is it one that pertains to the whole text?" Writers can try asking some of the questions we generated earlier, or can simply read the text and think, "The thought I have about this is . . . "

Say the text was "Papa Who Wakes Up Tired in The Dark" from Cisneros' *House on Mango Street*. Show children that you come up with a claim: "Although this text focuses on one moment, it uses that moment to show the whole of the narrator's life." Then push yourself to say how the text does this, or the reasons why it does this: "It does this by portraying the narrator's father and by revealing many of her family traditions."

In a similar manner, show children how a writer drafts a very quick literary essay. Let the children do the work of finding a story—or example—to build each topic sentence. Show them that often writers link two stories with some connections. Encourage children to quote a section and then unpack that quotation.

You'll only need to do a single paragraph together as a class, but this work should remind children of the overall task they're doing as they assemble their pieces into a draft. Remind them, too, that when writers decide to write a new draft of a chunk of material rather than merely stapling things together, this is cause for great celebration.

MECHANICS

You'll need to decide when and how you want to help children turn their rough drafts into final pieces. It is likely that you'll need to build another day or two into your unit of study, and that you'll read students' work in progress outside of the writing workshop, correcting some aspects of it and leaving other work to be done during and after editing conferences.

Most of the editing help children will require for this unit will not be unique to the unit. That is, they'll still be working on spelling, punctuation, logic, clarity, and the rest. But there will be a few issues that are unique to the genre, and I want to help you with these.

First, as I mentioned earlier in this session, you'll find that children want to include everything but the kitchen sink in their essays. If they collected four examples to illustrate that Jenny in "Boar Out There" has created a mythical idea of the boar, they'll want to include every example. You may find it helpful to suggest an ideal length for your children's literary essays so they have more motivation to select.

If you have a chance to do so, you'll find that children's essays benefit enormously from tightening, from consolidating. I doubt if you could easily convey the art of this in a minilesson, but you could certainly gather a small group of children together and show them that a three-page-long typed essay can become two and a half pages without actually losing any content at all. One way to consolidate texts involves eliminating redundancy using lists.

Harrison, for example, had written:

> Lupe overcomes her difficulties by squeezing an eraser 100 times. She overcomes her difficulties by doing "finger ups" for finger strength. She also overcomes her difficulty by practicing after dark even when she could be tired.

He took out redundancy, so now his draft read:

> Lupe overcomes her difficulties by squeezing an eraser 100 times, by doing "finger ups" for finger strength and by practicing marbles even after dark.

You'll also find that children need lots of help with citations. This is a time to review the conventions around quotations marks, but also you'll want to teach children how to pick and choose the most pertinent sections of a citation, using ellipses in place of the irrelevant material. For example, Judah wanted to show that Lupe changes from the start to the end of the story. She found sections of the story that suggested that at first Lupe wasn't strong. She was "a shy girl who spoke in whispers," and her thumb "was weaker than the neck of a newborn chick." In the sentence I just wrote, notice that, following Judah's lead, I excerpted only the tiny sections of "The Marble Champ" which made the point Judah wanted to make, and notice also that I needed to write some words that set up the excerpts. Judah must do similar work.

Let me explain more clearly. A child may want to show that Lupe encountered frustration when she first tried to play marbles. The child might identify this sentence from the text as relevant:

> She tried again and again. Her aim became more accurate, but the power from her thumb made the marble move only an inch or two.

If the child's topic sentence was: "Lupe battles frustration," the child can't simply attach the citation to the topic sentence, or the resulting text would be confusing:

> Lupe battles frustration. "She tried again and again. Her aim became..."

In your editing conferences, then, you'll need to teach children that writers tuck explanatory information into our sentences. This, of course, asks children to not only recognize places where more information is needed but also to have the linguistic dexterity to tuck subordinate clauses into texts:

> Lupe battles with frustration. One day, after pouring marbles onto her brother's bed, she set to work trying to flick one marble at another. "She tried again and again. Her aim ..."

As you meet with children in one-to-one and small-group conferences, remember that your children will probably be brand new at the complex work of inserting text references into an essay. They need not master this! Teach those who seem ready the gist of this work, and be ready to do as any editor might do and to insert a phrase, add a sentence into a draft. The final texts need to make sense, and when working with this brand-new and challenging aspect, you'll find that some children need your help in order to make their texts comprehensible.

PACKAGING AND POLISHING YOUR LITERARY ESSAYS

IN THIS SESSION, YOU'LL PASS ALONG SOME TRICKS OF THE TRADE WHICH WILL ALLOW CHILDREN TO TAKE THEIR ROUGHLY CONSTRUCTED ESSAYS AND MAKE THEM LOOK MORE PROFESSIONAL. SPECIFICALLY, YOU'LL SHOW THEM WAYS TO WRITE INTRODUCTORY AND ENDING PARAGRAPHS, TO IMPORT SOME SPECIALIZED LINGO, AND TO HANDLE CITATIONS WITH MORE FINESSE.

GETTING READY

- Examples of leads written for secondary-school essays
- Example of one child's process for writing and revising a lead, using an essay children have studied
- See CD-ROM for resources

Just as stories often rely on traditional beginnings, so, too, literary essayists can draw on the traditions of their field. When high-school and college students are taught to write essays on Hamlet and Beloved, teachers tell them to begin their essay with a few sentences which situate this essay within its larger context. Interestingly enough, this is exactly what I do in this minilesson—in fact, in this very paragraph! My writing is shaped like a funnel. First I talk abut texts in general, then narrow in to talk about the lessons older children are taught about literary essays. If you keep reading, you'll see that I continue funneling you, my reader, in toward the specific point I plan to make today. Specifically, today I try to teach children to write opening sentences which gesture toward situating their essays within larger contexts.

I also show children that once they've written an introductory passage, it's easy to write a corresponding closing passage, suggesting that it's 'no-big-deal' to write these components of a literary essay.

Finally, I invite children to spend any extra moments polishing their essays. They'll especially learn more about making citations and about using the specialized jargon of literary scholars.

MINILESSON

Packaging and Polishing Your Literary Essays

CONNECTION

Orient children by telling them that once they've constructed rough body paragraphs, they need to package and polish their essays. One way to do that is to write an introductory paragraph.

"Today, some of you will finish selecting and combining the bits that will make the mosaic of your first, second, and perhaps third body paragraphs. Once literary essayists have written, selected, and roughly combined the evidence to support our claims, then it is time to think about packaging and polishing our essays. One way we can do this is to write introductory paragraphs that prepare readers for our thesis statements (the thesis traditionally ends the first paragraph of a literary essay, setting readers up for what will follow)."

Remind children that they already have a repertoire of ways to start a narrative.

"You already know that narrative writers have a host of ways to begin stories. Sometimes narrative writers and storytellers begin by showing the character in action: 'I grabbed my sneakers and ran barefoot across the beach.' And sometimes narrative writers begin instead with dialogue': "Race you to the water," I said, and, grabbing my shoes, ran barefoot across the beach.' Some begin with classic story openings: 'Once upon a time' or 'Once, long ago' or 'One day, not long ago.'"

"Earlier this year, you also learned templates that writers of personal essays sometimes find helpful. You learned that essayists sometimes find it helpful to begin an essay by showing their journey of thought, saying something to the effect of, 'I used to think . . . but now I realize . . .' or 'I once believed . . . but recently I've come to think that . . .'."

Name your teaching point. Specifically, stress that literary essayists often write leads that contain broad statements about literature, life, stories, or about the essay topic. The introductory paragraph aims to put the essay into context.

"Today what I want to teach you is this. Literary essayists are usually taught to begin an essay by putting this particular essay and/or this particular text into context. We write a generalization about literature or stories or life—one that acts as the broad end of a funnel, channeling readers so they are ready for the specific point we set forth in our thesis."

COACHING

Chances are very good that children will need another day of composing their essays before they are ready for you to help them with their introductory paragraphs. Don't teach this lesson if few are ready for it, or your instruction will fall on deaf ears. Instead, use the extensions or your own sense of what your children need to provide another minilesson to help them go from folders to drafts.

TEACHING

Refer to the panoramic view at the start of some movies, and to the way the camera later zooms in on a single character making his or her way through that larger context, to help writers sense the function that lead paragraphs often play in literary essays. Share examples of leads written for secondary-school literary essays.

"You know how some movies begin by panning the whole landscape and then the camera seems to zoom in on some specific place—perhaps a winding country road—and eventually we see an old man cycling down that road. In a similar fashion, literary essays often begin by panning the whole landscape and then the camera zooms in. But in a literary essay, the landscape is not a hilly countryside and the camera doesn't zoom in on a single road. Instead, when a literary essay begins with a wide view, it often means the essay says something general about how literature tends to go, or about stories, or about life. Of course, the writer says something that provides the big-picture context for this particular essay, this particular journey down a road of thought."

"You will learn a lot more about this when you are in middle school, high school, and college. Let me read to you three leads that my sons wrote for their high-school essays. Remember, these were written by high schoolers, so they will be complicated, but see if you can sense how they begin broadly, talking about big topics, and then funnel down to the particular theory that the essay will develop."

- The desire for love and for money has motivated much of human history. Western literature is filled with novels which address the conflicting feelings a woman and her family feel when the woman must decide between marrying a man she loves and marrying a man who can provide for her financially. Many of the characters in Jane Austin's novel, *Pride and Prejudice*, personify one view or another of the advantages and limitations of marrying for love rather than for money.

- Some researchers suggest there are stages to accepting death or great loss. These stages include denial, anger, and finally acceptance. Characters in Chris Crutcher's book, *The Crazy Horse Electric Game*, go through these stages as they deal with a great loss in their lives.

- I am a lacrosse player. When decisions must be made in the heat of a game, our coach has always told us that the worse thing to do is to stall. It is always better to make a decision, however bad it may be, rather than to freeze in indecision. When I first heard this advice, I was skeptical. Now, after reading Shakespeare's *Hamlet* and Heller's *Catch-22*, I understand the wisdom of my coach's advice. A bad decision is always better than no decision at all, because every decision leads to some amount of progress, even if the progress comes, as in *Hamlet* and *Catch-22*, from mistakes made and lessons learned.

Here is another example, one I chose not to read aloud but which also makes the point: The headlines of recent newspapers spotlight our nation's desperate search for justice. Did our president knowingly deceive us about Iraq's weapons of mass destruction in order to take us into war? Was the office of the vice president involved in criminal deception to the grand jury? Questions about right and wrong are basic to what it means to be human. In the tragic play Hamlet, *Shakespeare explores this fundamental aspect of life. The play suggests that, in a world filled with corruption and betrayal, it is difficult to live as just people because our information is inevitably fragmented and because a person who walks this path is doomed to loneliness, unsure of whom to trust and therefore alienated from the world.*

Tell the story of how one child went about writing the lead to a literary essay that the children have already studied. Highlight the steps taken, including asking, "What is my essay really about?" and brainstorming a variety of choices.

"When Jill worked on her essay, she had already written her thesis:"

> Many people read Sandra Cisneros's essay 'Eleven' and think it's about a girl who has to wear a sweater she doesn't want to wear. But I think the story is about a girl who struggles to hold on to herself when she is challenged by people who have power over her.

"So she began with the idea that 'Eleven' tells the story of a girl who struggles to hold on to herself. Jill asked herself, 'What is the broader context—the larger landscape of kinds of texts—that this belongs in?' To answer that question, Jill needed to think about what she wanted to highlight in her essay. She could have said her literary essay about 'Eleven' was really about voice, or about girls, or school, or about people who struggle over power differentials. And depending on which of these she chose, she might have put her essay into a different landscape. Jill decided that she wanted to highlight—to pop out—just the idea that Rachel *struggles*. Jill gathered a cluster of friends, and together they brainstormed a bunch of possible lead sentences that talk about the big picture of characters and their struggles. They suggested these were possible leads:"

> • Whenever I watch a movie, I know there will come a part when the music changes and I need to worry about the character. That part is sure to come because in the movies, as in all stories, characters struggle.

> • My life is full of problems. Everywhere I turn, it seems that there are problems. When I read stories, I realize I am not alone. Characters in books, too, struggle with problems.

> • In school I learn from lessons that teachers teach but when I read stories, I learn from problems that characters encounter. When I see how people in books face their problems, I become better at facing my own problems.

"In the end, Jill wrote this as her lead:"

> In my life, not everything ends up like a fairy tale. I like to read books where characters are like me. They don't live fairy tale lives. We have the same kinds of problems.

To write a lead to a literary essay, it helps to be able to look at some thing—any item, really—and think of it as one instance of a larger category or class of items. In a small group, you may have to give some children practice at shifting between specifics and generalizations. Earlier I mentioned that you could teach children to realize that a fork is one instance of the more general category of a piece of silverware (or a tool for eating). A cat is one instance of the more general category of family pets or the feline category of animals or of companions. A rug could be thought of as a floor covering, a decoration, or a way to warm one's house. Help children see how in each of those instances, the thinker is shifting between a specific—a cat, a fork, a rug—and a generalization. Similarly, if one's thesis claims that "With determination and hard work, Lupe overcame her problem and became a marble champion," the author needs to think, "What is this an instance of?" The author might generate a list of possibilities, such as:

> • *In life, all of us face problems. The ways in which we respond to these problems reveal a great deal about our inner character.*

> • *Stories usually contain a character who yearns for something and struggles to achieve his or her motivations.*

ACTIVE ENGAGEMENT

Ask children to join you in thinking of the lead for the class literary essay by first thinking of the essay's larger landscape. Ask them to work with partners to generate lists of possible leads.

"Let's try writing introductory paragraphs by thinking about the lead to our essay on 'Spaghetti.' Remember, we first need to think about the general topic that our essay addresses, and we have some choices. The thesis is 'Gabriel is a lonely boy who learns from a cat that he doesn't need to be lonely anymore.' So we could say this is an essay about cats as companions (though I doubt that is really the main thing the essay addresses). Could you talk with your partner and generate a few other possibilities for the general topics? If you don't think this essay advocates cats as companions, then what general category would you file it under?"

The children talked, and soon I called on a few for suggestions.

"The essay could fit under the category of essays about animals that make a difference."

"The essay could fit under the category of characters who learn from surprising teachers."

"The essay could fit under the category of characters who change their attitudes."

"The essay could fit under the category of characters who feel as if they are misfits and find a way to belong."

"To write a lead for this 'Spaghetti' essay, we first need to decide which of these will provide the larger landscape for our essay, and that is up to us. Which do you choose?" I asked, and soon the class had decided that the essay would fit under the broad category of characters who learn a lot from animals. Once that choice was made, children worked with partners to brainstorm options, generating a list of several possible leads. In no time, the first paragraph was completed.

> Pet lovers know that animals are not just cute and companionable. They can change a person's life. In Cynthia Rylant's story "Spaghetti," Gabriel, a lonely boy, adopts a stray cat and learns that he doesn't need to be lonely anymore.

LINK

Remind writers that they now have a process they can go through to write a lead paragraph for a literary essay. Summarize the steps of the process.

"So, writers, when you have combined your material into a rough draft, you will want to begin packaging and polishing your essay. One way to package your essay is to work on an introductory paragraph. When doing so, begin by asking, 'What general themes might this essay address?' and come up with some options, as we did. Then, once you have decided on the landscape in which you want to set your essay, try different ways to draft a lead, and then choose one from those options. This is good work for you to do today, and whenever in your life you need to write a literary essay."

As practice for teaching literary essays, you and your colleagues may want to try imagining how you could turn these other options into possible lead sentences. When I coach children to do this, I sometimes bring out a pretend violin, puff my chest up, wave my arms, all in an effort to convey the sweeping, grand tune that many writers assume when writing a lead. Let's take "characters who learn from surprising teachers" as a case in point. For a lead, I might start:

> Throughout my life, I've had the opportunity to learn from many remarkable teachers. Few, however, have taught me as much as my scruffy little English cocker, Tucker. In Rylant's short story . . .

or

> Great teachers come in many shapes and sizes . . .

or

> Life is full of lessons, and oftentimes teachers come from surprising places.

or

> We attend school in order to learn from teachers, but many of us find that our most important teachers are those we stumble upon when we least expect to find them.

You'll need to decide on the actual logistics involved in helping children go from rough to final drafts. Can you ask children to use word processors and type their drafts at home, allowing you the opportunity to reread and edit them? If many of your children don't have access at home to computers, they'll need to write a rough draft at home, and in school, and then you'll still need to take their drafts home, edit them, and give children time to make final drafts. The scheduling of all this must be in your hands.

WRITING AND CONFERRING

Unpacking Evidence

I pulled my chair alongside Tyler, who had laid six or seven slips of paper out across his desk and now sat, immobilized in front of the intricate design. "What's up?" I asked.

"I got my first sentence," Tyler said, "and my evidence. But I don't know how to combine it so it goes."

"What's giving you trouble?" I asked.

"My big idea is that 'Eleven' isn't really a story. And I'm on the first reason—because it doesn't have a problem and a solution," Tyler said, then pointed to the lines he'd cited as proof:

> Mrs. Price says, "That is enough nonsense. Put the sweater on."
>
> "But"
> "Now"

Could also say:

> When Mrs. Price said, "Of course it's yours. I remember you wearing it," Rachel couldn't say anything. Her power was taken away from her.

"So why do you think it is hard to combine these?" I asked, but Tyler didn't have an answer.

"Tyler," I said. "Do you remember that when I taught you to collect ministories that illustrated your big idea, I told you that after you tell the story about one time, then you need to unpack the story, showing how it relates to your big idea? You need to say something such as, 'This shows that . . .' and 'This is important because . . .' Well, I'm realizing that I should have taught you that in fact writers 'unpack' almost any evidence that we include in an essay. And I think the reason you are struggling to combine your claim and your evidence is that you haven't really unpacked your evidence yet." Then I added, "What I mean by 'unpacking' the evidence is that you need to be able to take a quotation from the text (like those you have copied) and you need to talk about how that quotation serves as evidence for your point." Then I urged Tyler to take hold of one of his notes. "Hold this," I said, and talk to me about how this bit of evidence goes with the point that you are trying to make."

> MID-WORKSHOP TEACHING POINT   **Revising for Clarity and Cohesion**   "Writers, can I have your eyes and your attention? Earlier today I pointed out that after you have assembled a rough draft of your essay, you will want to begin packaging and polishing it. I gave you some pointers for how to write a lead paragraph, and later I will do the same for a closing paragraph. But meanwhile, it is also very important that you read over your draft and work on creating something called cohesion. Cohesion means stickiness, but I don't mean you need to pour glop on your essay to make it sticky! Let me explain what I do mean."
>
> "Earlier, I read you leads to literary essays that my sons wrote when they were teenagers. The really odd thing about grades 7 through 12 is that practically the only genre my sons wrote in was literary essays! So I tried to learn everything I could about that genre from their teachers, because it is not a kind of writing I see a lot in the world."
>
> "I won't forget the day I was walking down the school corridor with the chairman of Ridgefield High's very fine English department, and she said to me, 'The students really struggle with essays. And we are all clear about what the hardest thing is for them.' She continued walking, and my mind raced through all the possibilities: was the hard part
>
> *continued on next page*

Tyler read aloud his evidence:

> Mrs. Price says, "That is enough nonsense. Put the sweater on."
>
> "But"
>
> "Now"

"This shows she's really mean and gets mad?" he said, his intonation suggesting this was more of a question than an answer.

"Tyler," I intervened. "Remember, your point is, 'Eleven is not really a story,' and one reason for this has to do with Mrs. Price saying, 'That is enough nonsense.' How does that show that this isn't really a story?"

"Cause she keeps on getting mad at Rachel; she never stops," Tyler said.

"So, Tyler, that is important. The way you'd write this, then, might be like this," I said, and started to write in the air:

> "Eleven" is not shaped like a story because stories usually have problems and solutions, and in this text, there are problems but those problems don't have solutions. From the start of the text to the ending of it, Mrs. Price doesn't listen to Rachel. That problem never goes away, it is never solved. Even towards the end of the story, when Rachel protests, she only gets to say, "But" before Mrs. Price . . ."

Then I said, "So, Tyler, when you go to glue bits of evidence together, remember that you need to unpack the evidence. You need to talk about how that particular bit of evidence goes with the main point you are trying to make."

The next child I approached was Judah, who had already written a draft and was rereading it. She'd written this:

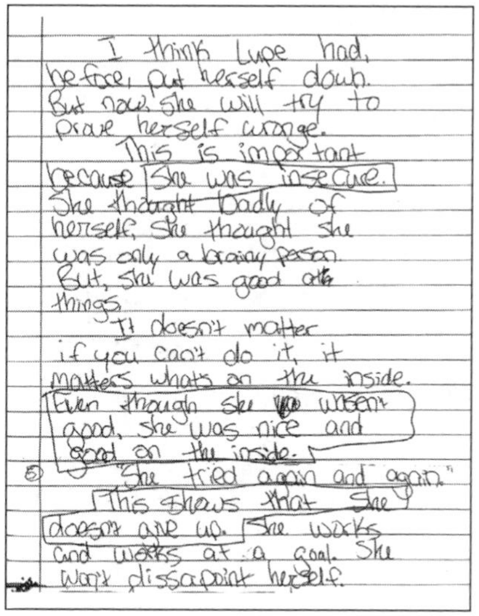

> I think Lupe had before, put herself down. But now, she will try to prove herself wrong.
>
> This is important because she was insecure. She thought badly of herself, she thought she was only a brainy person. But, she was good at things.
>
> It doesn't matter if you can't do it, it matters what's on the inside. Even though she wasn't good, she was nice and good on the inside.

developing insights about texts? Writing with correct control of conventions? Studding their essays with ideas? Then the department chair finished her sentence.' Yep, the hardest thing for all of them is writing transitions'.

"At that point in the conversation, we arrived at wherever she was going—I don't recall now where it was. But I do recall that she abruptly left me at that point. And I stood there in the hall, trying to get my brain around what she had just said. 'The hardest thing of all is writing *transitions*?' I thought. I wondered how that could possibly be, and frankly, I still wonder. But meanwhile, I want to be sure you understand transitions—because transitions are indeed one important way in which you can make sure that all the parts of your essays stick together."

"Strong essayists don't just use tape to combine our bits and pieces together to make an essay. We also use words. Sometimes the words function as bridges between one bit and the next one. In these instances, writers often use phrases that act as glue: *for example, another example, furthermore.* But writers also create cohesion with repetition. If I want to show that Gabriel is lonely, when I describe him sitting on the stoop, I will come right out

continued on next page

Fig. XIV-1 Judah's draft

She tried again and again. This shows that she doesn't give up. She works and works at a goal. She won't disappoint herself.

"So what are you working on?" I asked Judah.

"I got a draft started. I'm putting everything together and writing what I think about her," Judah said. "It is coming really good because I have most of a page already."

"How do you feel about what you've written?" I asked.

"Good because she is really good; she just doesn't know it," Judah answered.

"Judah," I pressed. "When I asked how you thought about your draft, I was really wondering how you think of this as a literary essay. Your answer was focused more on how you feel about Lupe. What do you think of this as a draft of a literary essay?"

"Good?" she asked, unconvinced.

"You don't sound too sure," I responded, "and that is okay. Because this is the first literary essay that you've written, so you are just figuring out now what makes a really good essay. There are a couple of things that matter a lot in a literary essay. Why don't I remind you of some of the criteria, and then you look over your draft and think, 'Do I have that already, or is that something I want to work on?' Okay?" Judah nodded.

"An essay always involves a claim. The writer needs to come out and say an idea, and readers should believe the idea matters to the writer," I said. "Do you think you have done that?"

Judah nodded. Then I pressed on, "And an essay needs to back those claims up with evidence that is convincing. Essayists often write with big ideas and then specific examples. Do you think you've done that?"

Judah reread her draft, her eyes scanning back and forth across the page. "I think I left that out," she said. "I have it but it is in my folders." I nodded, agreeing with her, and pointed out that sometimes in life when we are really persuaded of something, we assume others will buy into our ideas. But we always need to remember to be as persuasive as possible.

---

continued from previous page

and say that he is *alone*. I could describe his fantasy of sleeping out with the coyotes without using the term *alone*, but I will use that exact term—I will say, 'Gabriel imagined himself sleeping *alone* under the stars, surrounded only by wolves '(or even, by the *lonely* cry of wolves). I will do this because I know that repetition can act as a cohesive tie, as word glue. And when I have been giving a sequence of examples, I will sometimes remind readers that the upcoming example is just one more in a whole chain of examples. I might say, 'Not only does Gabriel sit alone on the front stoop of his building and think of sleeping alone among the coyotes, he also wanders alone down the street.'"

"I suspect that one reason high-school students still have trouble with transitions is that it is not easy to teach how to use words to tie an essay together. But I can tell you that it helps to reread your essay, trying to make it sound like it's connected. Sometimes as I read aloud, my voice tells me places where I can add cohesive ties. Then, too, I think it helps to read over your essay and pay special attention to the breaks in your text, and see if you can use words as tape to help with those breaks. Write in a word or a phrase, but reread the whole draft to see if your addition actually sounds right and works. And definitely get your partner or someone who has not yet seen your draft to read it over with you, pointing out little places where the pieces of your text—like pieces of a puzzle—don't yet fit smoothly."

SHARE

Writing Conclusions

Tell students that literary essayists craft their conclusions with care. List some choices writers have for their conclusions.

"Something terrible happened to me last night. I was watching a television show—an enthralling one. I kept wondering how it would all come together at the end . . . and it never did. Suddenly, the words came onto the screen: 'To be continued . . .'"

"Has that ever happened to you? It's an awful feeling, isn't it, to be left in the lurch?"

"So I want to take a few minutes to remind you that your essays need endings. You'll probably want to try three or four endings (just like you often try three or four leads)."

"Remember that we learned that literary essayists begin their essays with a generalization about literature or life in order to set up the broader context for stating a particular thesis about text? Well, the conclusions you write are just as important as the beginnings, for similar reasons. Literary essayists conclude their essays by reconnecting to that broader context, leaving readers with something to think about, to linger over—to carry around in their minds and perhaps to revisit later on in discussion with others."

"The conclusions you write matter especially because they are the last impression that your readers will be left with. The conclusion puts forth the final thoughts you want to emphasize about the text you have read. Remember that you have choices. For example, Judah returned to her thesis, emphasizing why the claims and evidence she used support that thesis. Adam linked the essay to himself, sharing the lesson he learned from reading the text. Both students, of course, made sure their conclusions still related to that broader context they introduced at the beginning of their essays."

"Constructing your essay is like constructing a building. All your hard work will be for naught if you have only a strong foundation and sturdy floors, but no roof! So, tonight, you will need to reread what you have drafted today and then make a strong final statement about your journey of thought."

HOMEWORK *Using the Language of Literary Scholars* Writers, we looked at some of the leads that high-school students used for their literary essays. I know you aren't in high school yet, but I'd like to teach you one trick that can make your essays look as if you are in high school! This is the trick: Your essay will look much more professional if you use the tools of your trade.

This is true for any endeavor. My niece and nephew raise and breed chickens. They are eight years old—they are twins—but they want to be taken seriously by other poultry breeders so they can purchase good birds from them and sell their birds for a good price. As a result, when Abigail and Hugh write and speak to adult poultry breeders, they use the words of their trade. They say things like this: "This bird has strong coloring on the undercoat, and its vent is clean and pink." Or they'll say to a breeder, "We are looking for a good showmanship bird, one with smooth legs and a good head." They answer inquiries by saying, "We have a hatch in February for the Rhode Island Reds and in April for the Call ducks."

If you want your literary essays to be taken seriously, you need to use the words of your trade. The main character, as you will recall, is the *protagonist*. The text is written in the voice of the narrator. The start of the story is its *lead*. You might describe a story by speaking of its *setting*, *plot*, *theme*, or *tone*. Tonight, read over your draft and see if you've used the words available to you, and make sure that you have included the vital information in your essay—the title, genre, and author's name of the text you are examining.

⊙ TAILORING YOUR TEACHING

If your students are having a hard time writing introductory paragraphs . . . you might enlist the whole class's help to create one for a story children know well. Take a simple childhood tale like *Cinderella* or *Jack and the Beanstalk* and prompt children to think of large, familiar themes. Tell children that the themes of fairy tales are repeated throughout literature. *Cinderella*, for example, which explores the notion of good triumphing over evil, and, more precisely, someone with little power triumphing over someone with significantly more, is mirrored in *The Lion, the Witch and the Wardrobe*; *Peter Pan*; *Skinny Bones*; *Pinky and Rex and the Bully*; *Dancing in the Wings* and *The Meanest Thing to Say*. Children might also notice that the character Cinderella is similar to other literary characters they know well—Harry Potter, for instance, is also adopted by reluctant family members, and *Ella Enchanted* is a modern-day Cinderella. Children might start to see additional themes: for example, an abused family member, forced to do housework wearing rags, rises above her situation with the help of a fairy godmother and goes, literally, from rags to riches. Once you have come up with themes, guide children to pick one and formulate a thesis statement. Then see if together they can move from this larger, more universal (or general) idea to say something specific about the book itself and its characters. Children might have an easier time doing this work for their own essays if they first do it for a story they've known since they were little.

If you have children who need help laying out their materials and deciding what to include . . . tell them that selection is a very important part of the art of essay writing. Just as a painter doesn't take all his or colors and put it on a canvas, but instead chooses a particular shade of orange and another of pink to draw a sunset, so too essayists realize the importance of selecting the material that will be the most powerful for their essays. You might ask your students to consider a time they went to an art museum and saw an exhibit in which only one piece of art was spotlighted in a large display area—a large painting or a single vase.

If you notice your children have a tendency to be redundant in their essays . . . caution them against using the same excerpt to support several arguments. Some use the same excerpt from the texts they're writing about to support several arguments, while others make the same point with three or four examples. Tell children that after they put their pieces together, to some extent, the challenge is to reread their essays with critical eyes, eliminating redundancy. Encourage children to think about what does and doesn't hold their attention. For example, if a character faced the same challenge over and over, or fought the same battle with the same enemy in every book in a series, they, as readers, would grow frustrated and bored. Remind children that just as they are hungry for new thoughts, ideas, storylines, so too are their readers wanting to be challenged by new ideas in each paragraph of an essay. Once you've made your point, move on to the next. The last thing you want is for your readers to be eyeing the clock. And sometimes less is more.

COLLABORATING WITH COLLEAGUES

In this unit of study, you will have helped your children develop many of the muscles that they'll need in order to write literary essays in middle school and also on standardized assessments. Before this unit can really pay off in those contexts, however, children need to be able to use most of what you taught quickly, writing a literary essay over the span of an hour or two, not a week or two!

With your colleagues, then, it will be important to think about ways in which you can transplant bits of this unit into other parts of the day, and ways in which you can help children do more of this work internally.

For example, look over the sessions that were geared toward helping children read thoughtfully, gathering entries that could, in the end, become seed ideas for an essay. The work that you invited children to do within the writing workshop is really work that thoughtful readers do on the run as we read, or in moments of reflection after we put a text down in order to mull it over and to talk it over. Could you imagine suggesting that children read their independent books with sticky notes at the side, marking places in the text where the character changes or acts out of character or learns a big lesson? Could you imagine suggesting that children always read with their own life issues like an open book before them, aware that oftentimes we can find help with our own lives in the books we read? These early sessions in this unit can surely nurture a culture of thoughtfulness around children's independent reading, their shared reading, and around whole-class read-alouds.

Then, too, you'll want to find opportunities for children to consolidate what they really want to say about a text into a claim that they believe is

thoughtful, provocative, and central to the text. After you read a chapter of your read-aloud book to the class, why not pause and say, "What claim would you like to put forth? Talk with your partner and see if you could get us started in a conversation by putting a claim, an opinion, in the middle of our community."

Children could become accustomed to weighing whether a claim feels central to the text and grounded in the text, and then they could learn to talk long about that claim. Talking long about an idea is a lot like writing long about the idea.

In the whole group conversation, you can coach children to do all that they learned in this unit of study. After a child cites an excerpt from the text, for example, you could ask, "Can you unpack that citation? How does it link back to the big idea under discussion today?"

Of course, children could do similar work around their independent books. If they read, jotting ideas on sticky notes, children could then have time after half an hour of quiet reading to look over their sticky notes "and prepare for a partner conversation." Meanwhile, you could teach children that the way to prepare for a partner conversation is not unlike the way they prepare for writing a literary essay or preparing for a whole-class talk. Readers scan their roles, review their thoughts, thinking, "What big idea do I want to put forth?" "How might I support this idea?" That is, they turn sticky notes into what the kids come to speak of as "boxes and bullets." Of course, those boxes and bullets take on new life when they are challenged, added to, and rewritten through spirited conversation.

LITERARY ESSAYS:
A CELEBRATION

IN THIS CELEBRATION, YOU AND YOUR COMMUNITY OF WRITERS WILL CELEBRATE THE LITERARY ESSAYS THAT YOU CHILDREN HAVE COMPLETED.

GETTING READY

- Children need to have created anthologies from their essays.
- See CD-ROM for resources

In the real world, there is a whole group of people who spend their lives thinking about the real message behind a beloved story, noticing the ways in which an author's craftsmanship supports the author's message. The people who do this are literary scholars, and they spend a good part of their lives writing essays about texts. For example, hundreds of literary scholars have written about the deeper meanings in Mark Twain's Huckleberry Finn. These literary essays are then circulated among the "club" of people who devote their lives to literary scholarship. This means that when these people talk and think about texts, they have all the advantages of being in book-club conversations with people who, like them, have pored over these texts . . . only they are not in the same room, let alone the same state, as those people. What this means is that what literary scholars actually do when they write about texts is they write in response to what others have said. A literary scholar might begin her essay on, say, Huckleberry Finn, by writing, "So and so has argued that although some may think Huckleberry Finn is a story about . . . it is really a story about . . . I want to partly agree and partly disagree with So and So's claim . . .

It is fitting, then, that your children celebrate their literary essays by circulating them among other literary scholars. The children in your class will already know each other's texts and interpretations of texts (because in fact, their ideas will have been coauthored through extensive conversations), so it will be important for your children's ideas to be circulated among a classroom full of readers who have read the texts under consideration and have become invested in thinking about those texts, but whose ideas are still just emerging. More specifically, the children in your class who have written about "Boar Out There" will collate their texts into an anthology of literary essays on this story, and this group of children will go to another classroom, listen in to a book talk about this story, and after a few minutes, offer their essays that extend or at least 'go-with' that child's reading of the story. "Read this," the author will say, "and mark it up. Get ready to cite it in your book talk." When the children in the book talk resume reading, they'll be asked to bring the views of the essay authors into the conversation, actually reading bits of the essays. All the members of the book club will be expected to talk back to the views of the absent (though, really, the eavesdropping) essayists using the same conversational prompts as they use to talk back to each other's ideas.

CELEBRATION

Before the actual celebration day, convene small groups of children whose literary essays addressed a particular text. Coach them towards compiling an anthology of related literary essays—rereading and sorting each other's essays according to an organizational structure they design.

"Writers, tomorrow we will publish our literary essays, and we will do so following the tradition of literary scholars. Across the world, there are people whose job in life is to do what you have been doing. They are professionals at writing literary essays, and we're going to publish just like they do."

"The pros at this work don't read their literary essays aloud at public readings or hold book parties, as short-story writers and poets do. Instead, these professional authors publish their essays in anthologies of literary essays. For example, I have here in my hand a book of essays about Mark Twain's famous novel, *The Adventures of Huckleberry Finn*. This book has a name on the spine, which is the name of the person who edited the anthology of essays."

"In our classroom, you will not only author articles, you will also coedit the anthology that brings together all the articles written about a particular text."

"So in a few minutes we're going to gather in small groups of coeditors. The four of you who wrote about Rylant's 'Boar Out There' will form one group, those who wrote about 'Eleven' will form another group, and so on."

"But before you can decide on the sequence of your articles and write a forward to your anthology, I need to tell you about your audience."

"Literary essayists write for other people who study literature. The average Joe on the street won't pick up this anthology of articles about Huck Finn, but people who are deep into a book club conversation about this novel will absolutely want to know what other smart readers think. So your essays need to go to other people who are deeply involved in thinking about 'Eleven' and 'The Marble Champ' and 'Spaghetti.' Those people are the children in Mrs. Rosenblum's class. They've been reading these same short texts, but they haven't spent as much time thinking about them as you guys have. Tomorrow, we will go to their classroom when they are in book club conversation. Those of you who've read 'The Marble Champ' will listen to those kids talking about that text . . . and then you'll give them your anthology, let them read your ideas, and you'll listen as they use those ideas in their continued book club. In that way, you'll see how it really works in the real world of writing literary essays!"

"So gather in your editorial circles."

On the day of the celebration, sit children from your room who have written about a particular text in a ring around the children from another class who've recently read that text. Launch book talks, with your children listening. After a few minutes, each of your children will give copies of his or her essay to two children.

Once the two classes of children had come together and everyone had taken their appropriate places, I convened attention. "Literary scholars: in science, when we study biology, we try to do as field biologists do, peering closely at drops of water and carefully recording what we see. Today, we will try to do as literary scholars do. Mrs. Rosenblum's class, you began studying some short texts yesterday, and I know you are just about to talk about those texts. We've studied the same texts, working for several weeks with them. We're going to listen in on your book-club conversations about these texts, hoping that there are ways that our ideas, written in our essays, might talk-back-to your ideas. So, right now, will Mrs. Rosenblum's book clubs get started?"

As the children talked, their teacher and Medea and I circulated, pointing out to the ring of listeners ways in which their ideas added onto or challenged the ideas the readers were discussing.

After a very short while, I asked for children's attention. "Mrs. Rosenblum's readers? We've been listening to your ideas about these texts—'The Marble Champ,' 'Boar Out There,' and so forth—and we have ideas we'd like to bring into the conversation. One way for that to happen is for you to move your chairs apart, and make space for us to literally squeeze into the circle. But among literary scholars, there is another very important way for people to bring ideas to a book talk. We write literary essays! Then we put those essays out into the world, often making anthologies of them or magazines of them. So, right now, the

Readers, please be sure to actually read the literary essays included in this book, noticing the way in which all the lessons of this book set children up to write this way. Spot Harrison's effort to write microstories which are angled to support his claim. Note how he tries to "unpack" his evidence, showing how it relates to his claim. Enjoy his efforts at an ending!

Literature often tells the story of underdogs who rise up in the end. The Mighty Ducks is the story of a rag-tag hockey team that ends up winning the state championship. Cinderella tells the story of the rejected youngest sister who ends up marrying the prince. "The Marble Champ," by Gary Soto, is also an underdog story. It tells not only about Lupe winning the marble championship, it also tells that she overcomes her athletic difficulties through hard work and family support.

Lupe overcomes her difficulties through the support of her family. For example, one dinner, Lupe asks her father to come to the marble competition. Her father drops his fork and drops into deep thought. He had finally planned to spend that very day playing racket ball, his favorite activity. But he looked into Lupe's eyes, thought about how important it was that she was risking

Fig. XV-1 Harrison's final draft

entering a sports competition, and announced he would be there. Lupe grinned. There are other ways in which Lupe's family showed their support. Her parents let her practice marbles even after dark, her brother gave tips on how to shoot marbles, and her whole family was there to encourage her when she was worried. Gary Soto shows how important family support was to Lupe. His story contains a full page description of the family dinner. This section was not important to the plot of the story but it needs to be in the story because it shows how supportive Lupe's family was to her.

Lupe also overcame her difficulties through hard work. Lupe' decision to work hard and succeed in sports was made when she lay in front of her shelf full of academic trophies and medals. She wished there was at least one trophy that showed that she could do sports – but there were none. She

Fig. XV-2 Harrison's final draft page 2

decided that she would work hard, day and night, to win a marble tournament. A bit later, she came home from school and immediately tossed down her backpack and got out her marbles. Let me point out Lupe usually came home from school and did her homework—that is why she had a shelf full of academic trophies. She put on a determined face, and started to flick her marbles. At five o'clock, she hadn't started homework. It's six o'clock, she had flicked 500 times, and she hadn't started her homework. At seven o'clock, she'll die if she goes on any longer. Final score—marbles: three hours; homework: zero hours.

Lupe overcomes her difficulties by squeezing an eraser 100 times for thumb strength, by doing "fingerups" for finger strength, and by practicing after dark even when she could be tired to improve her overall marble game.

Fig. XV-3 Harrison's final draft page 3

Gary Soto shows Lupe's hard work through repetition. For example, he says unnecessary lines like "Tried again and again," and "Practice, practice, practice, squeeze, squeeze, squeeze." These lines support my idea that Lupe is working hard.

I enjoy underdog stories because they make me have a feeling of strange success inside. I have experienced being an underdog, in soccer. But in the end, like Lupe, my soccer team succeeded. The hidden lessons I learned from this story taught me that even if you don't think about it, there is a part inside of you that says your parents are there; just remember who held you when you learned how to swim.

Fig. XV-4 Harrison's final draft page 4

writers who have been working with me want to give you their literary essays, and we're going to watch as you read them, and as you mark up points that you think you could bring into your book club. So, readers—you'll each get an essay, maybe two. And my class, just watch as people read your essays!"

After a few minutes, I said, "Would each literary essayists talk with someone who read your essay? Make sure they see the points that might be relevant in the essay to the book club conversation."

Restart the book talks. Only this time, encourage the readers to weave the views found in the literary essays into their book-club conversations. Remind your writers that they can nudge readers to reference their essays, whispering in to them.

"Readers, could you return to your book clubs. Only this time, make a point of bringing not only your own ideas to the conversation, but also the ideas you read about in an essay. And essayists, if you hear times when you think your ideas could be brought into a conversation, whisper a hint to the reader. Nudge them to cite your essay!"

"The talks here are amazing—and that is what happens when a group of readers can stand on the shoulders of so much thinking. That's the power of writing essays about reading."

As essayists talked, I circulated, encouraging children to use phrases such as "As one literary critic suggested . . ." or "In an essay on this text, so and so suggests that . . ." Encourage children to use conversational prompts—"I agree because . . ." "This is giving me the idea that . . ." to raise the level of the conversation.

Literary Essay to "Eleven" By Maxwell
Some people think that growing up is fun, or exciting, having birthday parties and blowing out candles. But smart kids know that growing up is not all fun. Your old clothes don't fit anymore, and you can't play the same games, and you need to worry about new things, like money or work. In the story, "Eleven," by Sandra Cisneros, Rachel comes to an understanding of what being eleven really feels like.

Rachel comes to understand that when you are eleven, you are also ten, nine, eight, seven, six, five, four, three, two, and one. In the story, Rachel sits at her desk, staring at the nasty red sweater Mrs. Price made her keep. She was disgusted with it, and wanted to cry like she was three. She tried not to let her three come out though. Why did she want to cry over a sweater? She thought she was eleven, old enough not to cry over something silly like a sweater. She then

Fig. XV-5 Max's final draft

realizes that she was not just eleven, but ten, nine, eight, seven, six, five, four, three, two, and one. There are other sections of the story where Rachel understands that when you are eleven, you're also all the ages inside. For example, she says "when you are scared and need to sit on your Mama's lap, that is the part of you that is still five." And "When you say something stupid, that is the part of you that is still three." Another section of the story where Rachel sees that she has all the ages is "When you are sad and need to cry, that is the part of you that is still three." And one more place is when she blabbed and stuttered to Mrs. Price when she wanted to say something. That was the part of her that was still four. Her understanding that when you are eleven you are also all the ages inside is important because the way Sandra Cisneros stretches out "10, 9, 8, 7, 6, 5, 4, 3, 2, and 1" instead of just saying "all the other ages"—she really wants to show that that is

Fig. XV-6 Max's final draft page 2

the most important part.
Something else that Rachel comes to understand is that turning eleven can be a let down I see this in the text here: Rachel expected to feel eleven on her birthday as soon as she woke up. But she did not. She opened her eyes and everything was just like yesterday but it was today. She went to school and expected to feel like a big eleven-year-old, cut instead has a terrible day. Mrs. Price forces her to wear a nasty, disgusting sweater. She cries in front of the whole class like she was three. At the end of the day, she just wanted it to be gone and forgotten. Other parts in the text where I see that Rachel understands being eleven can be a let down are "You don't feel eleven. Not right away. It takes a few days, weeks even, sometimes even months until you say eleven when they as you." And "You are not smart eleven. Not until you are almost twelve." And when she realizes that she does not know

Fig. XV-7 Max's final draft page 3

what to do when Mrs. Prices forces her to wear the sweater. She does not have enough ages yet. I can really tell that Rachel does not feel eleven because Rachel says "I'm eleven" or a variation on that a lot, and that shows that she really has to remind herself, because that is not the way she feels. Also, Sandra Cisneros made a list of examples at the end of the story of things that are far away like "I wish I was 102 or anything but eleven" and "far away like a runaway balloon" or like "a teeny tiny little o in the sky." This really shows how much Rachel wants the day to be over with. Because she did not have a happy birthday. She had a let down birthday.

Literature can help you understand things better. For example, I have come, through Rachel's thoughts and experiences, to a conclusion that growing up is not all birthday parties and blowing out candles. And I have learned that I should appreciate being young, while I am.

Fig. XV-8 Max's final draft page 4

ELEVEN

By Adam

In literature, authors write a lot about one character being upset and taking it out on another person. Sandra Cisneros' essay, "Eleven," is about a girl named Rachel who is mistreated by her teacher and in return mistreats her classmates.

Rachel is mistreated by her teacher. Mrs. Price finds an ugly, old sweater in the coat room and forces Rachel to put it on. Rachel says "That's not . . . mine." But Mrs. Prices moves on to the next math problem without understanding Rachel, saying "of course it's yours." Mrs. Price says, "I remember you wearing it once." This is mistreatment because Mrs. Price isn't respecting Rachel. Mrs. Price doesn't care about what Rachel has to say. Later, right before the bell rings, Mrs. Price pretends as if everything's ok, ignoring the real pain Rachel is feeling.

In return for Mrs. Price mistreating Rachel, Rachel then goes on to mistreat her classmates. Rachel thinks of her classmates in a derogatory way. An example of this is when Rachel commented, "Maybe because I am skinny, maybe because she doesn't like me, that stupid Sylvia Saldivar says" . . . I think it

belongs to Rachel!" Then later on, Rachel comments " . . . But the worst part about it is right before the bell that stupid Phyllis Lopez who is even dumber than Sylvia Saldivar says she remembers the sweater is hers." In both these examples, Rachel is calling her classmates dumb and stupid. She's doing this in her mind, but her feelings probably effect her actions too. Sandra Cisneros also shows Rachel mistreating her classmates when Rachel describes the sweater as smelling like "cottage cheese" and " . . . all itchy and full of germs that aren't even mine." This shows that Rachel is disgusted with wearing her classmate's clothes. The sweater, it turns out, belongs to Phyllis and she must feel awful, seeing Rachel cry over the fact that Rachel needs to wear her sweater.

This story teaches me that when someone mistreats a person, that person needs to protest so that they don't pass on their fury to other people. When someone gets mad at me, I sometimes don't protest and instead pass it on to someone else. Sandra Cisneros in "Eleven" teaches me to speak up.

Fig. XV-9 Adam's final draft

Fig. XV-10 Adam's final draft page 2

Fig. XV-11 Adam's final draft page 3

THE MARBLE CHAMP

By Judah

In literature, characters face challenges and learn to survive. In the short story "The Marble Champ" by Gary Soto, Lupe learns to overcome her difficulties by working hard and believing in herself.

Lupe overcomes her difficulties through hard work. Soon after Lupe decided to become skilled at marbles, she came home from school and decided to waste no time before playing marbles. But this wasn't just play. This was serious work. Lupe had never been good at sports. So this time she was determined to become good at marbles. She picked five marbles that she thought were her best. Lupe didn't practice on any old table; she smoothed her bedspread to make it into a good surface for her marbles. She really thought about what to do to get good at this sport. She shot softly at first to get her aim accurate. The marbles rolled and clicked against one another. Lupe was disappointed, but didn't give up. She decided her thumb was weak and decided to strengthen it. Lupe worked to get her thumb strong by spending three hours flicking at marbles. She worked to get her wrists strong by doing twenty pushups on her fingertips, and she worked to get her thumb even stronger by squeezing an eraser one hundred times. Gary Soto uses a lot of repetition to emphasize that Lupe worked hard to become good. For example, he wrote, "she tried again and again," and "Practice, practice, practice. Squeeze, squeeze, squeeze." Lupe overcame her difficulties, not only by hard work, but also because she believed in

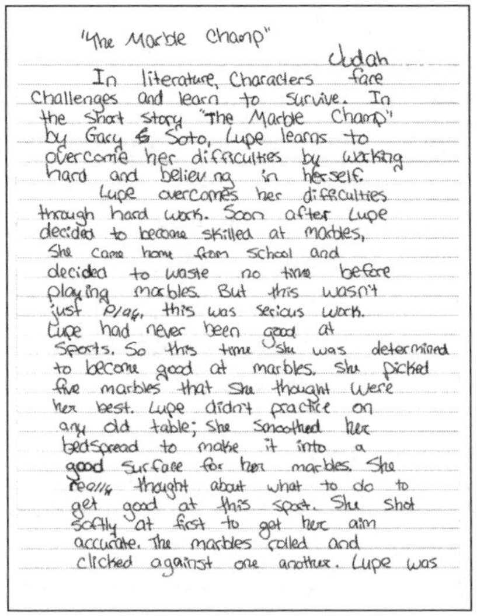

Fig. XV-12 Judah's final draft

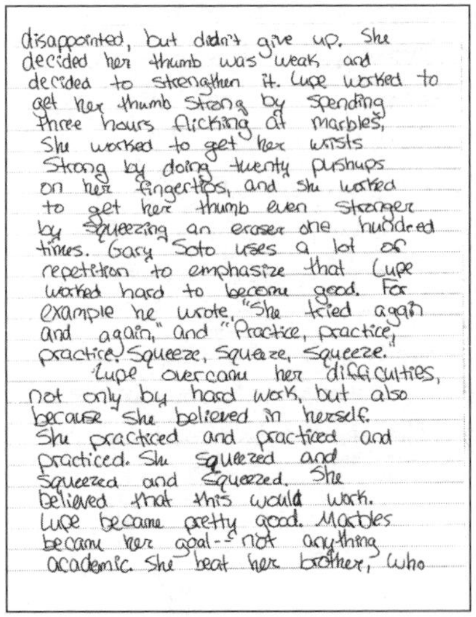

Fig. XV-13 Judah's final draft page 2

herself. She practiced and practiced and practiced. She squeezed and squeezed and squeezed. She believed that this would work. Lupe became pretty good. Marbles became her goal—not anything academic. She beat her brother, who played marbles. And, she beat a neighbor friend who, not only played marbles, was a champ. She believed in herself to play against them and she might win. The friend said, "She can beat the other girls for sure, I think." This didn't stop Lupe. It didn't even make her nervous! She kept going and still believed in herself. Lupe believed in herself to try and win the academic awards. Lupe believed in herself to work and try to become good. Lupe believed in herself to go to the games and try to win.

In the beginning, Gary Soto writes, "Lupe Medrano, a shy girl who spoke in whispers . . ." It is important to notice that Gary Soto is writing about a character who is complicated. He writes that she is shy. But she sits and looks at all of her awards. Then, as the story goes on, Lupe changes to a girl who believes in herself. In the beginning, Lupe was shy. Then, in the end, she shook hands with people who watched her, even a dog! At first, her thumb was "weaker than the neck of a newborn chicken." Then, after she exercised it, it was swollen because of the muscle. Her thumb was so strong, that when she shot, she shattered a marble. Gary Soto writes to make us think that Lupe is determined to become good at marbles.

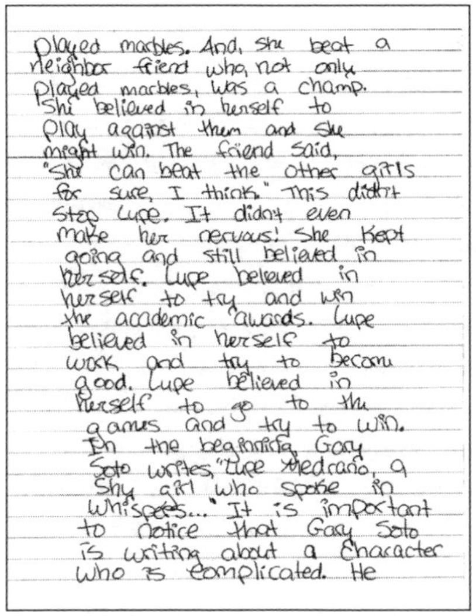
played marbles. And, she beat a
neighbor friend who, not only
played marbles, was a champ.
She believed in herself to
play against them and she
might win. The friend said,
"She can beat the other girls
for sure, I think." This didn't
stop Lupe. It didn't even
make her nervous! She kept
going and still believed in
herself. Lupe believed in
herself to try and win
the academic awards. Lupe
believed in herself to
work and try to becom
good. Lupe believed in
herself to go to the
games and try to win.
In the beginning, Gary
Soto writes, "Lupe Medrano, a
shy girl who spoke in
whispers..." It is important
to notice that Gary Soto
is writing about a character
who is complicated. He

Fig. XV-14 Judah's final draft page 3

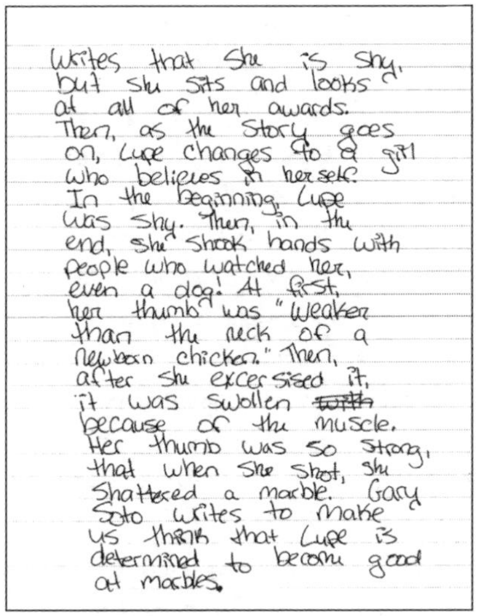
writes that she is shy,
but she sits and looks
at all of her awards.
Then, as the story goes
on, Lupe changes to a girl
who believes in herself.
In the beginning, Lupe
was shy. Then, in the
end, she shook hands with
people who watched her,
even a dog! At first,
her thumb was "weaker
than the neck of a
newborn chicken." Then,
after she excersised it,
it was swollen ~~with~~
because of the muscle.
Her thumb was so strong,
that when she shot, she
shattered a marble. Gary
Soto writes to make
us think that Lupe is
determined to becom good
at marbles.

Fig. XV-15 Judah's final draft page 4

A Literary Essay on "The Marble Champ"

By Ali

When I read I am often drawn to stories that are about people my own age who have problems that I might have, because than I can really feel how the character is feeling. In the short story "The Marble Champ" by Gary Soto a girl named Lupe has never been good at sports, but through determined effort she will do something she has never done before—win a sport.

At the start of the story Lupe had never been good at sports. She could not catch a high pop, kick a soccer ball, or shoot a basketball. One afternoon, Lupe lay on her bed staring up at the shelves that held her awards. Her awards were for spelling, reading, science, piano, chess and for never missing a day of school. Not one of her awards was for a sport. "I wish I could win something, anything, even marbles."

Gary Soto uses lists in the beginning of the story to convey the point that Lupe has been a winner. For example " . . . the school's spelling bee champion, winner of the reading contest three summers in a row, blue ribbon awardee in the science fair, the top student at her piano recital, and the playground grand champion in chess." Soto wants readers to notice that although Lupe has excelled in many areas in her life she has not been good in sports.

Through determined effort Lupe will win in a sport. One night after dinner, Lupe and her dad went outside. It was dark, but with a couple of twists the porch light went on. The light shone down on the circle Lupe had drawn earlier in the dirt. Lupe set the marbles inside the circle and she dropped down to her knee, she released her thumb. Even through she completely missed the marble she did not stop. She was determined to perfect her shot. She practiced again and again and again. It started to become a regular movement in her thumb. It was getting late and she continued to work her way around the circle. Dropping, aiming, releasing. Lupe prepared for the championship by squeezing an eraser 100 times, by shooting marbles for three hours, and by pushing up and down on her fingertips 20 times.

Gary Soto uses repetition to illustrate determined effort as an important part of Lupe's character. For example "Squeeze, squeeze, squeeze . . . practice, practice, practice." Repeating these words show how Lupe's determination to work hard in order to succeed.

From this story I have learned that determined effort can have surprising results. Lupe had motivation to succeed, but I don't think she was expecting to win her first game. I think she had prepared herself as best she could and she was going to try her hardest. What I realize is that having determined effort to always do your best is important, because it can help make your wishes come true.

Fig. XV-16 Ali's final draft

Fig. XV-17 Ali's final draft page 2

Fig. XV-18 Ali's final draft page 3